Browning's Dramatic

BROWNING'S DRAMATIC MONOLOGUES AND THE

POST-ROMANTIC SUBJECT

Monologues and the Post-Romantic Subject

LOY D. MARTIN

THE JOHNS HOPKINS UNIVERSITY PRESS

Baltimore and London

This book has been brought to publication
with the generous assistance of
the Andrew W. Mellon Foundation.

© 1985 The Johns Hopkins University Press
All rights reserved
Printed in the United States of America

The Johns Hopkins University Press, 701 West 40th Street,
Baltimore, Maryland   21211
The Johns Hopkins Press Ltd, London

The paper in this book is acid-free and meets the guidelines for
permanence and durability of the Committee on Production Guidelines
for Book Longevity of the Council on Library Resources.

Library of Congress Cataloging in Publication Data

Martin, Loy D.
    Browning's dramatic monologues and the post-
romantic subject.

    Bibliography: p.
    Includes index.
    1. Browning, Robert, 1812–1899—Criticism and
interpretation. 2. Monologue. 3. Romanticism—
Influence. 4. Marxist criticism. I. Title.
PR4238.M37 1985   821'.8   85-9796
ISBN 0-8018-2653-5 (alk. paper)

To my father, Loy Robert Martin

Contents

Acknowledgments

This book lay on my shelf in manuscript from December 1980 until the summer of 1984. In the winter of 1981, I decided to leave the profession of academic teaching and scholarship after nearly ten years and embark on a new vocation. The publication of the book seemed less urgent under these new conditions, and as there always seemed so much to do, I seldom thought of sending the book to a press. It is, therefore, to the repeated urging of John Bender and Laura Seitel that I owe the actual publication of these pages. I wish to thank them and also to thank Stephen Orgel, who recommended that I offer the manuscript to the Johns Hopkins University Press.

Several scholars have read all or part of the manuscript and made useful comments. For their encouragement and help, I wish to thank Herbert Lindenberger, Anne Mellor, W. J. T. Mitchell, Richard Strier, and Jeanne Vanecko. In lengthy written responses, Gerald Bruns and James Kincaid helped me believe in the book and saved me from some important mistakes. Eric Halpern, of the Johns Hopkins University Press, has ably led me through the submission and publication process and has given valuable aid in solving one of the book's most stubborn and vexing problems: its title.

In all, there are three very special debts that require a separate place in my acknowledgments. The first is to Wayne Booth, one of the few truly undefensive readers remaining for books such as mine. Wayne read my work before we ever met, understood what I was about when much revision was still needed, and later, as my colleague, kept my spirits and my belief in the book alive when they were very low. My second special debt is to Laura Seitel, who has read this book perhaps more carefully than anyone. For her loyalty and emotional support during the final stages of writing and for her unshakeable belief in the book's value, my gratitude is greater than I can say. Finally, I wish to thank my father. Since long before this book was imagined, he has given support of many kinds along paths that he did not always understand. For this trust no words of acknowledgment are adequate, and it is therefore to him that this book is dedicated.

BROWNING'S DRAMATIC MONOLOGUES AND THE

POST-ROMANTIC SUBJECT

Toward the Subject of the Dramatic Monologue

I   This book is about the dramatic monologue—how and why it was produced by Browning and a few of his contemporaries at a certain period in English literary history. This seems a simple enough topic, but it has entailed some complicated problems, not the least of which is understanding what we mean when we say that the dramatic monologue was produced. Materially, what a writer produces is books. He fills a certain number of pages with writing, and a printer reproduces that writing for consumption among the members of a community. This process is mediated by publishers, editors, booksellers, and reviewers, by makers of type and presses, builders of buildings, drivers of carts, makers and adjudicators of laws: in short, the social totality within which it is possible to say that a writer "produces." If we were addressing the question of why and how a given culture produces books, we could, of course, proceed in our research using established methods of economic history. But when we ask why and how a few writers "produce the dramatic monologue," we seem to be posing a different kind of question. "The dramatic monologue" is an idea, an abstraction, designed to tell us what is "in" some books but not in others, and to talk about its production involves us in different kinds of historiographic problems than we face in analyzing material production per se. In short, we are saying that, in addition to machines and food and textiles and books and roads, a society produces classifiable entities that chiefly emerge from, and are consumed in, human minds. Our questions have plunged us into the realm of ideology, or as Marx put it, "forms of consciousness."

To say it this way shows that the production of ideal commodities like dramatic monologues, laws, philosophical arguments, or religious doctrines adds a new set of complexities to the already complex business of material production. In this book, I am concerned with explaining what a dramatic monologue is, how it provides its reader (consumer) with a formal alternative to literary forms previously produced and largely abandoned as well as those that thrive contemporaneously with the monologue itself. In calling the monologue a form of consciousness, I might better have said "form of subjectivity," and it will soon become clear that any sense in which the monologue is an alternative to other forms is a sense in which it specifically constitutes and locates a certain kind of subject. To describe the monologue, therefore, will involve answering questions about the presentation of the subject in language: Are the boundaries of the subject physical, psychological, linguistic, ideological, or defined some other way? Are they defined at all? Is subjectivity unified or divided? What is the relation between subjective identity and temporal process? How do individual subjects generalize or specialize themselves? What relations are possible among subjects or between subjects and their environment? These are among the questions addressed in the chapters of this book, and they interact in a constant dialectic with those wider questions about how the monologue offers alternatives to other forms and why it is produced in a particular culture at a particular time. Indeed, this is a book full of questions. Sometimes my answers are partial; sometimes they are highly speculative and laden with more questions. Some of the best questions I cannot yet answer at all.

II

The preceding paragraphs locate in ideological production a set of complications added to the already complex system of material production in a given culture. This reverses the movement of much idealist criticism and scholarship, which considers the social and material "context" of a work of literature as a subordinate, and sometimes undesirable, added complexity that may or may not supplement the essential intelligibility of the work itself. But reversals like the one implied here have become more and more common during the past two decades. In concentrating on the social and material foundation of historical change, scholars of the present generation are, even when lost in the pleasure of interpreting the single poem, the children of our time. There is great, even dangerous, diversity among us, but from the most reverent philologian to the rampant deconstructarian, we seem to share a special sense of the ephemeral nature of whole cultures and their dominant struggles. However we may clothe our discourse in aesthetic jargons, we possess a fundamental curiosity about the dynamics of cultural change, a topic traditionally considered the province of the social sciences. As we look into selected aspects of cultural change—literary change being one of them—we encounter problems of historical explanation that direct our attention away from literature as an isolated aesthetic object (indeed even from an independent history of such objects) and towards its involvement in broader material conflicts and changes. Like any freshly growing discourse, however, ours suffers from the imprecision of the language available to us. What do we mean when we speak of poetry's "involvement" in material reality? What do we mean, as I asked at the outset, when we speak of the "production" of ideological forms?

The vagueness of these formulations intensifies a difficulty that readers of Marx have long encountered. Here, in one of the most famous passages of *The German Ideology,* Marx provides an apparently clear rationale for the kind of study that proceeds from the material to the ideological in its logic:

> The phantoms formed in the human brain are also, necessarily, sublimates of their material life-process, which is empirically verifiable and bound to material premises. Morality, religion, metaphysics, all the rest of ideology and their corresponding forms of consciousness, thus no longer retain the semblance of independence. They have no history, no development; but men, developing their material production and their material intercourse, alter, along with this their real existence, their thinking and the products of their thinking. Life is not determined by consciousness, but consciousness by life. In the first method of approach the starting-

point is consciousness taken as the living individual; in the second method, which conforms to real life, it is the real living individuals themselves, and consciousness is considered solely as their consciousness.[1]

Material life "determines" ideology, and ideology produces its "corresponding" forms of consciousness, but Marx does not explain just what kinds of relations are signified by these concepts of determination and correspondence. More than a decade later, he opens the same logical gap with regard specifically to literature and art:

> It is a well-known fact that Greek mythology was not only the arsenal of Greek art, but also the very ground from which it had sprung. Is the view of nature and of social relations which shaped Greek imagination and Greek art possible in the age of automatic machinery and railways and locomotives and electric telegraphs? Where does Vulcan come in as against Roberts & Co.? Jupiter, as against the lightning conductor? and Hermes, as against the Crédit Mobilier? All mythology masters and dominates and shapes the forces of nature in and through the imagination; hence it disappears as soon as man gains mastery over the forces of nature. What becomes of the Goddess Fama side by side with Printing House Square? . . . Looking at it from another side: is Achilles possible side by side with powder and lead? Or is the *Iliad* at all compatible with the printing press and even printing machines? Do not singing and reciting and the muses necessarily go out of existence with the appearance of the printer's bar, and do not, therefore, the prerequisites of epic poetry disappear?[2]

This passage is somewhat confusing. At first, the forms of Greek art "spring" from Greek mythology or ideology. This would correspond to the three-level model that Marx offers in *The German Ideology:* the forms of art "correspond" to ideology, and ideology is "determined" by material life. Hence Greek ideology (mythology) could not exist under modern material conditions, and Greek art could not exist without Greek mythology. Later, however, art seems directly dependent on material social existence, as when we are told that the epic depends on singing and reciting, which have been displaced by printing machines. But whether the connection between material reality and art or literature is direct or mediated by ideology, it remains essentially mysterious. In the section of the

Grundrisse just cited, the mystery is somewhat obscured by Marx's use of the negative construction. It seems plausible that Greek art could not emerge without Greek mythology or that neither could exist alongside modern science or mechanical means of reproduction, but Marx does not attempt to tell us why the actual material conditions of ancient Greece determine one kind of mythology or art and not another. He points out himself that Egyptian mythology necessarily leads to an art different from that of the Greeks, but Egyptian ideology is as free of modern natural science as its Greek counterpart, and Marx furnishes no positive method for explaining the form-determining power of distinct ideologies. Similarly, though we agree that the *Iliad* could not have been written in the nineteenth century, we cannot infer from Marx why singing and reciting should produce the form of the epic rather than something like the medieval romance or the modern fairy tale.

It is well known that the difficulty of defining the sense in which the ideological "superstructure" corresponds to a social and economic "base" troubled both Marx and Engels. Engels, in his letters, repeatedly insisted that the relation is not causal and that ideological forms can affect one another as well as the base itself.[3] Marx, in the very section of the *Grundrisse* from which I have just quoted, confuses the issue still further by asserting that "certain periods of the highest development of art stand in no direct connection to the general development of society, or to the material basis and skeleton structure of its organization."[4] Apparent retractions like this constitute what Hans Robert Jauss has called Marx's "idealist embarrassment," but they do not point to a withdrawal from the general position articulated in *The German Ideology*.[5] The *Critique of Political Economy* was intended as a summary of the *Grundrisse,* and in its preface, Marx reiterates his governing principle: "it is not the consciousness of men that determines their being, but, on the contrary, their social being that determines their consciousness."[6]

No subtlety of interpretation can conceal Marx's own confusion or ambivalence in thinking about the relation between the material totality of a culture and the specific forms of consciousness produced within that culture. As a result, this problem has been among the most fruitful in subsequent debates among Marxists. Perhaps the most well-known theory designed to specify the relation between literature or art and social reality is the so-called reflection theory, most ably defended by Georg Lukacs.[7] But the notion that art re-presents the processes of real history in idealized form has encountered nearly insuperable difficulties from the beginning. Some art appears to reflect no social reality at all, yet it is produced within distinct material circumstances. And except in certain brilliant applications, such as Lukac's "Narrate or Describe," reflection theories can deal easily only with content. The appearance and disappearance of literary genres, the characteristic structure of metaphor, the selective deformation of existing forms and conventions in all of the arts—these and many other artistic and ideological phenomena seem to require more supple theories of how forms of consciousness are produced than warmed-over mimetic accounts can provide.[8]

In the work of a theorist like Lucien Goldmann, we can find a clear recognition of the limits of reflection theories. Rejecting the dependence of such theories on the analysis of content, Goldmann claims that "the first problem that a sociology of the novel should have confronted is that of the relation between the *novel form* itself and the structure of the social environment in which it developed, that is to say, between the novel as a literary genre and individualistic modern society."[9] Unlike other Marxists, Goldmann does not stop at merely asserting a determinative connection between social conditions and ideology; he specifies that connection as one of structural homology: "The novel form seems to me, in effect, to be *the transposition on the literary plane of everyday life in the individualistic society created by market production. There is a rigorous homology* between the literary form of the novel . . . and the everyday relation between man and commodities in general, and by extension between men and other men, in a market society."[10]

The advantage of the concept of homology is that it can, by the methods of structuralist analysis, be explained or demystified. If the structure of society manifests itself as a system of communication, or *système de fonctions*—if, in other words, it is structured like a language—then the dominant structural elements of a given period will determine the form of any semiotic activity within that culture at that period. Reflection theories based on analysis of content always leave open the question of why we should expect art to represent reality rather than doing something else. Hence the circular idealism of Lukacs, for whom art *"ought to"* mirror social conditions and processes. Goldmann, on the other hand, frees the novel from particular content, removes it from the realm of individual volition, and gives an explanatory logic to Marx's claim that "life determines consciousness." The only question that remains is how true the logic is to Marx's conception.

Another way of posing the question is to ask whether a structure or *système de fonctions* corresponds to what Marx calls "life." This is a point on which Goldmann has been repeatedly taken to task. For Fredric Jameson, Goldmann's theory is yet another reflection theory in "sophisticated guise."[11] Jameson would be "only too willing to admit that the infrastructure is itself a sign-system" but complains that, as such, it cannot be identical with language and that for this reason its relation to "more overtly verbal [systems]" in the superstructure remains mysterious. Elsewhere he shows implicitly the weakness of a theory in which the structure of a form corresponds to the structure of yet another form that is, in itself, taken to be identical with reality. Refusing to choose between reflection theories that compare art to reality on the basis of content and structuralist theories that make the same symmetrical comparison in the equally abstract region of form, Jameson describes formal change in literature as an "adequation of form to content."[12] By this strategy, he is able to maintain the concreteness of the referent—material reality—apart from the ideological nature of the literary sign, while conceding that the concrete is nevertheless a structured set of relationships. Form and content as *signifiant* and *signifié,* are therefore both ordered entities, but entities that obey ordering principles different in kind. In a sense, this is equivalent to Saussure's insistence that the relation between signified and signifier is "arbitrary," where, in this case, "arbitrary" means that the adequation of form to content remains to be explained historically.

Marxists have traditionally experienced difficulty making a rigorous distinction between the ideal or "abstract" and the concrete or material. Without entering this debate, however, it seems possible to say that symmetrical concepts like "homology" or "reflection" imply an ontological or structural equivalence between the material and the ideal or between base and superstructure, an equivalence that, at the very least, fails to account for differential rates of change. As Robert Weimann, criticizing Goldmann, has said,

> Evidently, the concept of *histoire homologue* rests on the assumption that structural relationships "of the same type" exist within economic and aesthetic processes—an assumption which entirely disregards the fact (of basic importance to any literary history) that the novel of the nineteenth century possesses a capacity for survival and a quality of truth and value which the "homological structures" of contemporary economic life have not enjoyed. [13]

Weimann, by associating Goldmann's homologies with Barthes's *conscience paradigmatique* and with Lévi-Strauss's "system of signs," recognizes an idealist determinism in which concrete praxis cannot logically lead to systemic change:

> Here, as elsewhere, the structuralist is preoccupied with *le système:* he is concerned with *langue* at the expense of the social function and process of human speech (in questions, answers, dialogues, and the like) as related to the most varied forms of human activity. Consequently, the essential difference between language as a system of signs and language (*discours*) as an instrument of communication is blurred when the instrument and those who wield it are exclusively treated as "signs." [14]

Weimann's critique appears to be based on an appeal to empiricism, but its force is not, in fact, dependent on a positivistic use of counterexamples. It rests on the observation that Goldmann's homologous "levels" bear only a symbolic relation to one another. One structure stands as the model for another on the sole justification of considering them as being "of the same type." What weakens this kind of analysis is, not the claim that the two levels are not of the same type, but the recognition that no *discursive* relation is established whereby the model is transformed into the copy by a particular productive process at a particular time. A map, by one way of judging, may appear to resemble the territory it represents; by another way, it may show no resemblance at all. But whatever criteria we adopt, the decision about likeness and difference cannot offer an account of how and when and why the map was produced. Similarly, theories that are symmetrical and symbolic can never explain the discursive and complementary processes whereby an ideological entity is produced in certain material circumstances. When Marx maintains that life determines consciousness, he asserts a discursive relationship, and the gap or ambiguity in his formulation is a gap in discursive logic.

Another perspective from which to clarify the theoretical problem at stake here is that of Althusser. Symbolic theories of correspondence or homology always assume what Althusser calls a Hegelian conception of historical time. Since for Hegel all parts of a historical whole embody the Idea which is the essence of that whole, historical time must perforce be a "homogeneous continuity." Thus, for any given historical "present," the state of Idea that governs that present also governs all parts of the whole equally. We need only call that Idea by a name like *système de fonctions* and we have the structuralist version of Hegelian historiography. In Althusser's terms, "the Hegelian whole has a type of unity in which each element of the whole, whether a material or economic determination, a political institution or a religious, artistic or philosophical form, is never anything more than the presence of the concept with itself at a historically determined moment."[15] Such a moment Althusser calls an "essential section" of the historical continuum. Within such a section, whether it is an absolute present or a "historical period," the relations among economic, political, religious, artistic, or philosophical realities are fixed in concepts of symbolic equivalence. Changes in the relations among these different levels or "instances" of the whole lie beyond the Hegelian analysis and require a discursive articulation that Althusser identifies as Marxist: "As a first approximation, we can argue from the specific structure of the Marxist whole that it is no longer possible to think the process of the development of the different levels of the whole *in the same historical time.*"[16] Each of these levels retains its own characteristic temporal articulation and can be considered as "relatively autonomous" within the social totality. Politics, philosophy, art, science—all have their peculiar "time and history," and each of these continua is "punctuated in a specific way" according to "peculiar rhythms." Nevertheless, to say this is not, for Althusser, to assert the independence of these levels from the social totality. Indeed, "the specificity of each of these times and of each of these histories—in other words their relative autonomy and independence—is based on a certain type of articulation in the whole, and therefore on a certain type of dependence with respect to the whole."[17]

The observation of differential histories is not, of course, new with Althusser. Historians like Braudel and Febvre, art historians like George Kubler, and literary scholars like Claudio Guillen and F. P. Pickering have in different ways exploited the opportunities of a historiography based on the relative autonomy of differential time schemes.[18] What Althusser demands that these historians do not provide is the realization and articulation of dependence as a dialectical completion of the concept of independence: "we cannot be satisfied, as the best historians so often are today, by observing the existence of different times and rhythms, without relating them to the concept of their difference, i.e., to the typical dependence which establishes them in the articulation of the levels of the whole."[19]

In symbolic theories, relative independence is ignored in favor of a dependence that is paradigmatic for all elements of the superstructure. Althusser restores relative independence by making the mode of dependence different in different instances and by demanding a discursive historiography of the whole. Accordingly, he maintains that Marx's "theoretical revolution" was to attempt to think a differentiated or structured "effectivity of the whole on its parts."[20] To say, therefore, that the history of philosophy displays a relative independence of the history of economic relations is not to state an eternal truth about history that can be applied homologistically to relations between the economic base and politics, religion, art, or other distinct levels. The distinctness itself calls for historical explanation: "The history of philosophy . . . is not an independent history by divine right: the right of this history to exist as a specific history is determined by the articulating relations, i.e., relations of relative effectivity, which exist within the whole."[21] The task of the historian is, therefore, to discover just what relations articulate the ever-changing position of a particular history within a whole constituted by other histories with other rhythms and punctuations. Hence, to return to Marx's "life determines consciousness," we shall no longer search for a single explanation of "determines." "Life" in the sense of a social totality will exert a differential and changing "effectivity" on different forms of consciousness, thereby dialectically changing those forms. If the particular forms are literary, the literary historian will discover which temporal interactions within the structure of the social whole function in the production of literary works at a given "conjuncture," to use Althusser's term. As the historian perceives and specifies change in literary structures, the relations between structure and content and the dynamic interactions of genres, he will at the same time see shifts in the relevant intersections of the literary instance and other instances within the cultural whole. The articulation of these relations, however incomplete, will constitute the discursively historical explanation of literary change that symbolic theories of reflection or homology cannot provide.

Althusser's concept of a social whole that is at once in motion and structured has encountered its own difficulties, though not, I think, difficulties of the magnitude of those I have already discussed. Historians like E. P. Thompson have objected to Althusser's attacks on empiricism, and Thompson has been especially acerbic in rejecting Althusser's "structure" as an ideal construct having little to do with material history.[22] This is not the place to discuss and evaluate Thompson's critique in detail, but his consciousness of the machinelike quality of such models can help us to sharpen our awareness of what we, as literary historians, might do. Althusser's "structure," as well as the method suggested here, does imply, if not an essential Hegelian Idea, at least a substantial continuity pervading the social whole. Like the structuralists,

Althusser must assume that the interacting elements remain, at some level of generalization, entities "of the same type." One way of satisfying this demand is to say that all of the "instances" within the changing structure of the whole are, at base, processes of production. This once again raises the question of whether material production and ideological production can be considered as instances "of the same type." To consider them as essentially different is to annihilate the Althusserian concept of dependence, which we have seen to be dialectically necessary to the concept of relative autonomy. To open the ontological gap between material and ideological production is to condemn ourselves to seeking symbolic correspondences. In an earlier theoretical discussion of literary innovation, I have tried to show how such a gap fragments our account of the fundamental process whereby literary change takes place.[23] If we say that the transition between the writer's confrontation with existing texts and his production of a new kind of text includes a wholly psychological "moment of inspiration," or "displacement," we can offer no discursive account of literary innovation or change. The assumed divisions between ideology and materiality, mind and matter, the self and the other, the individual and the collective all preclude the continuity necessary to discursive history on the Althusserian model. These divisions inevitably lead to symbolic accounts of "reflection" or "homology" aimed at relating metaphorically or paradigmatically realms too alien from one another to interact directly in space and time. Critiques like Althusser's—or Wittgenstein's, in his attack on the theory of mental images—attempt to emplace a single complex human continuity of activity as the foundation of historical understanding.

Later, I will take the opportunity to discuss other challenges to the dualistic Cartesian epistemology, challenges compatible with Marxism but launched from the positions of cybernetics and communications theory. For now, however, I want to point out that Marxists themselves, especially those concerned with literary history, have begun to see the classic Marxist concepts of ideology and material production in new ways.

Raymond Williams, in *Marxism and Literature,* acknowledges the prestige of the hierarchy that separates ideology from material reality in order to subordinate the former within the concept of superstructure. But he attributes the strictest form of this separation to the Marx of *The German Ideology* and insists that the "naive dualism of 'mechanical materialism,' in which the idealist separation of 'ideas' and 'material reality' " predominates, "has in repetition been disastrous."[24] Williams traces this dualism to the distinction, emerging in strength in the eighteenth century, between society and culture. In a positive sense, this distinction allowed a growing awareness of the importance of material history—one from which Marx clearly profited. The problem lay in sustaining the separation between the "cultural" and the material: "Instead of making cultural history material, which was the next radical move, it was made dependent, secondary, 'superstructural:' a realm of 'mere' ideas, beliefs, arts, customs, determined by the basic material history."[25] In Williams's reading, the early Marx both tempts us to this "naive dualism" and at the same time offers an "emphasis on consciousness as inseparable from conscious existence, and then on conscious existence as inseparable from material social processes."[26] As evidence that Marx increasingly favored this holistic view of ideology and material production, Williams cites the following passage from *Capital:* "We presuppose labour in a form that stamps it as exclusively human. . . . What distinguishes the worst architect from the best of bees is this, that the architect raises his structure in imagination before he erects it in reality. At the end of every labour-process, we get a result that already existed in the imagination of the labourer at its commencement."[27] The point of this analysis to Williams, and the main claim of his book, is that "consciousness is seen from the beginning as part of the human material social process, and its products in 'ideas' are then as much part of this process as material products themselves. This, centrally, was the thrust of Marx's whole argument."[28] The last claim may be an overstatement, but Williams is right, I think, in seeing the advantages of treating ideology as part of material praxis and not as a static code apart from that vital activity.

Robert Weimann has attacked structuralist historiography for turning material reality into an ideal "system of signs," and Goldmann himself rejected the reflectionist reduction of formal systems

of signification, like novels, to their material "content." But both
the structuralist view and the one it attacks accept the distinction between form and content, between the architect's "structure in imagination" and the building he builds. Weimann challenges the split but
provides no theoretical alternative. Williams begins in a position very
close to Weimann's but furnishes the conceptual tool to effect the
"inseparability" that he finds asserted in Marx. That tool is an account of language as constitutive of both consciousness and material social existence. In his chapter on language, Williams, like Weimann, rejects the structuralist concept of language as an abstract
static system of signs and insists that it is first a social activity:

> Signification, the social creation of meanings through the use of formal
> signs, is then a practical material activity: it is indeed, literally, a means of
> production. It is a specific form of that practical consciousness which is
> inseparable from all social material activity. It is not, as formalism would
> make it, and as the idealist theory of expression had from the beginning
> assumed, an operation of and within "consciousness," which then becomes
> a state or a process separated, *a priori,* from social material activity. It is,
> on the contrary, at once a distinctive material process—the making of
> *signs*—and, in the central quality of its distinctiveness as practical con-
> sciousness, is involved from the beginning in all other human social and
> material activity.[29]

Williams does not deny the systematic nature of language; he
merely denies its static separateness, places it in motion as a part
of social process. This movement allows us, with Jameson, to
accept the notion that the social infrastructure is a sign system or,
with Althusser, to say that the social whole is a structure. Both
semiotic system and social structure, in the work of these writers,
are constitutive of social praxis and as such change in their most
fundamental systemic relationship as the productive activity of
women and men changes.

III

My account so far has been of a series of theoretical moments,
an artificial and simplified sequence to be sure. Its purpose has been
to bring us back to the point at which we began: the question of

what we mean when we say that Browning and his contemporaries produced the dramatic monologue. At the least, I think we can dispense with the formulation that says that the production of books is a material process while the production of dramatic monologues is an ideal one. Like Marx's architect, the poet's imaginative conception, constituted in language (not the final wording of the poems), is as much a part of the material production of his book as the setting of type, which is also conceived linguistically as an inseparable part of the activity of the typesetter. Hence there are no books without the constitutive imagined conception of what kind of books they are to be. This is the same as saying that any account of the production of literary works must include an explanation of why the writer came to select, modify, or invent the literary genres in which he wrote. Such an explanation will require clarity about the nature of literary productivity, a clarity that in turn must recognize language as both a process of production and the product itself, as at once a never-ending activity of signification and a collection of inscribed signs to be described and made intelligible. A book like this one needs, therefore, to adopt a dialectical alternation between attention to the discursive historical relations through which poems of certain kinds come into being and attention to the structures and meanings of the poems themselves. The concept needed to make this dialectical movement a theoretical unity is that of the poetic subject-in-language, continuously constituting and locating itself through the social activity of sign-making.

Much post-Saussurian theory posits or implies the existence of a transcendent subject, a kind of essential human mind that enters into an available system of signifying rules and produces discourse in accordance with these rules. However constrained, this subject remains a discrete individual or self that exists prior to its "expressions" in a language that is other than itself. In the article I alluded to earlier, I argued that for literary history to be written coherently, this transcendent subject must be replaced by one that is only constituted in the process of signifying. At that time, I found the necessary formulation of subjectivity in the work of Jacques Lacan. Lacan attacked the notion that the bivalent character of the

Saussurian sign meant that the linguistic signifier arbitrarily linked onto a transcendent signified that preexisted in the subject as a pure concept. Neither the signifier nor the signified resides as a static entity. Rather, signification involves a chain of signifiers such that the signified is always a previous signifier somewhere in the chain. As such the signified is demystified, stripped of its transcendence, as is the subject that is constituted by this process of signification. Language, in this view, is always becoming something other than itself, and the subject is no longer a transcendent and self-contained individual. Indeed, the subject is constantly being created from what Lacan calls the "discourse of the other":

> All that is language is lent from this otherness and this is why the subject is always a fading thing that runs under the chain of signifiers. For the definition of a signifier is that it represents a subject not for another subject but for another signifier. This is the only definition possible of the signifier as different from the sign. The sign is something that represents something for somebody, but the signifier is something that represents a subject for another signifier. The consequence is that the subject disappears . . . while under the second signifier appears what is called meaning or signification; and then in sequence the other signifiers appear and other significations. [30]

Already, a concept that opposes diachronic production to synchronic structure has been replaced by one that relates only different moments of social production. Here we can see the potential for resolving the opposition between *langue* and *parole,* or between the structured otherness of language and the immediate process of its enunciation. When I first wrote on literary innovation, I could already see the power of Lacan's theoretical breakthrough for challenging the division between self and other that had encumbered attempts to give a coherent account of literary change. Since then, these opportunities have been extended beyond the problem of innovative production. The Lacanian theory of the subject has now been used, by Rosalind Coward and John Ellis, as a model, not only for incorporating ideological production as material process, but for understanding how language can be both process and product. Salvaging Saussure to some degree, Coward and Ellis begin where Williams and Weimann leave off, while at the same time seeing that structuralist divisions between *langue* and *parole* or structure and product imply a transcendent subject. Their alternative echoes Lacan: "The concept of productivity implies that it is the play of difference of the signifying chain that produces signifieds; the fixing of this relation is provided by the positionality of the speaking subject, a subject who is produced in this movement of productivity. Man is constructed in the symbol, and is not pre-given or transcendent."[31]

This theoretical base allows Coward and Ellis to affirm that ideology—because it is the linguistic production of a certain subject—"is a material force."[32] In this, they align with Williams, Weimann, and Althusser, but they also are able to take important steps beyond the positions of these theorists. Departing from some traditional Marxist interpretations, Coward and Ellis deny that ideology is merely a collection of ideas and representations that distort social and economic reality in the interest of a dominant class. Instead, ideology, as a part of the material relations of production, constructs a certain subject and gives that subject a position from which coherent representations of reality are intelligible. For Marxism, the essence of the social totality is contradiction, and it is the business of ideology to obscure contradiction and make society as it is seem "natural." But Coward and Ellis insist that ideology does this, not just by constructing false representations of a naturalized social world, but also by introducing this "natural" homogeneity into a subject that takes up the position of a "self" or of the unitary (which is to say noncontradictory) "individual." Marx himself showed in *The German Ideology* the absolute interdependence of the ideology of bourgeois democracy and that of a unitary subject, an interdependence that makes both the social whole and the individual appear homogeneous but that results in contradiction: "Theoretical communists . . . alone have discovered that throughout history the 'general interest' is created by individuals who are defined as 'private persons.' They know that this contradiction is only a seeming one because one side of it, the so-called 'general' is constantly being produced by the other side, private interest, and by no means opposes the latter as an independent force with an independent history."[33] The contradiction between the interest of the collective and that of the individual disappears only when it is realized that neither the collective nor the individual is complete and homogeneous in itself. The concept necessary to negate this ideological representation is that of class interest. Class interest fragments the "general" collective of democratic society, and it renders the so-called private person merely a part of a class, now called "private interest." Hence the dominant class of capitalists (private interest) produces, not only the myth of "the people" or the general interest, but also its necessary contradictory antithesis, the myth of the "private person." In this and other similar passages, then, Marx shows how ideology constructs both a representation of the social totality and a subjective position from which that representation appears natural. The subject, by such a formulation, represents itself as unitary and homogeneous while in fact incorporating into itself an irresolvable contradiction, which is precisely *not* a contradiction between the individual and the general.

We can perhaps most easily see this contradiction by examining what Wittgenstein would call the "grammar" of the phrase "the individual." In a democratic grammar, we use "the individual" to mean both a person and a class: "Justice Smith is the individual on the Court most deeply committed to protecting the rights of the individual." In this sentence, the contradiction of the individual comes close to being a formal paradox in the sense Russell defined when he showed that paradox occurs when a class is taken to be a member of itself. In our sentence, "the individual" is a class of which "the individual" is necessarily a member. Our use of the phrase in this way both manifests and obscures a contradiction built into the fabric of all capitalist democracies.

The critical linkage in Coward and Ellis's sophisticated and powerful argument is the perception that the subject in modern democracies is constituted as an apparent coherent homogeneity and at the same time as an inevitable structure of contradiction. This subject can, in fact, be described in this way from a number of different perspectives. The most familiar—and the one Marx himself offers us—is the social perspective of ideology. Coward and Ellis also show, from the point of view of psychoanalysis—Lacan's psychoanalysis in particular—how the conscious image of homogeneous "identity" in which the subject locates itself gives way to contradiction through the antithetical working of the unconscious. The subject's unitary conception of itself becomes, then, what Lacan calls "imaginary":

> The subject in ideology has a consistency which rests on an imaginary identification of self: this is simultaneously a recognition (since it provides subject-ivity, enables the subject to act), and a misrecognition (a recognition which involves a representation in relation to forms which include the work of ideology). The consistent subject is the place to which the representations of ideology are directed: Duty, Morality, and Law all depend on this category of subject for their functioning, and all contribute as institutions to its production. The individual thus lives his subject-ion to social structures as a consistent subject-ivity, an imaginary wholeness. Ideologies set in place the individual as though he were the subject: the individual produces himself in this imaginary wholeness, this imaginary reflection of himself as the author of his actions.[34]

The psychoanalytic formulation also becomes, again through Lacan's theory of subjectivity, a linguistic or semiotic formulation that is necessary to complete the social formulation as well as to explain it discursively. It is only the beginning of an explanation to say that "in bourgeois ideology, a subject can represent itself as free, homogeneous and responsible for its actions because the social relations of capitalism are exchange-relations. For the social practice of wage labour to continue, these exchange-relations must presuppose a free subject."[35] What remains is to describe how the subject learns to construct itself as a free individual, and for this task, Coward and Ellis turn to the processes of ego formation within the bourgeois familial structure, processes that, in turn, involve the subject's inscription into the "symbolic order" of language.

Coward and Ellis try to show "how the contradictory processes of the individual subject are themselves constituted."[36] To summarize briefly their long chapter on Lacan would require disastrous oversimplification, but for present purposes, I think it will do to say that language, in their analysis, has two distinct roles. The first

is an ideological role: to create and position the subject as a homo-
genous totality. This role involves language as a conscious process
of communication:

> Ideological representations fix the category of subject as a closure, a struc-
> tural limit. The subject is constituted of, and in, contradiction, but social-
> ity necessitates that there should be a subject in order that any predication,
> and therefore communication, can take place. This (necessary) subject of
> sociality only ever appears in a specific ideological formation, that is it
> appears as the fixed relation of the subject to what it predicates, and this
> relation must necessarily be ideological. [37]

Over against this conscious, social role of language, there arises a
second role, hinted at in the passage on ideology. This is the constitutive role, which depends, not on the horizontal closure of
predication, but on the vertical openness of signification itself, the
continual "sliding" of signifiers in time. This is the process indicated by the passage I quoted from Lacan in which signification is
seen as a continual disappearing and incomplete reconstituting of
the subject. On this view the subject is always heterogeneous, at
once a self and an other by virtue of the dual nature of the sign
itself. And because the signified can only be a displaced signifier—
never a transcendent and absolute signified—the subject is always
an incomplete process rather than an identity as the ideological
position of the subject-in-the-sentence would suggest. In social
and economic terms, this subject that is both a self (the "I" in the
sentence) and an other (the symbolic relations that are language)
is also, as a transformation of the same contradiction, both a "force
of production" and part of a system called "the relations of production." This is, of course, the central contradiction or conflict
in the Marxist analysis of non-Communist societies. For the psychological dimension, Coward and Ellis turn to Lacan:

> In Lacan, this construction [of the subject-in-language] is a complex
> matter, since it involves a notion of the "splitting," or separation, of the
> subject: first from its sense of continuum with the mother's body; then
> with the illusory identity and totality of the ideal ego of the mirror stage;
> and finally a separation by which the subject finds itself a place in sym-

bolisation. It is this construction which creates the subject and the unconscious, and involves imaginary and symbolic relations.[38]

For Julia Kristeva, this splitting of the subject out into the symbolic (ideological, grammatical, logical, paternal) mode of language does not wholly obliterate or displace the more primitive place of meaning, which she calls *chora* or receptacle or mother. Thus, again, the subject remains divided or heterogeneous, constituted in contradiction. In Kristeva, however, we find a further important claim: that in poetic language, the contradictions embodied in a given social and family structure can be displayed, brought to consciousness. This amounts to saying that in poetic expression, ideology can be recognized for what it is along with the contradictions that lie beneath its apparent representations of homogeneity.[39]

Kristeva's claim raises once again the possibility of a relative autonomy for a particular instance of ideology, in this case, the literary. The relative autonomy of poetry would reside in its capacity both to retain and to defamiliarize the ideological constraints of its language. This defamiliarization is no more the representation of an object that we find in the accounts of the Russian formalists than ideology is a collection of "ideas about" the objective world. Poetry *may* defamiliarize objective or social reality, but its prior opportunity is to defamiliarize the subject itself. This is, of course, not something that poetry *must* do; the poem may well be produced as merely an explicit repetition of the ideology of consistency. This is the case, for example, with realist narrative, which according to Coward and Ellis, positions both the narrator and the reader as subjectivities for which action appears as naturally coherent and finally complete. Semiotically, this means that the relation between the signifier and signified seems neither arbitrary nor historically determined but fixed, natural, and therefore transcendent. By contrast, a work like Balzac's *Sarrasine,* as analyzed by Barthes in *S/Z,* "disturbs the positionalities upon which the representations of bourgeois society depend."[40] *Sarrasine* "calls attention to the productivity of [its] language,"[41] a productivity that involves the constant fragmentation, redistribution, and recombination of prior texts, both social and literary, that Kristeva calls "intertextuality." The subject positioned by this kind of language production is necessarily heterogeneous and constituted in conflict. The prior texts that supply its signifieds are stripped of their own ideological consistency and coherence; the text becomes no longer a boundaried product but a productive process of subjective defamiliarization.

The ideological positions available for locating subjectivity will be, at any given temporal conjuncture, multiple. They may be named with terms such as "author," "narrator," "singer," "speaker," "character," "persona," "interlocutor," "auditor," "actor," or "reader." Idealist critics, those whose role is to preserve ideological consistency and suppress contradiction, adopt whenever possible one of these subjective positions and ascribe coherent if differential "intentionalities" to whatever others appear either "in" or as the source of the work. An interpreter like Kristeva, on the other hand, finds within the convention of the novel's narrator, one who both narrates and cites, a conflict between the subjective positions of "actor in" and "auditor of" the fiction. [42]

Kristeva's work on the novel lies deeply in debt to the theories of "novelistic discourse" proposed by M. M. Bakhtin. [43] These two writers together might well help us to understand the relation between the novel as a major literary form in the nineteenth century and the emergence of the dramatic monologue as a minor but important form during the same period. For now, however, I shall merely point out that Kristeva's splitting of the novelistic subject presents the novel as a genre that retains the unitary position of completed intelligibility (author or reader) while it also reveals, in the convention of the narrator, the contradictions that lie beneath that ideological unity. This presentation of a dialectic between intelligible meaning and contradiction is the aim of interpretation in the chapters that follow. This purpose holds both at the level of genre (where Browning and his contemporaries discover contradiction underlying the identification of the author of a poem as a speaking subject) and in the interpretation of individual works. In the dramatic monologue, we shall find a form designed to give full force to the ideological desire for subjective unity while it denies, in its formal conventions, the possibility of fulfilling such a desire.

My explanation of how the monologue is produced will include some attention to contradictions embodied in language and style, some to the organization of social content, and finally, in chapter 6, an account of how these two axes intersect with a third, the psychoanalytic axis.

The interactions of these allogenic forces do not, of course, produce the dramatic monologue ex nihilo. Its intertextuality is also literary, and any satisfactory explanation of the form's specificity must see it as a narrowly defined Victorian transformation of Romantic literary strategies. Romantic poets confront the conflict between the notion of a divided subject and the desire for unity as directly as Victorian poets do, but their poetic responses are different. We need at least to begin to indicate what differentiates the Victorian poem from the Romantic poem in order to initiate the critical task of explanation.

IV

In *Natural Supernaturalism,* M. H. Abrams describes a set of concepts that, he says, "had wide currency in the age of Wordsworth and Coleridge":

> . . . the claim that man, who was once well, is now ill, and that at the core of the modern malaise lies his fragmentation, estrangement, or (in the most highly charged of these parallel terms) "alienation." The individual (so runs the familiar analysis) has become radically split in three main aspects. He is divided within himself, he is divided from other men, and he is divided from his environment; his only hope for recovery (for those writers who hold out hope) is to find the way to a reintegration which will restore his unity with himself, his community with his fellow men, and his companionability with an alien and hostile outer world.[44]

For the breakdown of any organic system, we might say there are two kinds of "restorations": replacements and repairs. For the Romantic poet, the first of these options most often seems the appropriate one. More modestly, the Victorians begin to experiment with the second. The Romantic seeks to reveal a plane of reality on which a humanly available wholeness is yet to be discovered. He facilitates a sublime breakthrough to a felt unity of matter and spirit. The open-ended and partial quality of alienated life in social time is superseded by a poetic reality that at least intimates the integration and closure that appear so lacking in post-Enlightenment Europe. This restoration of lost unity, along with the formal subjective consistency of the "lyric speaker" in Romantic poems, is an object of Romantic faith. But it is also conceived as a product. The poet makes something that simulates the unity of man and man, man and himself, or man and his environment, and the discrete closure of that product sharply distinguishes it from the lived reality it is designed to transform. In the words of Coleridge, "the common end of all *narrative,* nay, of *all,* Poems is . . . to make those events, which in real or imagined History move on in a *strait* Line, assume to our Understandings a *circular* motion— the snake with its Tail in its Mouth."[45] The circle and the line: one a whole, the other an open fragment, part of an indefinitely longer line, which is a broken one. The poem that attempts to be like "the snake with its Tail in its Mouth," will, of course, be concerned with formal symmetries, with consistency of medium, and with plausible closure. Such closure in the signifier may also be achieved only at the cost of exploding the coherence of other texts or genres, as when Keats builds the formal order of his great odes from the ruins of the Shakespearean sonnet, or as when Shelley, in *Prometheus Unbound,* creates the conditions for an objective world redeemed only to disturb radically, in act 4, the subjective position from which that world might be intelligible. But these are the contradictions and need their own analysis. The Romantic poem's ideological goal remains the sublime synthesis: for the mind, that poem will replace, as well as transform, the life it finds.

The other alternative, the non-Romantic one, is to repair the ragged edges of human fragmentation by reattaching whatever connective tissue can be preserved. Such a project will be more experimental. It will endeavor, not to simulate a complete whole, but to rationalize the relations among fragments. It will not aspire to a breakthrough to a higher plane of reality. Its medium, though distinct, will not be discontinuous with the stuff of that "strait Line" which is "real or imagined History." The poet who would pursue this kind of remedy will create not so much a well-boundaried product as an open-ended process, a process of speech refastening broken lines of interconnection between the alienated individual, his inner responding "self," other human centers, and even his natural environment.

The Victorian poet too has an ideological project that he can never entirely ignore or deny, however well he may acknowledge its contradictions. In a writer like Browning, we shall find, not only the desire for reconnection and disalienation, but the competing desire for individual autonomy as well. Gloomy poems like "Andrea del Sarto" or "Any Wife to Any Husband" or Tennyson's "Tithonus" have more to say about continuities and connections irrevocably lost than about successful "repairs." "Fra Lippo Lippi," on the other hand, presents an example of the apparently successful project of a moment's disalienation for a powerful individual. Whatever the particular instance, however, the problem remains the same: the desire for coherence in the system of social and natural ties arises only in concert with the desire for the individual autonomy, or "freedom," of the speaking subject, and the two stand in a relation of radical contradiction.

The ideological goal of the Victorian dramatic monologue is a transformation of that of the Romantic lyric. Its concept of homogeneity has shifted from one of wholeness to one of continuity. As the Romantic lyric perpetuates the illusion of discretely boundaried discourse, the dramatic monologue instantiates an open-ended discourse that only invokes traditional poetic devices of symmetry and closure ironically, in order to deny their traditional effects. The monologue is always, among other things, a deictic gesture toward the fading and uncertain vistas of a linear dimension of time and speech. Like Rabbi Ben Ezra, it seems to ask its reader to "grow old along with me!" Each poem seems to emerge without interruption out of a past that has been long in the unfolding. But that past has no palpable reality: it is ephemeral and lost. Poetically, within the monologue's convention, it cannot be represented. The poem itself may seem a late or final moment in a long sequence, but the sudden boundary that is the poem's beginning can often only express the faint desire for continuity:

No more wine? then we'll push back chairs and talk.
A final glass for me, though: cool i' faith!
We ought to have our Abbey back, you see.

("Bishop Blougram's Apology," 1–3)

Similarly, many monologues stretch the attention forward into a future beyond the moment of the text. Here too there is often a kind of plaintive eagerness:

Well, I could never write a verse,—could you?
Let's to the Prado and make the most of time.

("How it Strikes a Contemporary," 114–15)

Or, perhaps more familiarly,

Your hand, sir, and good-bye: no lights, no lights!
The street's hushed, and I know my own way back,
Don't fear me! There's the gray beginning. Zooks!

("Fra Lippo Lippi," 390–92)

Endings that seem to be beginnings and beginnings that conclude long conversations or chains of events—these are important parts of Browning's material for dramatic monologues, and one of my aims in these pages is to explain the formal innovations that result in these impressions. We shall see that they are far more tightly woven into the fabric of Browning's language and his art than a glance at first and final lines can show us now.

If Browning's monologues imply space-time continuities between the poem's moment and moments past and present that lie beyond the discourse of the text, they also generate a seamless transition between the language of speech and the language of poetry. Romantic theorists like Wordsworth, Coleridge, and Shelley had demanded that the poet choose between an artificial poetic language and the natural language of men. The dramatic monologue calls into question the antithesis behind the choice as it interweaves the most arbitrary assortment of formal verse gimmicks and conventions with the most colloquial and casual diction and speech rhythms. Here in "Saul," for example, the contrivance of anapestic couplets appears unconnected to any expressive purpose or generic constraint, yet Browning makes it seem a natural vehicle for direct Anglo-Saxon speech:

> I have gone the whole round of creation: I saw and I spoke:
> I, a work of God's hands for that purpose, received in
> my brain
> And pronounced on the rest of his handwork—returned
> him again
> His creation's approval or censure: I spoke as I saw:
> I report, as a man may of God's work—all's love, yet
> all's law.
>
> "Saul," 238-42)

As I shall argue at length in chapter 4, Browning posits a traditionally observed incompatibility between speech and poetic artifice in order to balance against it a seamless integration. Wordsworth had recognized in the poet's confinement within a specialized "poetic" idiom an alienating capitulation to the division of labor as a mode of social existence. His remedy was to release the poet—or lyrical subject—to speak a universal and homogeneous langauge that transcends time, place, and class. This is the extreme idealist solution. Coleridge well understood that Wordsworth's preferred poetic language is not the language of real peasants; it is a language of abstract peasants, removed from the world of "fragmentation, dissociation, estrangement" of which Abrams writes in the passage I quoted earlier. Browning's response is to create a subjective center for a discourse in which the poetic idiom (the specialist's language) need not be alien to the general idiom of a particular time and place. And since his speakers often represent cultures far distant in time and geography, he also challenges other prevailing nineteenth-century estrangements: that of a runaway present from its cultural and political past as well as that of a rapidly developing England from distant and exotic places.

The broadest pressure of all of these effects comes from an insistent examination of the strengths and weaknesses of communication as a binding social force. How much of the world, Browning seems to ask, can be put back together again by discovering potential but unrealized continuities among moments, places, persons, sexes, races, and classes? To ask this question, Browning experiments with a new set of poetic conventions. I can only call these conventions tentative devices of reciprocity and exchange. The simplest example might be just a question. Literature is, of course, full of questions, but in the dramatic monologue, the question is directed toward an interlocutor whose response, by the rules of the genre, cannot be heard. Hence the question raises the problem of reciprocity, but our attention is kept on the interrogative itself. To judge its fitness to complete a circuit, we must determine whether the possible answers that the interlocutor might give can be interpreted adequately by the questioner, indeed, what the importance of questioning per se is in the speaker's psyche. Questions are only one of the devices of reciprocity and subjective exchange, but all of them, as they help constitute the dramatic monologue, concentrate poetic energy on the fragility and potential contradictions of communication. They ask whether, in a given set of circumstances, networks of understanding and cooperation can be created or repaired.

In all of this, the individual speakers of the poems furnish hypothetical centers of being-in-language. But the language in which they have their being always fuses them with that which is outside themselves—other persons, other times, other cultures. The dramatic monologue, more perhaps than any other literary form, challenges the immense prestige of the Cartesian dualism of the self and the other. While it exclusively displays the unique individual, it allows him or her to exist only as an indissoluble part of something that is not himself or herself and thereby lays siege to the sovereignty of the *Cogito* as a basis for subjectivity. For Browning, the relation signified by "part of" is not a Romantic relation in which the ideal whole is manifest in the real individual; it is a relation entirely within the linear human history that Coleridge so emphatically contrasted with poetry. That which the self is part of is not a whole at all, but a kind of open system, "shading off" into an indefinite earthly distance. Accepting the integrity of the individual, the Romantic poet proclaims the impossible ambition: "I am adrift in the world alone, and I must have faith or vision enough to know that I am part of a great oneness." The Victorian might answer, "You were never alone. Because you insist on the sovereignty of the self, you cannot acknowledge those infinitely many tendrils that bind you to the other, bind you so tightly that the boundaries of your individuality are no more than dispensable metaphysical fictions. The fear of being adrift and estranged is really a wish that you might be sufficient unto yourself, the 'captain of your soul.' What you really fear is the brutal intimacy that the modern world brings on you with ever greater insistence, and in that fear you are the true man of your age." To Browning, modern individuals, including the Romantic poet, *create* their alienation as a wish fulfillment, as a division of labor, a contradictory self-reification. Their estrangement is not antithetical but identical to the metaphysical commodity that is the Romantic myth of wholeness. The vaguely located speaker of *Pauline* recalls a past in which Romantic abstraction seemed to relieve a real agony of being alone:

> And I was lonely, far from woods and fields,
> And amid dullest sights, who should be loose
> As a stag; yet I was full of bliss, who lived
> With Plato and who had the key to life:
>
> (*Pauline*, 433–36)

But even in the 1830s there was doubt that to be free and "loose / As a stag" and to seek the holistic "key to life" could be a lasting remedy. For Browning's fictional Romantic, the attempt led only to a more complete isolation:

> Oh, Pauline, I am ruined who believed
> That though my soul had floated from its sphere
> Of wild dominion into the dim orb
> Of self—that it was strong and free as ever!
> It has conformed itself to that dim orb,
> Reflecting all its shades and shapes, and now
> Must stay where it alone can be adored.
>
> (*Pauline*, 89–95)

Browning's leave-taking of Shelley (and probably of Wordsworth) in *Pauline* offers no alternative, either philosophically or formally, to the conformation of the soul to the "dim orb" of an ideal self. Still, the time was not far off when Browning, like Sordello, would confront the world of human interchange and posit a form of disalienation that is piecemeal and temporal. This does not mean that he discovered an image or a process to embody the wholeness, the internal consistency of the subject, that eluded the great Romantic visionaries. Unlike Sordello, he was able to invent forms of poetry as predicated communication, experimental discourses that could present powerful images of self-sufficiency only to torment them with irony, analysis, and the painful detailing of missed opportunities to reach beyond the self. Browning's speaking subject is always founded in contradiction. It is always both supremely idiosyncratic and inevitably incomplete, lacking a fixed identity. This is not just because that subject always requires a communicative process without closure to exist; it is also because the speaker of a dramatic monologue is always a fragmentary splitting off from the creative source of his or her discourse. This source, which, for reasons I shall explain later, I choose not to call "the poet," never appears as its *own* process of being-in-language. Conversely, the individual speaker can never wholly represent the unitary "author" of the poem. To be sure, the desire for such a subjective unity provides the occasion for the dramatic monologue, but even when the speaker is explicitly acknowledged as "R.B.," the desire is merely repeated, and the result is an addition, not a completion:

> Love, you saw me gather men and women,
> Live or dead or fashioned by my fancy,
> Enter each and all, and use their service,
> Speak from every mouth,—the speech, a poem,
> Hardly shall I tell my joys and sorrows,
> Hopes and fears, belief and disbelieving:
> I am mine and yours—the rest be all men's,
> Karshish, Cleon, Norbert and the fifty.
> Let me speak this once in my true person,
> Not as Lippo, Roland or Andrea,
> Though the fruit of speech be just this sentence:
> Pray you, look on these my men and women,
> Take and keep my fifty poems finished;

Where my heart lies, let my brain lie also!
Poor the speech; be how I speak, for all things.

(''One Word More,'' 129–43)

Browning here enters for a moment into the ideology of the ''true person,'' that fully realized self who speaks univocally in the absolute lyric present of the Romantic poem. Almost nostalgically, he wishes to write a poem different in kind from all of those monologues in which he speaks for a moment ''from each mouth'' but without hope of telling the whole range of his ''joys and sorrows, / Hopes and fears, belief and disbelieving.'' His poems, as fragments past and lost, have become public property—''all men's''— a condition he contrasts with ''mine and yours.'' But the meaning possessed as ''mine and yours'' is fully as divided as that which is ''all men's''; it requires an act of doubtful exchange between two. This duality is once again the fragile duality of the dramatic monologue. The unifying claims of bourgeois marriage may provide the incentive to attempt unitary intelligibility in actual material speech, but as soon as the subject begins to speak, as he believes, in his ''true person,'' he finds that the ''fruit of speech'' is just a sentence in which he offers once again his poems, ''these my men and women.'' The distinction between a discourse that is private and one that is ''all men's'' has collapsed. Despite the empty imperatives to ''let'' the true person speak—the heart and the brain unite—there can be only one ''poor'' speech ''for all things,'' a fractured speech (as the syntax of the last line dramatizes), which always requires the distinct responding other for its intelligibility to emerge.

This struggle between the subject as homogeneous ''true person'' and as heterogeneous and ''disappearing'' moment of speech or signification gives the dramatic monologue its form, a form that can never resolve the contradiction at its center. But it is precisely this uncommonly open access to the contradictions underlying the Victorian myth of the individual that gives the monologue its special value, its range of reference. Such poems, to be produced and consumed in the market, must, to some minimum standard, conform to the prevailing ideology's concept of what is real or natural speech.

At the same time, they must allow the contradictions to surface as they do not in the discourse of ideology. When Browning sacrifices coherence to contradiction too freely, his poems are rejected in the marketplace as obscure. The relations between signifier and signified are no longer fixed; they are continually being produced, and the subjectivity that produces new meanings must somehow be shared between "the reader" and "the author," a divided responsibility that Browning's readers often could not understand. The fact that Browning could not write poetry either to accept or reject the autonomy of the individual as constitutor of coherent meaning began in an inability either to accept or reject the influence of that supremely important and supremely "subjective" predecessor, Shelley. In the next chapter, I shall indicate how an early dramatic monologue arises out of conflicts with the Romantic model that are already present in *Pauline*. These conflicts involve constraints on the language of poetry that, in turn, adjust continually to the changing relation between the poet and the market for his poems. Chapter 2, therefore, will concern Shelley and Browning's departure from his example as a prehistory of the dramatic monologue.

The Genesis of the Monologue

I   For simplicity, it may be useful to locate the following rather complicated argument on two axes: an axis of literary production within a social totality and the "relatively autonomous" axis of literary history.[1] In order to make such an exposition as coherent as possible, I have decided on a few rather arbitrary constraints. First, I have limited my attention to Browning for the bulk of these chapters. This choice is artificial, since Browning did not invent the dramatic monologue by himself, and in chapter 7 I shall indicate briefly how other Victorian poets may be understood in light of my more detailed account of Browning. Second, in this chapter, I have represented the relation between poetry and the social totality as the relation between art and the market, or art and "the public." This is schematic and leaves open many questions about the complex intellectual and ideological dimensions of Victorian life. Some of these questions will be addressed in later chapters, but some will, for the time being, be left open. Third, I have begun by considering the monologue's emergence in literary history in light of Browning's relation to Shelley, his principal early poetic model. This choice temporarily neglects the fact that all poets define the kind of text they are writing, whether consciously or not, in relation to many other kinds of texts. The resulting intertextuality of any writer's work will involve both texts of kinds easily identified as "past," or anachronistic at the poet's own conjuncture (e.g., Shakespeare's tragedies for Browning), and texts with which the poet's own work competes or cooperates in the contemporary marketplace. An exhaustive account of the complex intertextuality of the dramatic monologue is not, however, the immediate goal of this book.[2]

For the present chapter, then, it has seemed necessary to simplify. The next section interprets an early Browning monologue as a response to perceived ideological dilemmas intrinsic to the Victorian marketplace. This is intended as only part of an explanation of the form's particular features. In section 3, I shall add to it a description of Browning's even earlier adherence to and departure from the lyricism of Shelley, a transitional process preceding the experiment of the monologue and best represented in *Pauline*. This process is, of course, also affected by social and material conditions, conditions that determine how a young poet positions himself in relation to his predecessor. Hence our discussion of the literary historical axis will return us to questions about how Browning was able to perceive his public as distinct from the ways in which Romantic poets perceived theirs. First, however, I want to concentrate on a fairly early example of the monologue in order to see what sorts of social forces the genre responds to.

II

At the end of the last chapter, I cited a passage from "One Word More" that points to an unresolved conflict between the desire to be a unified "true person" in speech and the inevitably fragmentary and interactional nature of speech itself. This conflict is not a new one for Browning in 1855; it has troubled him for many years by then, and it entails special problems for the artist. I think this conflict—or contradiction—provides both the seed and the structure of the dramatic monologue, and in 1845, Browning wrote a poem that, perhaps more than any other, articulates the logic by which the monologue came into being. "Pictor Ignotus" looks both backward through the agonies of *Pauline* to Shelley and forward to the mature monologues of *Men and Women* and beyond even to the sixties and *The Ring and the Book*. The simplest thread of this continuity is the issue, always deeply disturbing to Browning, of the artist's relation to his public. Is the value of the artist's product finally a private value established only within the "dim orb of self," or is it an exchange value, a value conferred only by the willingness of the community to commission or buy? The comfortable answer of the good democrat—"some judicious balance between the two"—merely obscures these opposing imperatives, and the agony of "Pictor Ignotus" may be read, on one level, as a denial of the real possibility of a negotiated resolution.[3]

"Pictor Ignotus" begins and ends as an assertion of personal freedom. The syntax of the poem as a whole culminates in the claim of all great individualists: "I chose my portion." The unknown painter can imagine only two impediments to his freedom of action: the infirmity of his own "soul" or "flesh" and the supernatural imposition of "fate." Both of these he discounts. His "soul springs up" at the thought of the action he has not taken, and he insists that his flesh would not have shrunk from "seconding" his soul. Similarly, he argues, "Never did fate forbid me, star by star / To outburst on your night with all my gift / Of fires from God . . ." What remains is the simple structure "I could have, but I chose not to."[4] But what is this "I," this free will that chooses to produce "monotonously" a product that no one will praise? That "I" begins the poem as a first person singular subject, immediately distinguished from both a second person and a third:

> I could have painted pictures like that youth's
> > Ye praise so.

"I," moreover, is a subject, nameless in itself, that locates its freedom of choice in the product it chooses to produce. The "Pictor Ignotus" is an Italian painter of the sixteenth century, a period in which the realist representations of "that youth"—doubtless Raphael—were rapidly displacing the conventional symbolic figuration of medieval religious painting. The unknown painter claims that he could have painted in the new mode, that he lacks neither the knowledge nor the skill

> > > to scan
> > The license and the limit, space and bound,
> > Allowed to truth made visible in man.

And, like that youth ye praise so, all I saw,
  Over the canvas could my hand have flung,
Each face obedient to its passion's law,
  Each passion clear proclaimed without a tongue.

This knowledge and this skill he summarizes as "all my gift / Of fires from God," and later he addresses God in recognition of the abundance of the gift:

O human faces, hath it spilt, my cup?
  What did ye give me that I have not saved?

Much of the ironic force—or, as I shall prefer, the contradictory force—of this poem seems to me to grow out of a hidden kernel within these lines, a kernel that is, in fact, a subtle pun. In short, I think the intertextuality of this particular poem concentrates here on a trace of the Gospel according to Saint Matthew and, in particular, on the parable of the talents.[5] It is the unknown painter's claim that he has chosen not to exercise his "talent," and that talent is a "gift" from God. He is, in other words, both free in his choice of "portion" and not free in that his choice can only be exercised with regard to that which is given by an other. In the gospel, the cruelty of this contradiction is made clear to the third servant only too late. A "talent" is, of course, both an intrinsic quality of a "true person" and, in its older meaning, an externality, a gold coin. The parable of the talents is worth quoting entire:

For the kingdom of heaven is as a man traveling into a far country, who called his own servants, and delivered unto them his goods. And unto one he gave five talents, to another two, and to another one; to every man according his several ability; and straightway took his journey. Then he that had received the five talents went and traded with the same, and made them other five talents. And likewise he that had received two he also gained other two. But he that had received one went and digged in the earth, and hid his lord's money. After a long time the lord of those servants cometh, and reckoneth with them. And so he that had received five talents came and brought other five talents, saying, Lord, thou deliveredst unto me five talents: behold, I have gained beside them five talents more. His lord said unto him, Well done, thou good and faithful servant: thou hast been faithful over a few things, I will make thee ruler over many things: enter thou into the joy of thy lord. He also that had received two talents came and said, Lord, thou deliveredst unto me two talents: behold, I have gained two other talents beside them. His lord said unto him, Well done, good and faithful servant; thou hast been faithful over a few things, I will make thee ruler over many things: enter thou into the joy of thy lord. Then he which had received the one talent came and said, Lord, I knew thee that thou art a hard man, reaping where thou hast not sown, and gathering where thou has not strewed: and I was afraid, and went and hid thy talent in the earth: lo, there thou hast that is thine. His lord answered and said unto him, Thou wicked and slothful servant, thou knewest that I reap where I sowed not, and gather where I have not strewed: thou oughtest therefore to have put my money to the exchangers, and then at my coming I should have received mine own with usury. Take therefore the talent from him, and give it unto him which hath ten talents. For unto every one that hath shall be given, and he shall have abundance: but from him that hath not shall be taken away even that which he hath. And cast ye the unprofitable servant into outer darkness: there shall be weeping and gnashing of teeth.[6]

The gospel's ambivalence toward active and passive paths to salvation and toward money and wealth runs deep. Ruthless usury may serve as a metaphor for entry into the kingdom of heaven, while elsewhere, "It is easier for a camel to go through the eye of a needle, than for a rich man to enter into the kingdom of God." Browning's Pictor Ignotus appears as a kind of recapitulation of the wicked and slothful servant. If God has given him the talents that he claims—the vision of real human faces and passions—his only response has been to keep them quietly to himself: "What did ye give me that I have not saved?" But what does the shadow text of Matthew make of the poem? The monologue in no way raises the religious issue of the speaker's salvation. Is Browning merely telling us that the unknown painter is either despicable or pitiable for not having committed his talents to action? Does the poem trivialize the gospel by casting into the outer darkness of the world's forgetting anyone too sensitive or too cowardly to risk innovation? I find the poem, like the gospel, much more complicated and difficult to interpret than this. If the parable of the talents institutes a troubling compatibility between assuring one's own fate and oppressing others through usury, Browning's poem foregrounds the incompatibility between maintaining the integrity of the self and submitting that self to the exchange values of trade.

The difference between the vexations appropriate to the gospel and those appropriate to the poem lies in the two terms of the pun on "talents." When talents are coins, external to the self, as in the gospel, the problem lies in equating the riches of the world with the riches of the soul or of heaven. When talents are internal, qualities of the individual himself, the problem lies in the fact that, to preserve a distinct identity long enough to acquire a name—to be "known"—requires an external splitting off of a part of one's self (one's talents) in the form of a product. To be whole is to be known as such, but to be known, one must become fragmented or self-estranged by placing one's internally constituted talents at risk. Semiotically, this contradiction is embodied in the very act of naming. My name points only to me; it signifies my discrete individuality. Yet, in Lacan's terms, it signifies this subject, not for itself and not for another subject, but for another signifier, other—many other—names that are not "mine." As such, my name is both a part of me and a part of "that otherness which is language." The first major contradiction of Browning's poem lies, then, in the fact that the Pictor Ignotus's very distinctness as an individual depends on his being "unknown" or unnamed—depends, indeed, on his not being "like" that youth whose name we know is Raphael. In brief, if he is unknown, he cannot be identified as the "one who speaks to us"; if he speaks to us "as himself," he cannot be unknown. He is an impossibility; he is a fiction. It must be someone else who authors his discourse.

All of these contradictions can be articulated only from within an ideology that renders the individual identity as discrete and homogeneous and that represses the alienation of the individual from the product that, through his talents, he produces. We can read the poem called "Pictor Ignotus" only as the product of someone's labor, but that someone cannot be the painter himself. The immediacy of the painter's own "presence" in the discourse is an illusion designed to mask the alienation of the product—the poem—from the "true person" that is its author. The gift of the poem's speaker is to proclaim human passion "without a tongue," but the gift of verbal proclaiming originates the poem itself and must reside in a hidden or "distant" source. That poetic gift is one that is at once invested and saved, exchanged and hoarded. Within the ideology of the parable of the talents, there is only a choice between investing and saving talents, and it is this essential choice that the Pictor Ignotus shares with the servants of the rich lord. In short, Browning's painter can have his existence only in a poem that in itself calls into question the intelligibility of the fundamental choice he makes. We may wish to ask what features of the painter's ideology will make his choice appear natural or intelligible but will also yield to questioning.

The painter's fantasy of his own success and fame takes its natualness in the text from another text, which offers a historical or "true" example. That text is Vasari's *Lives of the Painters* where, in the "Life of Cimabue," Vasari describes a celebration of the painter nearly identical to the one Browning's unknown painter imagines for his painting as it arrives in some "glad aspiring little burgh":[7]

> Flowers cast upon the car which bore the freight,
> Through old streets named afresh from the event,
> Till it reached home
>
> (31–33)

The Pictor Ignotus's fantasy seems natural and reasonable because it is a reimagining of the rewards garnered by painters whose names, like Cimabue's, have been preserved. But this is all predicate. The ideology of the unknown painter's fantasy is hidden, not in the predicate, not in the object, but in the constitution of the subject itself. We know from Vasari how Cimabue's product was celebrated, but in Browning's account, it is not just the painting, duly alienated from its producer, that collects praise and veneration. Indeed, in this daydream, the product and the producer become indistinguishable; each is equally "the subject":

> Nor will I say I have not dreamed (how well!)
>   Of going—*I, in each new picture,*—forth,

As, making new hearts beat and bosoms swell,
    To Pope or Kaiser, East, West, South, or North,
Bound for the calmly-satisfied great State,
    Or glad aspiring little burgh, it went,
Flowers cast upon the car which bore the freight,
    Through old streets named afresh from the event,
Till it reached home, where learned age should greet
    My face, and youth, the star not yet distinct
Above his hair, lie learning at my feet!—
    Oh, thus to live, *I and my picture,* linked
With love about, and praise, till life should end,
    And then not go to heaven, but linger here,
Here on earth, earth's every man my friend,—
    The thought grew frightful, 'twas so wildly dear!

                                    (25–40; emphasis mine)

The painter, as subject of his projection, becomes immediately
identified with the painting itself ("I, in each new picture").
Later, when the painting has traveled through the "calmly-satisfied
great State" and the "glad aspiring little burgh" and has "reached
home," veneration from both young and old "greet / My face." Here
the fusion of the producer with the product emerges in the ambiguity of "My face": is the painter thinking of his own face or one
he has represented from his overflowing cup of human faces? The
distinction is unnecessary, for it remains "I and my picture" together who are "linked / With love about, and praise." To this point,
the ideological veil is intact: the relation between the signifying
fantasy and its signified (Vasari's text, the previous signifier) continues to seem natural; the text is a realist text. Only at the
moment that "life should end" does the realist text terminate, the
signifier depart from its signified, and the ideological coherence of
the dream dissipate. The unknown painter has so far denied the
possibility of being alienated from his painting that, even after
death, he insists on a supernatural "lingering" on earth to share
the love and praise lavished by "every man" on his work.

At this point, however, the strain is too great; the fantasy of
universal love, unsupported by the consistency of the realist text,
gives way to fear that the painter's public will not turn out to be
homogeneous in its admiration. The painter realizes that his paint-

ing, if it is to be praised like the painting of "that youth," must stand the test of an aggressively heterogeneous public. It must, in other words, take its value from exchange in the marketplace.

Browning's placing of his Pictor Ignotus in the sixteenth century becomes important at this juncture. In the Quattrocento, the "consumer" for a painter's work was indeed relatively individual and homogeneous in nature. Paintings were produced on commission, and the contracts that set the painters to work typically stipulated in advance much of what the painting was to depict and even exactly what materials were to be used. To return to the parable of the talents, the catastrophic ejection of the slothful servant from the kingdom of heaven results from his inability to infer the proper course of action, which his lord does not prescribe. In the contractual relation between patron and painter in the fifteenth century, no such misunderstanding was possible. When Fra Fillipo Lippi assures his patron, Giovanni di Cosimo de' Medici, that he "shall always do what you want in every respect, great and small," he does so with the certainty that the latter will make his wishes explicitly clear.[8] Such security of communication requires, of course, a stable code, and that code, for Quattrocento painters, was the code of symbolic religious painting, the language of "Virgin, Babe and Saint." By contrast, the code of emerging realist conventions, while still perhaps allegorical or abstract, is nevertheless relatively indeterminate. Kristeva has identified these two codes as the "symbolic" and the "semiotic" and has pointed to the historical transition from the one to the other as the condition for the emergence of the realist form of fiction known as the novel.[9]

Socially, the semiotic code arises in conjunction with a form of production in which the product is made without a prior and unambiguous mandate from a unitary consumer. This is the form of the modern or bourgeois market, where an artisan like a painter must risk his own appraisal of what the public wants by completing his work previous to any commitment to purchase it. Like the faithful servant in the gospel, he invests his talents, both internal and external, on the gamble that his appraisal of public demand will be accurate and his audacity will be rewarded. His success will depend on his correctly predicting the relations between signifier and signified that will strike his public as natural. When the subject of his painting is a material one, as in portraiture, the ideological naturalness of his representation will be measured in terms of mimetic likeness. When the subject becomes more abstract, the artist will gain favor in the marketplace, not by offering once again a fixed vocabulary of symbols, but by creating a fresh metaphor that will seem "just right":

> And, like that youth ye praise so, all I saw,
>   Over the canvas could my hand have flung,
> Each face obedient to its passion's law,
>   Each passion clear proclaimed without a tongue;
> Whether Hope rose at once in all the blood,
>   A-tiptoe for the blessing of embrace,
> Or Rapture drooped the eyes, as when her brood
>   Pull down the nesting dove's heart to its place;
> Or Confidence lit swift the forehead up,
>   And locked the mouth fast, like a castle braved.
>
> (13–22)

It is important to recognize in this passage the fact that the difference between symbolism and realism is not the difference between the abstract and the concrete. Both are abstract, but symbolism simply makes an arbitrary equivalence between the sign and its referent, an equivalence that, in the case of Quattrocento painters, can even be agreed upon contractually in advance of execution. The semiotics of realism, on the other hand, demand a "naturalization" of the abstract, a discovering of an apparently material signifier that seems the true companion of its conceptual signified. This requires a consensus on the ideological plane, a homogeneous communal apprehension of what relations between signifier and signified qualify as apt. Such a consensus, were it possible, would leave the producer or artist free to remain unified and wholly invested in his or her representations. The contradiction lies in the fact that the ideology of the free market system also forbids intersubjective consistency in the form of consensus. The market is democratic. "Different people like different things." "Every individual is entitled to his or her opinion." In short, the contradiction faced by the realist painters addressing the opening market of the sixteenth century and after is the fundamental contradiction underlying the concept of taste. Either side of this contradiction seems, independently, as natural as daylight. On the one hand, as Hume would have it, "The great variety of taste, as well as of opinion, which prevails in the world, is too obvious not to have fallen under everyone's observation." On the other hand, as Hume would also have it, "It is natural for us to seek a standard of taste; a rule by which the various sentiments of men may be reconciled."[10]

For the artist, the public is a subjectivity both unified and divided, and it is the oscillation between these two views that Browning's Pictor Ignotus articulates when he imagines first an exhilarating and then a terrifying response to his pictures. First, he will paint his picture. Then he will submit it to the whole social spectrum, from pope and kaiser to humble burgher, from "learned age" to callow youth. And he will find a consensus of praise. But then the vision changes, not to one of universal censure, but to one of multiplicity and divided response: "This I love, or this I hate." The problem lies in the painter's partial vision of his dilemma. He can see clearly, if only through his oscillation of fantasy, the contradiction in which the realist code demands a predictable consensus that the free market precludes. "The subject" that will judge his art is constituted by the homogeneity/heterogeneity paradox, and this much is clear to him. What remains hidden is the fact that all subjectivity is so constituted in his world. His own choice, between investing and hiding his talents, between participating in or withdrawing from the market, between being *in communitas* or being alone, between being immortalized ("named") or being forgotten—all of these formulations of his choice presuppose, as the parable of the talents does, the homogeneity of himself as subject.

The "I" that identifies with "each new picture" is an individual entity; it must either be located "in" the picture or alienated "outside" it. If the painter's identity is fused with his product, and if that product is preserved by being valued, the painter himself may gain a kind of immortality. But the cost is intolerable; he becomes, like a slave, a commodity that can be bought and sold, judged capriciously and coldly cast aside. Rather than elevating his painting to the level of the human, the realist painter in vogue degrades the human to the level of reified ornament, casually procured:

> These buy and sell our pictures, take and give,
> Count them for garniture and household-stuff,
>   And where they live needs must our pictures live
> And see their faces, listen to their prate,
>   Partakers of their daily pettiness,
> Discussed of,—"This I love, or this I hate,
>   This likes me more, and this affects me less!"
>
> (50–56)

To the public that buys and sells pictures, the painter's work is a mere object. But for the painter, who has truly submitted his talents in the marketplace, the painting still contains his animate identity; unapprehended, it continues both to "see" and to "listen." Painting and painter achieve the condition, not of product and its alienated producer, but of the unified and conscious slave on the block.

"Wherefore I chose my portion." The Pictor Ignotus will "save" his talents, talents given definition—even their existence—by the market and its language. To save them, in other words, is finally to lose them, and the painter's boast of an inner cup of human faces that overflows becomes finally an idle one. He chooses not only to withdraw from the market in which the merchant "traffics in my heart": he chooses also to abandon the only pictorial language in which he can participate in a human community. He returns to the symbolic "series, Virgin, Babe and Saint," a dead language that can only be repeated endlessly without hope of response. It is only the semiotic code that takes its meanings from the reciprocities of communication, reciprocities indispensable to the perpetuation of the signifying chain.

For the symbolic medieval code out of context, there can only be stasis: "With the same cold calm beautiful regard." But even this stasis is contradictory. The Pictor Ignotus has escaped the judgment and the buying and selling by withdrawing himself from his paintings and thus from all human activity. But in doing so he has merely identified himself with those paintings again in a new and even more chilling sense. The most essential fact of his own isolated humanity—the slow decay of his physical body—has now become simultaneously the essential feature of the paintings themselves:

> The sanctuary's gloom at least shall ward
>   Vain tongues from where my pictures stand apart:
> Only prayer breaks the silence of the shrine
>   While, blackening in the daily candle-smoke,
> They moulder on the damp wall's travertine,
>   'Mid echoes the light footstep never woke.
> So, die my pictures! surely, gently die!
>
> (63-69)

The choice is a cruel one. The painter may either risk his total identity in the innovative style that the community demands or he must "stand apart" with his pictures and thus lose his identity altogether—become nameless because unknown. Again the contradictions abound. To do that which is new means to strike out an individual path, to present one's own personal vision. Logically, this would be a departure from the knowledge and values of the collectivity. Yet this is precisely what the community demands in order to confer its recognition and praise. To conform to what the community already knows is, paradoxically, to "stand apart," to alienate oneself from that community. These are the contradictions that underlie the bourgeois myths of progress and personal ambition: they are a transformation of the contradiction Marx articulated in *The German Ideology:* the interest of the individual and that of the community as a whole both oppose and require one another.

Traditionally, critics have read "Pictor Ignotus" as offering a judgment on its speaker. He is seen as a coward, as "frightened of the world's rough handling" or as "totally [lacking] ambition."[11] Such judgments, of course, do little more than match the ideology of the critic to that of the poet, and the result is that critics have found "Pictor Ignotus" a slight piece—simple by comparison with later monologues by Italian painters like "Fra Lippo Lippi" or

"Andrea del Sarto." But these dismissals overlook the fact that Browning's placing of the Pictor Ignotus in the sixteenth century raises problems different from those familiar in the anthology pieces. Browning's painter in this poem speaks wholly from within the ideology of the unified ego, and the poem itself raises that ideology to consciousness through a second level of contradictions in its own form. Whether the poem's speaker paints in the old style or the new, symbolically or realistically, he remains a unitary presence either wholly submitted to or wholly withdrawn from the market system that is his only society. Browning offers no clear preference between the polarities of his choice. Instead, he presents the speaker in a literary form that denies the homogeneity of the subject.

The monologue does this in two ways. First, it removes the subjective consistency of the speaker's immediate public, his projected auditor. At first he seems to speak to someone (singular or plural?) who praises the young Raphael. Later, though the discourse seems uninterrupted in time, he concludes the monologue by addressing the youth himself:

> O youth, men praise so—holds their praise its worth?
> Blown harshly, keeps the trump its golden cry?
> Tastes sweet the water with such specks of earth?
>
> (70-72)

More important, the monologue fragments the subjective unity from which, since Aristotle, the lyric discourse has been assumed to emanate. As the interlocutor is indeterminate and at the same time distinct from the poem's implied "reader," so the speaker remains deprived of an identity—a name—and is not the "author" of his own discourse. If, as Rosalind Coward and John Ellis maintain, bourgeois ideology "positions" the subject as a homogeneous center in which contradictions seem to disappear and meaning is intelligible, Browning has given us a poem—an ideological discourse—that positions no unified subjects and that deprives us of a center from which the speaker's choice can be definitively judged. The choice of the unknown painter is only a meaningful choice from within the position that the monologue refuses. For the artist who creates the monologue itself, the literary style of realism appears only in order to be defamiliarized. The speech itself seems realistic because it is the common idiom of nineteenth-century English conversation. But its very naturalness alienates it from the sixteenth-century Italian subject that it pretends to represent. The indices of its reference conflict; although the poem appears an unbroken signifying chain, its chain of signifieds is double, and the sign as it unfolds can never be consistent or homogeneous.

As Browning saw so clearly in "One Word More," the individual who writes a dramatic monologue can never be either wholly embodied "in each new monologue" or wholly withdrawn into a fixed symbolism. His discourse is always already the "discourse of the other"; by the time his subjective product can be judged and bought and sold, he is already occupying a different subjective position, speaking from another mouth.[12] The dramatic monologue is, in the fullest and most conscious sense, the product alienated from its producer. "Pictor Ignotus" represents the hopeless position of a producer who is psychically incapable of accepting his own alienation. He, as a possessor of talents (the "forces of production"), literally ceases to exist. His disappearance, moreover, is nothing other than the productive coming-into-being of alienated art: the monologue itself. The alienation of the artist from his art is seen, therefore, not as a weakness of will or spirit, not as a lack of commitment or ambition; it is seen as the only way for the artist to exist and produce within the capitalist market. "Pictor Ignotus," it is true, only faintly outlines the potential of the dramatic monologue itself. But this poem, perhaps better than any other, makes explicit the logic of the poet's need to bring the dramatic monologue into being.

III

The dramatic monologue is not merely produced ex nihilo in certain social and economic conditions; it is produced as an alternative to other, related, kinds of writing. The logic of "Pictor Ignotus" suggests that the monologue stands for Browning as an alternative to the polar choice between symbolic and realist modes. In "Pictor Ignotus," these modes are represented as two different styles of Italian Renaissance painting. In the next section, I want to indicate why it seems appropriate to identify Shelleyan lyric poetry with the repetitional style of the Pictor Ignotus's "Virgin, Babe and Saint" and how Browning was drawn away from this kind of poetry toward the dramatic monologue. This will require a digression of some length on Shelley himself, and in order to provide continuity between Shelley and the Browning of *Pauline,* I shall concentrate my analysis on the structure of metaphor, the poet's relation to his public, and his relation to other poets. The latter two categories will, of course, also allow us to return to the problems raised by "Pictor Ignotus."

By the time Browning wrote his first published poem, *Pauline,* he had been accustomed to think of himself as a poet for many years, and he had been deeply influenced by powerful models. At the age of twelve, he completed a volume of verse written in imitation of Byron. He read Wordsworth, Coleridge, Shakespeare, and Milton, was introduced to Keats, and read fragmentarily among many other authors in the volumes of his father's substantial private library. Most important, at fourteen, his poetic course was permanently altered by the discovery of Shelley. Much of his early verse Browning later destroyed, leaving little record of what genres he experimented with in the years preceding *Pauline.* It is safe to infer, however, that in the journey from adolescent imitations to the invention of an important English poetic genre, the dramatic monologue, Browning's earliest publications represent a middle or transitional stage.[13]

Even *Pauline* and *Paracelsus* are generic hybrids. Browning himself calls *Pauline* a "fragment of a confession," and Robert Preyer identifies that poem, along with *Paracelsus* and *Sordello* as only impure examples of the "spiritual confession or monodrama."[14] That the confessional lyric of Byron and Shelley provided Browning's earliest models there seems little doubt, and useful research by A. Dwight Culler suggests that the Continental monodrama may have been of nearly equal importance in the years preceding *Pauline* and *Paracelsus.*[15] Thus *Pauline* is not an experiment in a particular Romantic genre. It is, as J. V. Cunningham says all poems must be, a "simultaneity of literary kinds."[16] Nevertheless, the poem contains many examples of the discursive and poetic conventions that Browning tried to adopt from his predecessors, enough at least to illustrate the process whereby he began his movement toward formal innovation.

If we cannot measure Browning's early departures from Shelley within a single genre, we can narrow the focus and compare the two poets within a shared procedure: the making of metaphors. In *Pauline,* I shall be concerned with the structure of the long simile in which Browning compares his enduring worship of Shelley to the worship of a "sacred spring." That passage itself bears several clear traces of Shelleyan texts, while it also adumbrates Browning's mature procedure, which, I shall argue, remains essentially unchanged thirty years later in the central metaphoric gesture of *The Ring and the Book.* To understand metaphor as Browning uses it, however, we need to understand it as Shelley uses it. I have referred previously to symbolic representation in opposition to discursive, semiotic, and realist modes of signification. My analysis of Shelleyan metaphor is, in part, meant to clarify that distinction and to demonstrate some of its potential richness. Initially, it may seem farfetched to interpret the "Pictor Ignotus" as Browning's fantasy projection of himself had he not pulled away from Shelley. I hope that by the end of this chapter, the idea will have gained in plausibility.

Among other things, metaphor is a means of representation. The best illustration I know of the distinction between symbolic and discursive representation is an ancient one. It is an argument, reported by Flavius Philostratus in his *Life of Appolonius of Tyana,* over the proper method of representing the gods in sculpture.[17] Appolonius, a Greek, criticizes the Egyptian practice of representing gods by figures of lower forms of life like animals. Thespesion, an Egyptian, complains that a Greek sculptor like Pheidias is presumptuous in depicting Zeus as a man, since no one has ever seen Zeus. Appolonius replies that the imagination can "conceive of its ideal . . . with reference to the reality" that is available to the senses. Thespesion doubts this connection between sense and ideal and maintains that the Egyptians respect the infinite distance between gods and men by representing "their forms as symbols of a profound inner meaning, so as to enhance their solemnity and august character." The disagreement is clear and logically unresolvable. The Greek believes that the relationship between higher and lower realities is a discursive one that can be articulated rationally in language: something like, "Zeus looks like a fully developed young man of surpassing physical beauty." In more fully elaborated versions of this kind of certainty, gods and men do battle, maneuver politically, love and hate one another in the continuous time and space of Greek culture's most authoritative fictions. The Egyptian, on the other hand, interprets the lower and higher realities of men and gods as ontologically discontinuous in every way. Thus for him, human representations of the gods are wholly arbitrary, and men need to acknowledge that fact by choosing symbols that make no claim to noble elevation in the purely human scale. The important point is that this debate offers, not a choice between earth and heaven, between materialism and idealism as the ultimate source of value; it offers a choice between two different ways of relating the material to the ideal. Either that relation is structured in a differentiated articulation or it is merely a gap, an unfilled ontological space between a world discourse of arbitrary signifiers and a transcendental signified different in kind from any possible signifier.

If Browning, in 1845, still viewed Quattrocento painting with a "comparatively undiscerning" eye, as Leonee Ormond suggests, he may well have read the stylized depiction of "Virgin, Babe and Saint" as essentially symbolic.[18] Relative to more realistic styles, these representations may have seemed to him pessimistic about the painter's ability to naturalize the relation between pictorial conventions and their divine referent. And Shelley is certainly pessimistic about the possibility of representing ideal reality, since he proposes metaphor—or simile—as an alternative to direct knowledge:

> What thou art we know not;
> What is most like thee?
>
> ("To a Skylark," 31-32)

This question introduces the famous series of similes in "To a Sky-lark," one of Browning's early favorites among Shelley's lyrics. To see why these similes represent an essentially symbolic mode of representation, we need to glance briefly at Shelley's carefully formulated conception of poetic metaphor.

"Reason," Shelley tells us, "respects the differences, and imagination the similitudes of things."[19] Poets, rich in imagination, employ this power of perceiving similitude to intuit as an intellectual unity a holistic, and finally homogeneous, universe. Speaking of poets, he says,

> Their language is vitally metaphorical, that is it marks the before unapprehended relations of things and perpetuates their apprehension until the words which represent them become, through time, signs for portions and classes of thought instead of pictures of integral thoughts; and then if no new poets should arise to create afresh the associations which have been thus disorganized, language will be dead to all the nobler purposes of human intercourse.[20]

Metaphor encodes perceptions that time attenuates. The important "relations of things" are permanent; they are merely unapprehended "before" and fragmented "through time." Shelley organizes the knowledge of reality according to a three-level hierarchy: there are "things," the differentiated *noema* of the world known through the senses; there are "portions and classes of thought," or *dianoia,* discursively organized by the subjective intellect; and there are "integral thoughts," a kind of pure *noesis,* or intuition of a unified reality. Poetic language moves beyond things to classes by discursively articulating similitudes, but Shelley also asks the poet to do more, to "create afresh" relations that become neglected and disorganized in time. Classes are still subject to the constraints of time and space, and Shelley, throughout the *Defence of Poetry,* leaves no doubt that the poet aspires to a noetic intuition of reality abstracted beyond the temporal: "A poet participates in the eternal, the infinite, and the one; as far as relates to his conceptions, time and place and number are not."[21] The *Defence* prescribes no method, but in Shelley's own poetry, the progression from portions and classes of thought to pictures of integral thoughts is the progression from simile to metaphor.

When, near the beginning of "To a Skylark," Shelley asks the unseen minstrel "What is most like thee?" this demand for a simile follows the admission that a direct sensory or noemic apprehension of the bird is impossible: "What thou art we know not." In place of such knowledge, the poet will give likenesses; he will, in other words, align *noema* with *noesis* and assert, on faith, a similarity. To this end, Shelley answers his own demand for a simile:

> Like a poet hidden
>   In the light of thought,
> Singing hymns unbidden,
>   Till the world is wrought
> To sympathy with hopes and fears it heeded not:
>
> Like a high-born maiden
>   In a palace-tower,
> Soothing her love-laden
>   Soul in secret hour
> With music sweet as love, which overflows her bower:
>
> Like a glow-worm golden
>   In a dell of dew,
> Scattering unbeholden
>   Its aereal hue
> Among the flowers and grass, which screen it from the view!
>
> Like a rose embowered
>   In its own green leaves,
> By warm winds deflowered,
>   Till the scent it gives
> Makes faint with too much sweet those heavy-winged thieves:
>
> Sound of vernal showers
>   On the twinkling grass,
> Rain-awakened flowers,
>   All that ever was
> Joyous, and clear, and fresh, thy music doth surpass.

(36–60)

Here we can distinguish how metaphoric relationships establish two levels of cognition above the mere naming of things. On the first abstracted level, each particular—poet, maiden, glow-worm, and rose—is related in a separate simile to the skylark. Beyond this, however, each simile is related metaphorically to the other similes, creating a similitude among similitudes. Like the unseen skylark, the poet is hidden, the maiden abides in a "secret" bower, the glow-worm is "screened" from view, and the rose is covered by its surrounding leaves. From each comes an emanation, a flow, which the world perceives without perceiving the source. To return to Shelley's own terms, not only are there "before unapprehended relations" among disparate items in the universe, there are also unapprehended relations among the relations. To perceive these is to go beyond separate acts of classification to participate in a single "integral thought." To say "X is like A" is to create a class. But by saying, in effect, X is like A, X is like B, X is like C, and X is like D and by equating the likenesses, Shelley is able to say metaphorically that the relation, XA *is* the relation XB, *is* the relation XC, and *is* the relation XD, implying an indefinite extension of the paradigm to other particulars. The poet's language, in other words, while always referring to the world, can articulate many thoughts that, on examination, turn out to be but one thought. Simile shows relations of which metaphor confirms the transcendent or sublime meaning. Simile asserts a perceived or apparent equivalence; metaphor projects an ontological equivalence subsumed finally in "the eternal, the infinite and the one."

So far, "To a Skylark" would seem to offer a model for the task of interpreting the infinite to the finite world that Shelley so confidently assigns the poet in the *Defence*. But Shelley's poetry is, even when it repeats the claims of the *Defence,* a poetry of frustration. The lyric subject, alienated from his public in the relation of teacher to pupil, can never fulfill the promise of interpreting the world in a complete and integral thought. That whole knowledge is invested in the unrepresentable skylark, who knows no pain and has access to truths deeper "than we mortals dream." The attempt of mortals to represent the skylark's perfect knowledge results only in contradiction:

We look before and after,
    And pine for what is not—
Our sincerest laughter
    With some pain is fraught—
Our sweetest songs are those that tell of saddest thought.

Yet if we could scorn
    Hate and pride and fear;
If we were things born
    Not to shed a tear,
I know not how thy joy we ever should come near.

(86–95)

As humans, we "come near" the skylark's "joy" only paradoxically by being, unlike the skylark, bound in time and conflict. This paradox serves to interrupt the discursive continuity between the temporal, or material, productivity of the poet's speech itself and the skylark's ideal knowledge of a homogeneous universe. The assertion that the "portions and classes of thought" re-presented in the sequence of similes open metaphorically onto a univocal or "integral" thought must, in the end, be an assertion of faith. Moreover, the fundamental symbolic disjunction between heterogeneous representations creates a corollary paradox for the poetic subject itself. That subject is a split, or ambivalent, subject. It seeks to locate itself within a discourse that mediates between a knowledge and a material world that have already been denied discursive connection. The result is that the subject speaks, but he speaks of knowledge he cannot have to a world that cannot hear him. For Shelley, this empty space of the subject is signified by the desperate concept of the half:

Teach me half the gladness
    That thy brain must know,
Such harmonious madness
    From my lips would flow
The world would listen then—as I am listening now.

(101–5)

The poem's conclusion is conditional: "If you would teach me half your gladness, I would have a discourse for communication with the world." But the "integral thought," the "all that ever was" comprehended by the skylark, cannot be divided or it deteriorates to become "portions and classes of thought."

Like many of Shelley's poems, "To a Skylark" reaches ambivalently toward two goals. One goal is discourse, community, history; the other is truth, certainty, definition. At the end of "Mont Blanc," for example, we are told that the pure abstraction, Power, dwells in the mountain "silently," without a voice, while before, the poet has asserted, "Thou hast a voice, great Mountain, to repeal / Large codes of fraud and woe." The force offered to mediate this simultaneous presence and absence of discourse is the mind, the imagination. But the imagination's role is invoked at the end of the poem, not as a positive certainty, but as a question, an ambivalence:

> And what were thou, and earth, and stars, and sea,
> If to the human mind's imaginings
> Silence and solitude were vacancy?
>
> (142-44)

Similarly, at the end of "Lines Written among the Euganean Hills," Shelley finds the alternative to the Sea of Pain, not in the real temporal cities of Venice and Padua nor in pure abstraction, but in the imagination's mediation of the idea of paradise and some real material "calm and blooming cove." But such a place is not the residence of a transcendent unitary poetic subject. It also demands community, first the community of a few trusted friends, but then, by extension of desire, the paradisal cove becomes the reforming place for the entire "polluting multitude." By the time the fantasy is fully extended, however, it can only be expressed in a series of wistful predications of "may," coupled with the claim that if such a bower existed and if it could contain the polluting multitude, then

> Every sprite beneath the moon
> Would repent its envy vain,
> And the earth grow young again.
>
> (371-73)

Such imaginings of paradise regained emerge directly from the contradiction between private and collective values that the impossible bower embodies. This is the very contradiction that underlies the contradiction of a poetic univocal truth, which can only be possessed by a homogeneous subject ("the poet") but which must be communicated ("taught") through the discourse of the community. It is the contradiction embodied in Shelley's desire for the poet to participate in the "eternal, the infinite and the one" and yet be a political force in his time.[22] The latter unresolvable paradox becomes perhaps even more clear in Shelley's political poems in which the more concrete the occasion of the poem the more its principal figures move toward universalized personifications:

> I met Murder on the way—
> He had a mask like Castlereagh—
>
> ("The Mask of Anarchy," 2.5-6)

The ambivalence of which I am making such a great point is not, it is important to stress, an ambivalence of loyalty toward the "concrete" or the "abstract" object. The symbolic relation between the material and the ideal poles of reality—a relation that ultimately grounds itself in the contradiction between private and general interests—results chiefly in an ambivalence concerning the positioning of the subject itself. The Shelleyan poetic subject submits to a kind of nonspace between what Bakhtin and later Kristeva call "monological" and "dialogical" discourse. The monological is the univocal discourse of definition, truth, denotation, logical analysis. The dialogical is a "doubled" discourse in which the word takes its meaning in relation to two different subjective positions. In the epic, for example, discourse is monological, unfolding a singular representation of an object world by a unitary subject. By contrast, the novel requires citation, an intermittent discourse in which each word represents both a "character" (subject of utterance) and an "author" (subject of enunciation). In this kind of discourse, "the writer can use another's word, giving it a new meaning while retaining the meaning it already had. The result is a word with two significations."[23] This giving to a word a second meaning in addition to its "own" meaning must be a giving for someone other than the author or narrator. Hence the term "dialogical" discourse as opposed to the "monological" in which a subject gives a single meaning to a word that need be only for the subject itself. In dialogical discourse or narrative, "by the very act of narrating, the subject of narration addresses an other; narration is structured in relation to this other. (On the strength of such a communication, Francis Ponge offers his own variation of 'I think therefore I am': 'I speak and you hear me, therefore we are.')"[24] In Shelley, the lyric subject seems suspended in ambivalent or split desire, a desire directed on the one hand toward an "integral thought," a truth that can only be thought in a monological or univocal discourse, while on the other hand, toward dialogical exchange with the world or community. In Shelley's life, this suspension is expressed in his inability to locate himself either within the English social or cultural community or wholly as an exile. In his poetic persona it is expressed, not only in the division between philosophical and political poetics, but also in the contradiction between the models of poet-as-madman and poet-as-man-of-the-world.

In brief, the subject in Shelley's poems seems caught in an unconsummated quest for the discursive conditions of its own existence or location. Its discourse can no longer be the monological discourse of the homogeneous "present self," as in Wordsworth or Coleridge, and yet it has not yet undergone the dialogical split between subject of enunciation and subject of utterance that we find in Browning. When we put the matter this way, we can see Shelley's subject as no longer merely suspended but historically transitional.[25] Nowhere is the direction of this transition more clear, along with many of the terms that it incidentally includes, than in "Julian and Maddalo."

First and most obviously, Julian, who speaks—who is the subject of utterance—is neither distinctly identical with nor distinctly divided from the poem's subject of enunciation. He is neither Shelley, the Romantic autobiographical lyricist, nor the fully realized "speaker" of the dramatic monologue.[26] Accordingly, he divides himself between the leisure, vacation world, an exile's world, of Venice and the practical world of London, a world of responsibilities and "connections." Venice is a place of beauty and horsemanship and pleasure and solitude; and it is a place that gives space for abstract philosophical disputation, the kind in which Julian and Maddalo engage. The two friends go to observe a maniac in the Venetian madhouse in order to resolve their disagreement over free will and fate, but they find there not a philosopher nor even an exemplum of clear significance.[27] What they find is a singer, a writer, a poet. The maniac has been driven insane by the failure of a love affair. At times his language seems the pure monologue of reverie; at other times it is divided, dialogical, directed both to himself and to the woman who has abandoned him. Gradually his story unfolds. He has come to Venice with the lady from the world of his affairs. But somehow the love that flourished in that world flounders in this. From the failure of love comes ruin, both of the mind and of the maniac's fortunes. His madness consists in an inability to live in either world, for the reason that he cannot discursively connect the two. Love itself had been the medium in which he had hoped to construct the discourse that would disalienate the activities of productivity and pleasure, and love in turn has not only deprived him of pleasure, it has made his material ambitions and political alliances meaningless to him as well:

> Nor dream that I will join the vulgar cry,
> Or with my silence sanction tyranny,
> Or seek a moment's shelter from my pain
> In any madness which the world calls gain,
> Ambition or revenge . . .
>
> (362-66)

The maniac's inability to return to either world (he will not "bear removal" from the madhouse) is also a suspension between the two kinds of discourse that I have called monological and dialogical. In the former, he can only pose a metaphysical question that he cannot definitively answer: "What Power delights to torture us?" In the latter, he addresses to the lady the communication of a pain that he simultaneously labels as "uncommunicable":

O Thou, my spirit's mate
Who, for thou art compassionate and wise,
Wouldst pity me from thy most gentle eyes
If this sad writing thou shouldst ever see—
My secret groans must be unheard by thee,
Thou wouldst weep tears bitter as blood to know
Thy lost friend's incommunicable woe.

(337–43)

The maniac's language, neither monologue nor dialogue, neither philosophical truth nor communicational exchange, is according to Julian, "such as in measure were called poetry." And Julian, though he "never was impressed so much," finds the subjective place of that poetry one he cannot finally enter. At first, he fantasizes that he might stay in Venice, enjoying its pleasures, its beauties, its books, and its tranquility. Paradoxically, he imagines that if he were able to enter wholly into the subjectivity of the maniac, study "all the beatings of his heart," and gain entrance to "the caverns of his mind," he "might reclaim him from his dark estate." But he sees in this "idle thought" not only attraction but danger. Finally, the "chief attraction" of his life in London is that he "sought relief / From the deep tenderness that maniac wrought / Within [him]." The maniac's suspended position, making of the fleeting recreational world of Venice an unnaturally perpetual lyric present, cannot become, for Julian, a place of identification. Julian's choice is in effect between becoming the maniac in the place of poetic discourse and returning to a different kind of "friends" in London. The discourse in London is one of interaction, not identification. Instead of occupying the mind of another, Julian, the man of the world, is "connected." He chooses, in other words, between the discourse of poetry on the one hand and either the discourse of the world's affairs or that of philosophical certainty on the other. Poetic discourse fails to locate the alienated subject in a world where all "real" subjectivity must be alienated. Sanity requires two discourses, that of Venice and that of London, that can never be resolved, but poetry requires a metaphorical unification of discourse, a unification that renders the poet necessarily "in-sane," a madman. Hence, though Julian's idle dream "made for long years impression on [his] mind," nevertheless, he tells us, "The following morning, urged by my affairs, / I left bright Venice."[28]

"Julian and Maddalo" locates poetic discourse in exclusion of both public and private worlds, but because it is related to both of them through desire, it institutes a nondiscursive, or symbolic, mode of relating them to one another in its representations. We have already seen the bare structure of this mode in "To a Skylark"; elsewhere it becomes more clear how such parallel constructions serve to mediate the duality of the material and the abstract. In the *Meno,* Socrates asks his interlocutor to define virtue. Meno replies with particular examples of virtue that only "puzzle" Socrates because they contain no account of the abstract and immutable essence of virtue itself. The Aristotelian answer to this dilemma is to allow the category of particulars to emerge as prior to the definition of the "universal" concept that defines the category. In either case, concrete and ideal entities demand a discourse of explanation to connect them. For Shelley, the discourse of explanation disappears because the distinction between the heterogeneous catalogue and the unitary concept disappears. The catalogue itself, with its stanzaically or metrically structured entries, comes to contain both concrete and abstract entities in symbolically parallel positions. Shelley may pose the Platonic question, "What art thou Freedom?" but his response is a series of stanzas that neither define nor enumerate exclusively. Rather, in some stanzas, the answer is material:

> For the labourer thou art bread,
> And a comely table spread
> From his daily labour come
> In a neat and happy home.
>
> Thou art clothes, and fire, and food
> For the trampled multitude—
> No—in countries that are free
> Such Starvation cannot be
> As in England now we see.
>
> (The Mask of Anarchy, 55.224–25)

In others it is pure abstraction: "Thou art Wisdom," "Thou art Peace," "Thou art Love." By this symbolic discourse, the subject is placed as neither monological philosopher nor dialogical polemicist, neither the Byron and Shelley of the Italian palace disputations nor the Byron and Shelley of London affairs and the Greek wars of liberation. Such poetry, in its time, truly "moulders," to use the term of "Pictor Ignotus." Because it wakens only "echoes the light footstep never woke," the world ignores it. This is part of what fascinated Browning in Shelley's career, and I think that this sense of a poetic subject suspended, not quite out of historical time and not quite in it, leads directly into the confusing ambivalences of *Paracelsus* and *Sordello* as well as early creations of the dramatic monologue like the "Pictor Ignotus."

The Shelleyan ambivalence only suggests a *desire* for a splitting of the poetic subject in dialogical discourse. In truth, Shelley's fantasies of both philosopher and legislator assume the positioning of a homogeneous and unitary subjectivity.[29] Browning, by opening the ideological consequences of ambivalent suspension, actually performs the division between subject of enunciation and subject of utterance that Shelley only adumbrates in poems like "Julian and Maddalo" or (even more faintly) "Epipsychidion." Stylistically and generically, this meant finding alternatives to Shelley's symbolic mode; and in order to understand the early stages of Browning's departure (which precede his principal generic innovation), we need to establish for comparison the stylistic basis of Shelleyan lyrics like "To a Skylark."

Richard Ohmann, invoking a fundamental distinction of Saussurian linguistics, has argued that a speaker or writer "usually gravitates, albeit slightly, either to combination or to selection" as a favored way of making simple sentences into more complex ones.[30] Ohmann calls those who favor the horizontal or syntagmatic axis of combination "continuity-seekers," and those who lean toward vertical or paradigmatic selection he designates "similarity-seekers." Shelley, as we might expect, is chiefly a similarity-seeker, but a glance at Ohmann's examples from the prose of George Bernard Shaw reveals some interesting differences between Shaw and Shelley. Here is a typical passage from one of Shaw's essays:

> The whole range of Shakespeare's foibles: the snobbishness, the naughtiness, the contempt for tradesmen . . . : all these are the characteristics of Eton and Harrow.[31]

Shaw elaborates the sentence vertically through accumulations of representative nouns or phrases, broad selections of traits that fit in the category of "foibles." The basic unit being accumulated in Shaw's prose is usually, in other words, a lexical unit, even when a brief phrase or clause is called for. To understand the sentence, we must see immediately that snobbishness, naughtiness, and contempt are all foibles. In Shelley, however, the basic unit of selection or similarity is a syntactic unit, elaborate in its own internal combinational logic. Accordingly, in the similes of "To a Skylark," the principle of similarity is not to be found in the definitions of "poet," "maiden," "glow-worm," and "rose" but in the repetition of the phrase structures that unfold their immediate environments and actions. The syntax of each stanza locates each item spatially through a prepositional phrase beginning with "in" and thus denoting enclosure. The nouns are then further modified by participial phrases. These phrases vary considerably in structure, but each identifies the process by which the subject's mysterious emanation emerges from the secret enclosure into the public world.

We can say that in terms of linguistic combination, more complex structures are contexts for less complex structures. The word gives significance to the phonemes it organizes, the phrase or clause to its words, and the sentence to its constituent phrases and clauses. Up to the level of the phrase, Shelley develops the context syntagmatically with almost all relations determined by syntactic continuity. It is only in establishing the next higher level of context that a competition arises between further principles of combination, in the syntax of the whole sentence, and a new principle of selection in the paradigmatic repetition of phrase structures. At this level, the selection axis clearly dominates. Aside from the fact that the entire main clause is temporally deferred for the reader, this dominance can be demonstrated in two ways. First, the sentence that contains the skylark similes suffers from what amounts to a solecism, albeit one that generally goes unnoticed. The phrases, "like a poet," "like a maiden," and so on, grammatically modify "music." But the music is not like the poet, it is like his hymns, and the poet in turn is like the skylark, not its music. The logic of syntax has clearly broken down in this sentence, and yet the organizing prestige of the main clause has been so diminished by the syntactic parallelism among modifiers that the inconsistency seems a trivial detail in a passage of great communicative clarity. The second indication of the power of paradigmatic association is the tendency of most readers to link the "vernal showers / On the twinkling grass" to the preceding series of similes despite the fact that the showers stand in apposition to the object and not the subject of the sentence. This mistake is induced by the preposition "on," which corresponds to "in" in the structure of the other phrases, and, probably to a lesser degree, by the participle "twinkling," which also has its counterpart in the preceding stanzas.

To summarize then, Shelley does not "prefer" similarity relations to continuity relations in this passage. He merely affirms that the former function as context to the latter and thus represent a higher order of reality. As discursive *dianoia*, syntagmatic displacements are finite, particular, and analytic, enforcing distinctions between subject and object. They signify "portions and classes of thought," while paradigmatic relations generalize and synthesize, symbolically absorbing the subject / object (or ideal / material) antithesis into a higher noetic unity expressed in the near oxymoron "pictures of integral thoughts." Thus, beyond the noemic level of the direct word, or the naming of "things," Shelley's sentences, like his metaphors, often operate on two further levels of progressive abstraction.

Shelley's characteristic habit of sentence elaboration alters only slightly when it is not reenforced by prosodic and stanzaic patterns of repetition. Examples can be found on any page, but some of the central metaphors of *Prometheus Unbound* can illustrate how a somewhat different syntax from that of "To a Skylark" obeys the same underlying principle of order:

> ... and meanwhile
> In mild variety the seasons mild
> With rainbow-skirted showers, and odorous winds,
> And long blue meteors cleansing the dull night,
> And the life-kindling shafts of the keen sun's
> All piercing bow, and the dew-mingled rain
> Of the calm moonbeams, a soft influence mild,
> Shall clothe the forests and the fields, ay, even
> The crag-built deserts of the barren deep,
> With ever-living leaves, and fruits, and flowers.
>
> (3.2.114–23)

Shelley creates metaphors to challenge traditional distinctions between "classes of thought": fire and water, water and earth. The intimacy of water and light appears in the participial modification of "showers" by "rainbow-skirted." "Meteors cleansing" attributes a function to fire that is normally associated with water. And the "dew-mingled rain" of moonbeams once again makes a water and a light image into a unity. Finally, "The crag-built deserts of the barren deep" extends the domain of water to include the details of a singularly dry terrestrial landscape. The principle of paradigmatic repetition is once again syntactic, the participial modification of the noun that signifies the class of thought being challenged. Moreover, as in "To a Skylark," one of the repeated phrase structures occurs in the complement of the main verb, allowing the central paradigm to compete with the distinction between subject and object in the syntagma. The main clause, "The seasons clothe [the world]," is once again suppressed, and this suppression is further enhanced by added lexical cataloguing in the predicate (forests, fields, deserts, ... leaves, fruits, flowers). Shelley's sentence structure projects a complexity arising from the parallel listing of discrete tableaux. The separate contexts in the list do not significantly interact in time and space, despite allowances for action within each nominal group and despite the dynamic main verb, "shall clothe." Instead, the groups are related through similarities exacted by parallel phrasing and through their common participation in the abstract principle of mildness.

One last example. In the preface to *Laon and Cythna,* Shelley gives us a clue to the link between these linguistic orders and the more specialized orders of literary genres. He describes what he calls a "narrative":

> The poem . . . is narrative, not didactic. It is a succession of pictures illustrating the growth and progress of individual mind aspiring after excellence and devoted to the love of mankind; its influence in refining and making pure the most daring and uncommon impulses of the imagination, the understanding, and the senses; its impatience at "all the oppressions which are done under the sun"; its tendency to awaken public hope and to enlighten and improve mankind; the rapid effects of the application of that tendency; the awakening of an immense nation from their slavery and degradation to a true sense of moral dignity and freedom; the bloodless dethronement of their oppressors and the unveiling of the religious frauds by which they had been deluded into submission; the tranquillity of successful patriotism, and the universal toleration and benevolence of true philanthropy.[32]

The list goes on to include many more items. The discursive norm of a sentence consisting of subject, verb, and complements has once again virtually given way before the symbolic juxtaposition of phrases and clauses. Shelley tells us that his poem is a narrative and begins explaining its contents with two terms of process, "growth" and "progress." But these hints of displacement are quickly swallowed by the real generic principle of the poem as Shelley sees it: *Laon and Cythna* is a "succession of pictures." Shelley's account includes no narrative links between these pictures; they merely signify repeating examples of noble social virtues. This way of understanding a poetic genre is, of course, embedded in the syntax of the characteristically Shelleyan nonsentence. That syntax governs Shelley's execution of those classes of discourse called poetry, and therefore, his concept of poetry might be superimposed with little distortion over our own account of Shelleyan syntax. The following passage differentiates "poetry" from the inferior form of the "story":

> There is this difference between a story and a poem, that a story is a catalogue of detached facts, which have no other connexion than time, place, circumstance, cause and effect; the other is the creation of actions according

to the unchangeable forms of human nature, as existing in the mind of the Creator, which is itself the image of all other minds. The one is partial, and applies only to a definite period of time, and a certain combination of events which can never again recur; the other is universal, and contains within itself the germ of a relation to whatever motives or actions have place in the possible varieties of human nature. Time, which destroys the beauty and the use of the story of particular facts, stripped of the poetry which should invest them, augments that of poetry, and for ever develops new and wonderful applications of the eternal truth which it contains. Hence epitomes have been called the moths of just history; they eat out the poetry of it. [33]

The diachronic unfolding of language, by virtue of its inscription in a particular temporal sequence, points always to a partial reality. Both the discursive story and the reality it signifies are continually in the process of being effaced and can never be reconstituted in time. Moreover, the very discursiveness of the story, its dependence on metonymic combination, locates its subjects in systems of displacement: commerce, exchange, social interaction, politics. This is why, when Julian, the man of affairs, returns to Venice many years after eschewing the opportunity of entering the poetic subjectivity of the maniac, he returns with a different desire, the desire for a "story." Maddalo's daughter first tells the maniac's "mournful tale" as a group of essential details, epitomes. Julian, however, demands more: "Child, is there no more?" Of course, there is more. She has given him only the poetic part. "Like one of Shakespeare's women," she has told him only the kind of details that might have been inferred from the maniac's own mode of speech: "They met—they parted." Julian, the product of his own choice to return to his affairs, now demands "connections," a more discursive, explanatory account:

> Something within that interval which bore
> The stamp of *why* they parted, *how* they met.

III

I have tried to show the force of Shelley's claim that the language of poetry is "vitally metaphorical," and I have suggested that the symbolic structure of his metaphorical language positions a homogeneous subject that nevertheless cannot unify the worlds of thought and things discursively. We shall see that for Browning the dramatic monologue is a discursive mode of representation, and that he deconstructs, in a number of ways, the homogeneity of the speaking subject.

The poetic subject of *Pauline* remains much like the subject of "Julian and Maddalo," neither decisively monological nor dialogical. Just as in "Julian and Maddalo," it never becomes clear in *Pauline* whether the discourse is "doubled," locating a subject of enunciation separate from the subject of utterance, or univocal. For Shelley, this uncertainty reveals, I think, a discomfort with the dilemma of the poetic nonsubject in poems like "To a Skylark," an unresolved straining toward a liberating split. But however much he has complicated and raised to consciousness the contradictions underlying the lyric voice, Shelley can radicalize poetic form and language to no degree further than we find in "Julian and Maddalo." For Browning, the moment of the Shelleyan movement is only a beginning. Even in the poem that begins where Shelley left off, a look at Browning's syntax and the structure of his metaphor reveals an initial movement away from the symbolic mode. This movement, on the level of language, is a shift toward elaboration along the syntagmatic axis of combination and involves a freshened quest for continuity and connection. The quest projects a desire, and the desire emerges from, among other sources, a specific anxiety, appropriate to the 1830s, about the continuance of a poetic tradition that relies on the uninterrupted appearance of new and discrete "great poets."

Writers like Wordsworth, Coleridge, and Shelley posed difficult theoretical questions about the poet's role in society but always under the assumption that there would be an elite of great writers. Indeed, Shelley finds his own age especially well endowed with "such philosophers and poets as surpass beyond comparison any who have appeared since the last national struggle for civil and religious liberty."[34] By the 1830s, however, England seems a world suddenly without great poets in it. The deaths of Keats, Shelley, and Byron and the withdrawal of Wordsworth correspond to a time in which serious doubts have arisen as to whether fresh poetic genius can develop at all in modern materialist England. Such doubts advanced the Romantic anxiety about exclusion to an important new level and generated a new kind of discourse among critics. The *Edinburgh Review* (no doubt in the person of Francis Jeffrey) recalls the sense of "discovery and enterprise" that accompanied the first Romantic experiments but laments in bewilderment their subsequent disappearance:

> Then came, in rapid succession, the poetical miracles of our age: we lent our charmed senses to the witcheries of Scott, the passion of Byron, the high metaphysics of Wordsworth, the wonderful and unearthly melodies of Shelley; and, when the unexampled richness of that period had wasted itself in excess of luxuriance, we still listened for a space to the prolonged echoes of inferior yet sweet minstrelsy. The popularity of the art was maintained, and poetry continued a matter of common literary interest, through the exertions of many who attained not to the first rank, after these had become silent. Those were times in which critics flourished, and bore a part . . . in the general prosperity of the commonwealth of the Muses. But they are past, and no visible tokens seem to announce their return. Even while many of our best poets are yet alive, poetry herself is dead or entranced.[35]

The review goes on to attribute the decline in poetry to the general changes in English cultural life that turn attention to practical triumphs and render the "wonders of the imagination . . . cheap and vulgar."[36] This is only one example of a theme that recurs often in Victorian criticism for at least two decades, and the sense of a lacuna in English poetic history is often accompanied by a frustrated desire to reestablish some kind of continuity with lost greatness. Thus, while the Romantics strove to resemble the great poets of the past after the Augustans had struggled to surpass them, Victorians began to feel at least a partial need to reestablish human contact, to re-create the continuous "current of ideas" that Arnold said the modern poet could "nowhere find" in the immediate literary environment.[37]

This, I think, is the relevant context for the opening lines of Browning's famous invocation to Shelley in *Pauline:*

Sun-treader, life and light be thine for ever!
Thou art gone from us; years go by and spring
Gladdens and the young earth is beautiful,
Yet thy songs come not, other bards arise,
But none like thee: they stand, thy majesties,
Like mighty works which tell some spirit there
Hath sat regardless of neglect and scorn,
Till, its long task completed, it hath risen
And left us, never to return, and all
Rush in to peer and praise when all in vain.

(151-60)

The great poet is gone and none replaces him. There is a yearning here, and the irony that Browning perceives derives from the fact that while Shelley lived, he was unappreciated, whereas now, when an audience comes forth, no poets arise, so that "all / Rush in to peer and praise when all in vain." But Browning has not always been so certain that others shared his love of Shelley. A passage of eleven lines follows in which he explains how he had long admired Shelley before he had realized there were others with similar feelings, "Scarce deeming thou wast as a star to men!" Now, however, he knows that Shelley has been heard and revered. Browning, in other words, has momentarily set aside Shelley's own anxiety about the collective conditions in which the poetic subject's discourse might become dialogical. Though he returns to it later, his own logically prior anxiety concerns the possible absence of the poetic subject itself. Browning has taken the first step in denaturalizing the ideology of the "great poet." He has seen that under certain conditions, the great poet may not come into being, despite the fact that an audience (which may include himself) now eagerly receives such poets. Hence it becomes appropriate to read poems like "Pictor Ignotus" as attempts to discover what kind of poet or artist can come into being in a world where the Romantic integral subject no longer appears. The bitter irony is that the audience that is now prepared to take Shelley to its heart may not know how to receive the sort of poetic subject that becomes possible after Shelley.

This last contradiction, which I think Browning already recognized when he wrote *Pauline,* is finally internal to the poet himself; it actually initiates the splitting of the subject that brings the new kind of poetry into the world. This is true because Browning is at once a part of the audience that idolizes Shelley and the subject of a discourse that departs from Shelley's own. Nothing could present this ambivalence more clearly than the metaphor of the sacred spring, which restates Browning's discovery of comradeship in worship. This metaphor, in several ways, resembles Shelleyan metaphor, while in others, it anticipates a very different kind of metaphor characteristic of Browning's later work. It represents, in other words, a moment of uncertainty in which Browning is straining both to use and to escape Shelleyan metaphoric language. Moreover, in its very patterns of thinking about past poets, it embodies the Victorian desire to reestablish a lost continuity. Browning tells us he has worshipped Shelley,

> As one should worship long a sacred spring
> Scarce worth a moth's flitting, which long grasses cross,
> And one small tree embowers droopingly—
> Joying to see some wandering insect won
> To live in its few rushes, or some locust
> To pasture on its boughs, or some wild bird
> Stoop for its freshness from the trackless air:
> And then should find it but the fountain-head,
> Long lost, of some great river washing towns
> And towers, and seeing old woods which will live
> But by its banks untrod of human foot,
> Which, when the great sun sinks, lie quivering
> In light as some thing lieth half of life
> Before God's foot, waiting a wondrous change;
> Then girt with rocks which seek to turn or stay
> Its course in vain, for it does ever spread
> Like a sea's arm as it goes rolling on,
> Being the pulse of some great country—so
> Wast thou to me, and art thou to the world!
>
> (172-90)

Some affinities with Shelley are obvious, especially the use of the river, which is so central to poems like "Alastor" and "Mont Blanc" and to the philosophical speculations of Shelley's essays and correspondence. The symbolic potential of the river's source fascinated Shelley, and he often called these originating fountains "sacred" as Browning does. They may also be symbols of past poetry or the poet's thought, as when Shelley reminds Maria Gisborne

> how we sought
> Those deepest wells of passion or of thought,
> Wrought by wise poets in the waste of years,
> Staining their sacred waters with our tears.
>
> (170–73)

Here the Shelleyan metaphor again creates an analogy between the speaking poet and other "wise poets": as the passions of the latter provide the hidden wellspring of a stream, so the quest for passion yields a similar outflowing of waters in the tears of Shelley and his friend. Thus both the modern poet and the poets he reads are parts of that repeating metaphoric projection of which the "poet hidden / In the light of thought" and the skylark are also parts.

Browning's image of the wild bird is also a common one in Shelley, as is the tower in the town and the general landscape surrounding the river "girt" with stones and "embowered" by trees. The Browning passage is not an imitation of any particular poem in Shelley, but if it has a principal antecedent, it is probably "Mont Blanc." Browning's river is "Like a sea's arm as it goes rolling on, / Being the pulse of some great country," while in "Mont Blanc," "one majestic River, / The breath and blood of distant lands, for ever / Rolls its loud waters to the ocean waves." Browning's "sacred spring" may be read as a phonetic transformation of the "secret springs" in Shelley's poem, from which "The source of human thought its tribute brings / Of waters." This connection is rendered all the more appropriate by the fact that Shelley's metaphoric equivalent of these secret springs of thought is a "feeble brook" that empties into a great river.

I mention these details because it has often been assumed that the influence of Shelley had, in Mrs. Orr's terms, "passed away with [Browning's] earliest youth."[38] *Pauline* is not a poem of

Browning's earliest youth, yet some identification with Shelley clearly remained important to him. Nevertheless, even the poem's most Shelleyan moments reveal an organizational logic that renders the text of Shelley a dying, if not already dead, letter.

The Shelleyan model elaborates by repetition, and the single most conspicuous repetition in the Browning passage is the word "some," which appears six times in the nineteen lines. This is a Shelleyan favorite. The best example from "Mont Blanc" occurs when the poet, addressing the Arve ravine, states that "One legion of [his] wild thoughts" seeks "In the still cave of the witch Poesy . . . Ghosts of all things that are, *some* shade of thee, / *Some* phantom, *some* faint image." Phrase repetition, though simpler than in our earlier examples, implies an unbounded extension of the catalogue to signify "all things that are." Shelley frequently employs indefinite determiners with nouns in these catalogues, perhaps because they present items more as representative than as unique. The determiner, "some," in the "Mont Blanc" passage corresponds to the indefinite article in the series "Like *a* Poet . . . Like *a* high-born maiden . . . Like *a* glow-worm . . . Like *a* rose." We could interchange them to get series beginning with "*a* shade of thee" and "*some* Poet" without significant grammatical or semantic disturbance. In the skylark similes, repetitions other than the indefinite article dominate the effect, but when those more elaborate parallelisms are absent, Shelley intensifies the determiner function by repeating "some."

The lines that contain the first three instances of "some" in Browning's invocation to Shelley seem to me, if taken out of context, indistinguishable from many of the most typical passages in Shelley's own writing. Browning compares his discovery of Shelley to the discovery of a sacred spring and indicates his delight in converting occasional other readers to his devotion by extending the metaphor:

> Joying to see some wandering insect won
> To live in its few rushes, or some locust
> To pasture on its boughs, or some wild bird
> Stoop for its freshness from the trackless air.
>
> (175–78)

The indefinite determiners introduce three nouns in parallel phrases, and the nouns have a readily discernable level of semantic equivalence; each is a figure for a person discovering the joys and sustenance of the sacred spring of Shelley's poetry. We might, from this observation, want to generalize as we have done for Shelley by saying that Browning is creating a paradigm that becomes ontologically inclusive in the final line of the metaphor: "so / Wast thou to me, and art thou to the world!" But if we were to stop here, we would seriously distort the metaphor as a whole.

Internally, Browning's three parallel phrases each link an animal (insect, locust, and bird) to its new-found natural environment (rushes, boughs, and freshness [water]). Syntactically, this relation is provided by the same participle plus infinitive construction in each case: "won to live," "[won] to pasture," and "[won to] stoop." Moreover, the "environment series" (rushes, boughs, freshness) has already appeared in the preceding three lines: water in the sacred spring itself, the long grasses that cross the spring, and boughs in the small tree that "embowers" it. In this wider context, however, it is possible to see that these noun sequences are not of the same type as the Shelleyan sequence, poet, maiden, glow-worm, rose. Despite the parallelism of the second four lines, the first three lines establish a chain of association among the nouns that is syntagmatic rather than paradigmatic, as it was in the skylark similes:

> As one should worship long a sacred spring
> Scarce worth a moth's flitting, which long grasses cross,
> And one small tree embowers droopingly—
>
> (172–74)

The sentence unfolds a physical landscape in which the water, grasses, and tree are spatially contingent features. This is still metaphor, but it is, to risk our own oxymoron, "metonymic metaphor" in its inner structure, since parts interact extensively in a visual panorama rather than reembodying a single abstract relational pattern. The item "grasses" and "tree" are the subjects of relative clauses that modify, rather than parallel, the initial term, "spring."

The result is that when we come to the next four lines, with their obvious syntactic parallelism, these details retain their character of being spatially organized and temporally accumulated in a continuous landscape and thus incorporate the insect, locust, and bird into the same matrix. Shelley's paradigmatic stanzas display no such descriptive continuity from one nominal group to another.[39] He is more interested in the similarity / difference relations among representatives of human, animal, and vegetable nature than in locating these details relative to one another in space and time. Browning, though he retains vestiges of Shelley's technique, replaces these discrete categories, and the poet's implied struggle to reach a higher perception of equivalence among them, with a single expanse in which each detail gives way naturally in time and space to the rest. Hence the other three occurrences of the determiner "some" do not display the same apparent symmetry as the first three. The first one designates the river itself, which is diachronically revealed "downstream" from the original spring. The second occurs in an awkward half-simile, really a modifying clause for the river's banks, which functions to locate them in temporal flux by saying that they appear to be "waiting a wondrous change." And the third and last introduces "some great country," which displaces the banks "untrod of human foot" in the poet's metaphoric journey down the river.

I said in my analysis of the skylark similes that the process of outward flow was a repeating principle in the world and thus the ground of the central paradigm. For Browning, there is only one river, one flow, and it signifies the movement from one state of consciousness to another in time. This concern with nostalgia, process, and change is deeply embedded in the diction of the entire passage. Not only has the poet worshipped "long" at the sacred spring, the spring has also been "long lost." The woods do not merely stand by the river, they have been there a long time, and they "will live" in that place as opposed to more populated regions. The banks give the impression they do only at a particular time of day while they appear to be waiting for change. The river itself, like the metaphor that gives it being, "does ever spread" as it "goes rolling on."

Most important, this passage reveals a stylistic tension between a syntax of symbolic repetition and a syntax of displacement. The metaphor is genuinely transitional in the history of literary discourse, clinging to the earlier model while somehow being impelled toward a new mode. This new mode grows from what Walter Benjamin might have called an "allegorical" syntax, one that, like history itself, "takes on meaning only in the stations of its agony and decay."[40] The typological or symbolic syntax found in Shelley produces a language of mystic signs, temporal in their own succession but pointing to another order, another logic into which they do not themselves directly penetrate. The "fading chain of signifiers" may recall to mind a world that also fades, but Shelley strains toward a faith in another dimension of reference as well. By contrast, Browning's language, even from the early 1830s, steadily measures and manifests the temporal and corporeal rhythm of the lives it creates. Shelley "marks" the presence of a reality that he proceeds, at the same time, to mystify and hypostasize. Browning's sentences "mark off" that reality and so make concrete its unfolding in discourse itself. Hence Browning can begin *Paracelsus* with a line that embodies the continuity of three moments, displaying the indisseverable coreality of life and the syntagm that re-presents it: "Come close to me, dear friends; still closer; thus!" This line begins the non-Romantic history of a would-be Romantic hero. *Paracelsus* has begun to be non-Romantic, not because it escapes Romantic subjectivity; it is still, in Browning's own term, the history of a "mood." But it treats that mood in its "rise and progress."[41] The poem reveals "action in character," and since character is only made of speech, the action, the "stations of . . . agony and decay," is necessarily interior to the speech. It is not at all clear how well Browning understood this implication in 1835. What is clear, and what I hope to show in detail, is that the sentence as an unfolding constituent of the life that gives time its tragically metonymic meaning becomes the foundation of the dramatic monologue.

Earlier, I suggested that Romantic metaphor was at least partly generated by a specific anxiety about the poet's role in his public world. One outgrowth of this anxiety is a poetic desire, the desire to repeat the hidden skylark's perfect song in a form accessible to men. I also pointed out that Browning's metaphor is preceded by a passage of lament at the absence, not only of Shelley himself, but of any subsequent poets worthy to replace him. This too is an anxiety, one that Browning shared with many of his contemporaries. But Browning's desire is not like Shelley's desire. Shelley lives in a world well supplied with great poets, who suffer from neglect. Thus he develops metaphoric projections in poems like "To a Skylark" and the "Letter to Maria Gisborne" and in essays like the preface to *Prometheus Unbound* and the *Defence of Poetry* whereby the modern poet becomes analogous to his ancient predecessor as both preserver of vital language and giver of wisdom. This is what I have called the symbolic mode of representation. In *Pauline,* however, the poet is not presented as desiring to resemble another poet; he wishes to make contact, to re-create a continuity that has been lost in time.[42] Thus he fantasizes discursively, trying to distend some ephemeral vestige of the lost past to inhabit the present in the person of Shelley: "The air seems bright with thy past presence yet." The poet recognizes the oxymoron in "past presence," and yet he persists in his fantasy:

> But thou art still for me as thou hast been
> When I have stood with thee as on a throne
> With all thy dim creations gathered round
> Like mountains, and I felt of mould like them
> And with them creatures of my own were mixed,
> Like things half-lived, catching and giving life.

$$(162-67)$$

In Browning's projection, he stands with Shelley in contiguous space, and his own creations are "mixed" almost as though synchronically with Shelley's own. This discursive mixing, this permeability of the poet's creations allowing past and present to flow together in an exchange of life, is the quality sought in predecessors by many other Victorians beside Browning. The *Edinburgh Review,* for example, complains in 1836 that Byron's poetry lacks just this capacity for mixing and is therefore not a congenial model for the Victorian poet: Byron's poetry "stands . . . by itself, a pyramid of black and dazzling marble—proud, monumental, barren; while all our poets of any really creative character, conscious of possessing, and determined to retain their personal identity, seem to be turning elsewhere for those assimilating and pervading qualities which are destined to feed them in their growth."[43] Victorian poets need to "assimilate" and be "pervaded" by their models, and Browning is no exception in his longing for Shelley. Still, there is a dimness to his vision; Shelley can only be brought to a kind of half-life through the intensity of abstract desire. The story must be told again; it must be made more alive through metaphor. Hence Browning gives his fantasy a local habitation in the nineteen lines I have been analyzing. The metaphoric juxtaposition there is not between one poet and another, or between the emanations of two poets as in the "Letter to Maria Gisborne"; it is between the predecessor poet and a more accessible allegorical sign of him. Browning is not likening himself to Shelley; he is trying to make Shelley less distant from him. He cannot literally draw nearer; his creatures and Shelley's can never truly "mix" in the medium of historical time, and he can never walk with Shelley in the same "landscape." So he invents a metaphoric landscape, a "country" in which the figure for himself and the natural symbol of Shelley— Shelley's "own" image of the great river—interact contiguously in time and space. This is still fantasy, but the restatement brings Browning nearer the ideal of human contact with the lost poet. His fictional country begins as a private world of nature, the sacred spring, and through an unbroken following of the water's course, the discrete poetic subject is brought back to that social world of men that had been so empty of poets. But now Shelley, abstracted in time and space by the image of the river, has survived in the world of men: "so / Wast thou to me, and art Thou to the world!" This last is not an analogical or symbolic relation; the subject designated by "me" is a material part of that structured totality that is "the world."

The desire for commerce with Shelley remained with Browning long after he ceased trying to speak Shelley's language. Frederick Pottle was not wrong to "catch still the incredulous longing in Browning's voice" when the poet wrote, "Ah, did you once see

Shelley plain / And did he stop and speak to you, / And did you speak to him again? / How strange it seems and new!"[44] Nevertheless, as profound as this affinity was (along with the subsequent revulsion from Shelley's personal morality), it would be a mistake to infer that the problems of accommodating and rejecting poetic models are restricted to a single "poetic father." A poet goes on evolving complicated intertextualities as his career develops, and in Browning's case, I would stress the fact that the apparent discontinuity between his own period and the poetically relevant past continues to condition his response to other models and sources long after Shelley has ceased to be important. He continues to use metaphor to explain his use of earlier texts, and those metaphors display the features and bear the implications that were progressive in the example from *Pauline*. What does change is the nature of the models Browning chooses. In his earlier works, he used his Romantic predecessors as they used their own models: as a source of diction, imagery, and poetic phrasing. But as he experimented with post-Romantic literary forms, he drew on his reading mostly for subject matter. The most celebrated instance is, of course, that "Old Yellow Book," which prompted him to write his most ambitious poem, and the title of that work introduces Browning's most famous metaphor.

In the opening verse paragraph of *The Ring and the Book,* Browning explains how ancient goldsmiths forged a gold ring. They made the hard gold soft by alloying it with honey and wax. Then they formed it into the shape of a ring and repurified the gold by drawing off the honey and wax with acid. This, he explains, "signifies" the way *The Ring and the Book* was written; the Old Yellow Book is the raw gold, Browning adds a certain "something" of his own to make it malleable, and his own poem is produced like the goldsmith's ring.

> From the book, yes; thence bit by bit I dug
> The lingot truth, that memorable day,
> Assayed and knew my piecemeal gain was gold,—
> Yes; but from something else surpassing that,
> Something of mine which, mixed up with the mass,
> Made it bear hammer and be firm to file.

Fancy with fact is just one fact the more;
To wit, that fancy has informed, transpierced,
Thridded and so thrown fast the facts else free,
As right through ring and ring runs the djereed
And binds the loose, one bar without a break.
I fused my live soul and that inert stuff,
Before attempting smithcraft, on the night
After the day when—truth thus grasped and gained—
The book was shut and done with and laid by

(1:452–66)

Though the language has changed a great deal since *Pauline,* and the youthful attempts to think analogically like Shelley have been abandoned long ago, this metaphor nevertheless displays a surprising similarity to that earlier metaphor for the poet's confrontation with his source. It has a narrative syntax and structure, moving through a process of physical transformation, and it offers a model of engagement, rather than resemblance, between the poet and the antecedent text or writer. Browning, as enunciatory subject, "mixes" something of his own with the "inert" gold of the book, just as "creatures of [his] own were mixed" with the dead Shelley's creations in *Pauline.* Moreover, we find that the temporal path of the metaphor moves from the discovery of a private treasure toward the presentation of that treasure, in a more accessible version, to the world at large. Hence Browning begins his poem by invoking the "British Public, ye who like me not," and ends with a transformed address to the "British Public, who may like me yet." The process of smithcraft, like the journey down the river, is designed to bridge the gap between the private knowledge of the poet and the collective consciousness of his audience, something that, as we have seen, Shelley could only desire. But as in *Pauline,* this is more than an attempt to gain favor with the reading public. Browning's poem and his metaphor are more deeply an effort to reestablish linkage with a lost past. The paragraph that first addressed the British public continues as follows:

Truth must prevail, the proverb vows; and truth
—Here is it all i' the book at last, as first

There it was all i' the heads and hearts of Rome
Gentle and simple, never to fall nor fade
Nor be forgotten. Yet, a little while,
The passage of a century or so,
Decads thrice five, and here's time paid his tax,
Oblivion gone home with her harvesting,
And all left smooth again as scythe could shave.
Far from beginning with you London folk,
I took my book to Rome first, tried truth's power
On likely people. "Have you met such names?
Is a tradition extant of such facts?
Your law-courts stand, your records frown a-row:
What if I rove and rummage?" "—Why, you'll waste
Your pains and end as wise as you began!"
Every one snickered: "names and facts thus old
Are newer much than Europe news we find
Down in to-day's *Diario*. Records, quotha?
Why, the French burned them, what else do the French?
The rap-and-rending nation!"

(1.408-28)

The reality of the story in his book is lost forever beyond a gulf of temporal discontinuity. This is the context for the metaphor of the ring, just as the sense of disjunction between the generation of great Romantic poets and the world of the 1830s was the context for the metaphor of the river. Like Shelley's Julian, Browning's first response to an ancient story is to desire further knowledge, to find the contiguous reality beyond the account. He would have the participants in his murder plot become real people with verifiable histories. But the intervening centuries are a barrier, an irrevocable and violent dissociation. The old book may point to a reality, but it will forever be a reality that cannot be known, that cannot be seen. It is from this absence, and this desire, that the metaphor of the ring and the poet's mixing of fancy with fact to make "just one fact the more" derive. Whatever contact with the distant but tantalizing past has been lost, the poet must reconstruct through a process of discursive fusion; he desires, as Browning says in the final lines of *The Ring and the Book*, to create a "rare gold ring of verse" linking "our England to his Italy."

In the thirty years between *Pauline* and *The Ring and the Book*,

Browning gave us the greatest examples we have of the form known as the dramatic monologue. This chapter has almost closed the intersection of two axes that locate that genre in both literary history and the social system of Browning's time. I say "almost," because my preliminary remarks on poetic discourse are not yet an account of poetic genre. The social axis has been drawn, albeit lightly, through "Pictor Ignotus," allowing me to suggest that the dramatic monologue grows, in part, from an anxiety about kinds of artistic production that require a homogeneous subject in the place of their intelligibility. The literary historical axis already traces the course of an anxiety about discursive and historical continuities. We can see how these two anxieties may involve one another, but I have not yet shown their intersection in the dramatic monologue itself. To do that, I need a much more detailed account of the monologue's characteristic organization, including the ways in which that form is constituted by the kind of discursive poetic language I have begun describing. Hence the next three chapters concentrate on describing the monologue. By way of clarifying the meeting of the two axes that have schematized this chapter, I shall present the genre in three analyses: an analysis that examines the problems of continuity and the boundaries of discourse, an analysis that investigates the splitting of poetic subjectivity, and an analysis that extends the Shelleyan ambivalence concerning the monological and dialogical potential of poetic discourse itself.

THREE

The Being Written

I   Shelley's metaphoric movement
from *noema* to *noesis,* from "things" to "integral thoughts," corresponds very closely to the experience of the Romantic sublime. Sublimation, Thomas Weiskel tells us, "melts the formal otherness of things and reduces them to material or to substance. The formal properties of the perceived particular are canceled and replaced by their 'significance,' values assessed and assigned by the mind."[1] This replacement institutes what I have been calling the symbolic relation between the material and the ideal. Formal otherness, for Shelley, may consist in the participation of things in formal categories (earth, air, fire, water) or, linguistically, in their limited range of potential combinations within the sentence or semiotic chain. Their reduction to "matter," a metacategory akin to Shelley's "all things that are," is a reduction only in the sense of a descent into the dark night of the poetic soul, that essential relinquishing of articulated purpose in time and space necessary for the ascent toward the transcendent "integral thoughts" or sublime awareness of the mind's infinity. That infinity is conceived as a logos, a unified timeless presence to which all speech and all writing aspire through metaphor. This logos or absolute presence is the transcendent and ontologically distinct signified that the linguistic signifier represents through the symbolic mediation of mind.

In the language of Browning's early poems, we observe the beginning of a process of desublimation that ends in the creation of the dramatic monologue. The speaker of *Pauline,* along with Paracelsus and Sordello, can be described as a poetic subject that aspires to, but fails to experience, the Romantic sublime, a subject that began and has now abandoned a quest for self-contained homogeneity:

Oh Pauline, I am ruined who believed
That though my soul had floated from its sphere
Of wild dominion into the dim orb
Of self—that it was strong and free as ever!

(89–92)

Already the speaker understands the conformation of the "soul" to the "self" as a contingent act, a choice. The subject, initially split between a "dim orb of self" and a "sphere of wild dominion," has become perversely bound into a unity. In the lines that follow, that unity is described metaphorically, but the metaphors themselves, a sequence of dream narratives, reestablish the divided self in two ways: by projecting a dramatic exchange between two within the dim orb of self and by separating the subject who speaks to Pauline from the subject of the dreams. This latter separation is the most violent; at first the self is a "fiend" who entraps a "soul" in the form of a swan, after which the self becomes a female witch who seduces a god. The guilt and sexual ambivalence of this passage articulate the speaker's "ruin." He has sought the absolute present, the sublime transcendence, of unitary mind; but the process of thought that finally represents his subjectivity is the dream, a multiple narrative that images neither a changeless present nor a consistent subject.

This radical de-sublimation, of which we find only the first hints in the early poems, finds its ultimate projection in the dramatic monologue, or as I shall argue later, in the sequence of dramatic monologues that make up the books Browning wrote. The literary historical argument of the preceding chapter can be restated by saying that the intellectual processes of both sublimation and de-sublimation are, in part, linguistic. Browning's sentences do not lend themselves to the experience of the sublime because they struggle against the illusion of absolute presence, against what Derrida calls "The Written Being."[2] The Romantic project was always to signify "Being" by the written, but Browning abandons this attempt in favor of displaying "The Being Written" as a discursive vehicle for denying the cultural and personal isolation of an absolute present.

This chapter describes Browning's mature display of the process whereby the subject is "being written." Chapter 4 explains how the remarkable doubling of discourse in the monologue both splits the poetic subject and challenges the alienations implicit in specialized language. In Chapter 5, I shall look at the ambivalent incorporation of intersubjective exchange in the monologue's movement toward dialogical discourse.

II

The myth of transcendent presence may be located, through its furthest reduction, in the copula, in the static tyrannizing *Fiat* itself. This suggests concentrating on predication, and the opposition "The Written Being" / "The Being Written" becomes a linguistic pun based on the capacity of the copula to express the extreme poles of presence and dynamic process. On the one hand, "to be" is the essence of nonchange and nondisjunction; on the other, it is also the indispensable first component of the progressive form, *be + verb + ing*. This latter form, as in "Robert is writing," is a form of representing, not only process as opposed to stasis, but a process without discreteness or marked boundary. My argument is that Browning frequently presents the moment of speech (or writing) more as an ever-emerging fragment than as an inscribed signifier with its implied transcendent signified. Though the progressive form of the verb itself is one way of doing this, Browning has many ways, and my description of his writing as "progressive" may be taken as a useful heuristic metaphor. In any case, the following analysis will suggest that the dramatic monologue represents the discovery of a literary form capable of fictionalizing the acts of speech and writing as never-complete, never-present, never-structural unfoldings of the world-in-discourse. The dramatic monologue does not, indeed, have a structure in the sense that the Romantic ode or sonnet may be said to have a structure. What it has is a project, and part of that project is a linguistic and ethical denial of stativity as the basis of knowing the world.

As a beginning, it may be useful to indicate a little more fully the implications of progressive predication. The *be* + *verb* + *ing* form is what linguists call progressive "aspect." Aspects, according to Bernard Comrie, "are different ways of viewing the internal temporal constituency of a situation."[3] Perfective aspect, as in "Robert wrote a poem," "indicates the view of a situation as a single whole, without distinction of the various separate phases that make up that situation."[4] By contrast, the progressive, or imperfective, "pays essential attention to the internal structure of the situation."[5] In a sentence like "Robert is writing a poem," the action is not a whole; it is incomplete, and it is viewed from inside the time sequence in which it occurs. The sentence tells us that at a particular time, an action is in process, but it implies an indefinite temporal extension beyond the verb's "moment" in which the beginning and the ending of the act presumably take place. This perspective corresponds here to the perspective implied by the phrase "The Being Written," itself a generalization of the progressive verb phrase. In perfective sentences, the verb's moment and that of the action coincide as though the one enjoyed an ontologically certain "fit" with the other. Progressive sentences imply that the speaker's utterance intrudes its intervals while recognizing that action does not contain those particular intervals within itself. Such sentences, in other words, call into question the reality of absolute presence, reducing it to a grammatical choice located in the verb's aspect. Perfective aspect "perfects" the situation it re-presents. Progressive aspect leaves it "imperfect," allowing for the temporal openness of the referent.

Although I am using the concept of progressive aspect here as a simplified schema for understanding the organization of the dramatic monologue, the relation between language and form is not entirely metaphoric or homologistic. The syntax on which Browning builds the monologues is, indeed, rich in progressive predication. Moreover, Browning also achieves the effect of the progressive, the concentration on articulating temporal continuities freed from the boundaries of discrete presence, by several other characteristic means of elaborating the predicate. One of these simply involves shifting the progressivizing function from the main verb to participles that modify it:

He walked and tapped the pavement with his cane,
Scenting the world, looking it full in face.

("How it Strikes a Contemporary," 10–11)

Though the two main verbs, "walked" and "tapped," are perfective, the modifying adverbial phrases are transformations of two sentences containing verbs of progressive aspect: "He was scenting the world" and "He was looking it full in face." These implicit progressives modify the main verbs precisely by placing them within a dynamic situation of unbounded continuous duration.

Another typical way that Browning blurs the boundaries of action is through modification by temporal adverbs. Subordinate progressives like the ones cited from "How it Strikes a Contemporary" function much as the phrase, "any more," functions in the first line of "Andrea del Sarto": "But do not let us quarrel any more." The progressive, as Comrie suggests, "looks at the situation from inside, and as such is crucially concerned with the internal structure of the situation, since it can both look backwards towards the start of the situation, and look forwards to the end of the situation."[6] Andrea, as he begins his monologue, is inside the situation, he looks backward to a time when quarreling began, and he pleads for a future time when the process will end; the situation's "internal structure" is his entire concern. Of course, many syntactic constructions can create this and similar effects. I shall be discussing the three that seem to me the most frequent and the least ambiguous in Browning's poetic language: *verbs of progressive aspect; present participles of dynamic verbs used as adverbs;* and *adverbial phrases signifying temporal proximity.*

By way of showing the relation of these stylistic devices to familiar dimensions of Browning's verbal strategy, I should like to begin by looking at the opening passages of "Fra Lippo Lippi." In that poem, a speaker attempts to change his relation to a listener, and the parameters of the change can be described in terms of progressive predication. The initial relationship between Lippo and the constable who apprehends him in the street is based on the executive power of the officer. Lippo is in trouble, and his immediate need is to interrupt the exercise of the constable's power.

This he does by invoking a social context in which the asymmetry is reversed:

> Aha, you know your betters! Then, you'll take
> Your hand away that's fiddling on my throat,
> And please to know me likewise. Who am I?
> Why, one, sir, who is lodging with a friend
> Three streets off—he's a certain . . . how d'ye call?
> Master—a . . . Cosimo of the Medici.
>
> (12–17)

Instead of only one power relationship (officer / miscreant), there is now also a second, inverted relationship (patron's favorite / public servant), which exists simultaneously and prevents temporarily the consequences of the constable's initial advantage. Lippo accomplishes this correction of the power imbalance by placing himself and his captor syntactically in parallel: the noun phrases "your hand" (metonymically representing the officer) and "one" (pronominally representing Lippo) are modified by relative clauses of similar structure. The similarity derives chiefly from the fact that both verbs carry progressive aspect ("is fiddling" / "is lodging"). Linguistically, Lippo characterizes both himself and his captors according to the internal structure of an open-ended situation. For Lippo, the doubtful sequel of the unfinished action could be disastrous, and he wishes to influence that outcome by suggesting that the sequel might as easily be disastrous for the officer. The present moment for both antagonists is, in other words, rendered fragmentary and uncertain by verb phrases that adopt an interior, or progressive, perspective on incomplete action.

Lippo's strategem works, but he knows his victory is only temporary. Freeing himself from that "gullet's gripe" is not the same as exonerating himself or avoiding the consequences of arrest. He must do more than instill a prudent caution in his captors; he must gain their sympathy. Hence he attempts to transform the two, offsetting power asymmetries into a single symmetrical solidarity relationship (comrade / comrade):

Tell you, I liked your looks at very first.
Let's sit and set things straight, hip to haunch.
Here's spring come, and the nights one makes up bands
To roam the town and sing out carnival,
And I've been three weeks shut within my mew,
A-painting for the great man, saints and saints
And saints again. I could not paint all night—

(43–49)

Comrade/comrade

Lippo's invitation to the officer to share vicariously in his experience depends on several of the syntactic features that relate to progressive aspect in their interiorizing effect. In the first two lines quoted, for example, the temporal adverbials, "at very first" and "now," connect the present with a specific beginning in terms of the comradely feeling that Lippo wishes to instill in his listener. Lippo would pretend that the discontinuity between a relationship based on power and one based on solidarity has been misleading, that he has entertained "solidarity feelings" for the officer throughout their acquaintance. The second two lines establish a public temporal context, nighttime in the spring, within which the officer can sympathize with a monk's dilemma. Moreover, what the officer is invited to feel vicariously is tedium, the passage of three weeks with only the repeated painting of "saints and saints / and saints again" for occupation. Here again, the projection of an interior temporal contour into Lippo's experience is achieved through the adverbials, "three weeks" and "all night," along with the crucial phrase, "A-painting for the great man, saints and saints / And saints again." The importance of this phrase is both semantic and syntactic. First, Lippo has transformed "the great man," his patron, from a powerful ally to a mild adversary viewed from within the new solidarity relationship. And the rhetorical basis for this shift is his implicit request that the officer identify with him in his private trials. This means imagining what it would be like to sit in a room painting for three weeks with no apparent end of the situation in sight. This is, of course, the approach to temporal "situation" characteristic of progressive aspect, and the participial phrase that identifies painting as Lippo's activity is accordingly a transformation of the sentence "I *have been painting* saints and saints and saints again." To put the matter succinctly, the rhetorical shift from the expression of two public power relationships to the expression of one private solidarity relationship is marked syntactically by the replacement of two parallel progressive time sequences with one such sequence that is imaginatively shared by the poem's speaker and implied listener.

These passages, and the linguistic patterns that constitute them, raise the question of how habits of language can be related to literary genre. Theoretically, this is a difficult issue, one that I have attempted to treat elsewhere.[7] For the present argument, I want only to claim that the two levels of discourse are related, that the dramatic monologue, in one of its principal functions, creates a poetic moment for a certain subject and for a certain duration that is viewed internally and that is indefinitely continuous with an implied extratextual past and future of unmarked extent. In chapter 2, I argued that Browning's language was responsive to anxieties about continuities in time, and I suggested that these anxieties revised Shelley's concerns with metaphoric significance. Significance is, of course, a function of presence, and the dramatic monologue attempts to demystify the ideology of presence by probing the difficulties of temporal retention and protension. At the heart of this project is the denial of boundaries between past and present and between future and present, and this denial is intrinsic to the complex of verb-forming and verb-modifying practices that I have attributed to Browning's language. To adopt the immediately relevant linguistic metaphor, Browning, by writing dramatic monologues, discovered an inclusive form for the manifestation of imperfective predication. We shall see that this "refusal to perfect" in the predicate becomes also an uncertain resistance to the discrete and noncontradictory homogeneity of the subject itself. For as John Ellis and Rosalind Coward have pointed out, the subject "only ever appears as the fixed relation of the subject to what it predicates, and this relation must necessarily be ideological."[8] The ideology in question, and the one that represents the subject in the social totality of Victorian England, produces the individual "as an identity (a point of self-reference) rather than a process."[9] The dramatic monologue, I would argue,

brings this ideology to consciousness in its full range of contradictions. The subject-as-identity appears, to be sure, as a unitary
"speaker," but at the level of predication—of social being and becoming—it is not just a few verbs but whole discourses that paradoxically take on something like "progressive aspect."

Dramatic monologues are temporal fragments, and when we
speak of a poem as a "fragment," we are largely making an inference from the way it either begins or ends, or both. Thus it is not
surprising that examining the opening lines of several of the monologues in *Men and Women,* we find characteristic modes of verb
modification, along with other syntactic traits, signifying an immediately contiguous past out of which the poem's moment grows.
The first two lines of "Andrea del Sarto" supply an apt example:
"But do not let us quarrel any more, / No, my Lucrezia; bear with
me for once." The two temporal adverbials, "any more" and "for
once," refer to a habitual situation preceding the moment of
utterance. Moreover, the relation between that relevant past and
the linguistic present is one of continuity, however episodically
manifested. Quarreling is an ongoing process, and Browning indicates this experiential continuity by implying a linguistic continuity: a first clause preceding the poem and linked to it by the
coordinating conjunction "but." This retention of an always disappearing line of past discourse is just one method Browning uses
to begin monologues in the midst of an unbroken temporal stream,
but even this limited technique takes several forms. The speaker of
"A Light Woman" reveals a story already in progress when he begins "So far as our story approaches the end, / Which do you pity
the most of us three?" Answer may also be made to something
said by a person apparently addressed by the speaker: "Escape
me? / Never—" ("Life in a Love"). In another variation, the speaker
may begin by referring to someone else's discourse in the third
person: "My first thought was, he lied in every word." In this
example, from "Childe Roland to the Dark Tower Came," the
contradiction between the initiatory boundary of the poem and
the absence of a coinciding boundary to the ostensible experience
has been focused in the adjective "first." Roland's "first" thought
is indeed the first of the poem, but syntagmatically, the sentence

seems to be an incomplete portion of the pattern, "My first thought after he said X was Y," where X has been omitted or deferred in the text of the poem itself.

Reference to an immediate linguistic past is not the only way Browning's initiatory devices create their characteristic effects. When Fra Lippo Lippi exclaims "You need not clap your torches to my face," he refers to an action that has presumably already taken place. Other speakers invoke extratextual knowledge, using temporal adverbs to locate that knowledge in time relative to the utterance: "I said—Then, dearest, since 'tis so, / Since *now at length* my fate I know" ("The Last Ride Together"; emphasis in this and following examples in this section is mine). Bishop Blougram's well-known "No more wine?" questions an interlocutor about a decision already expressed and also, in an important corollary to the typical pattern, looks forward with uncertainty to the immediate future. Many of these devices are protensive in this way, raising questions as much about possible succeeding events as about past ones. Thus "In Three Days" begins with the coordinating conjunction, which suggests unbroken discourse prior to the poem's present, but it rapidly shifts to the future tense for the verb, which is as usual modified by a temporal adverbial phrase: "So, I shall see her *in three days.*"

Browning has many incidental ways of indicating a retained contiguous past as well as a protended future. These local devices, however they differ, seem to be built out of remarkably regular habits of verb modification:

> Said Abner, "*At last* thou art come! *Ere* I tell, *ere*
>   thou speak,
> Kiss my cheek, wish me well!"
>
> ("Saul")

> They give thy letter to me, *even now:*
> I read and seem as if I heard thee speak.
> The master of thy galley *still* unlades
> Gift after gift; they block my court *at last*
> And pile themselves along its portico.
>
> ("Cleon")

Stand still, true poet that you are!
 I know you; let me try and draw you.
Some night you'll fail us.

("Popularity")

I wonder do you feel *to-day*
 As I have felt.

("Two in the Campagna")

Let us *begin* and carry up this corpse.
 Singing together.

("A Grammarian's Funeral")

Stop playing, poet! May a brother speak?

("Transcendentalism: A Poem in Twelve Books")

My final example is a command predicated on the interior point of
view characteristic of progressive aspect—it responds to a situation
signified by the sentence "The poet is playing." In the example
from "A Grammarian's Funeral," I have italicized "begin." In one
sense, present tense verbs of initiation belong in my list of progressive forms because they specify a location within a temporal
succession. Coming at the beginning of the poem, however, this
implication is somewhat weakened. If true monologues present a
poetic beginning that is not an experiential beginning, a poem that
"begins" with the clause "Let us begin" would seem not to conform. But this is not the case with "A Grammarian's Funeral." Its
beginning is, in fact, a continuation, and we know this because the
object of the verb "carry" is "this corpse." Though the act of
carrying may be only about to commence, a situation predates it
in which a corpse—some corpse—exists.

 Here we should briefly expand our account to consider deictics
and definite determiners as they appear in Browning's idiom.
Deictics are "pointers," usually adjectives (like "that" or "these")
or adverbs (like "there") that effect directional verbal gestures.
The accepted classification of determiners has been usefully summarized by Elizabeth Traugott as follows:

> *The* and *a* are usually called the "definite" and the "indefinite" article,
> respectively. Their prime function is to signal what assumptions the

speaker is making about what knowledge is common to him and the speaker. For example, if I say to you:

2.86 Do you want the ticket?

And you don't know anything about any tickets, you nevertheless know that I assume you know about some tickets; so you can reply:

2.87 What ticket?

But if I say to you:

2.88 Do you want a ticket to "Dracula, Prince of Denmark?" no such assumptions apply, and 2.87 would be inappropriate.

The assumes the noun has been referred to before, or is what is loosely called, "given, known material."[10]

The definite article, in other words, implies a time previous to the utterance that is epistemologically shared by the sender and the receiver of the linguistic message. Deictics such as "this" function in part to give a spatial dimension to a "world" that is experientially prior to the utterance and continuous with it temporally. Thus when we read, as an opening line, "Let us begin and carry up this corpse," we immediately wonder "What corpse?" and the effect is fundamentally different from that of a discourse that commences "Let us begin and offer up a prayer."

Not all definite determiners imply a shared past knowledge or experience; or if they do, the sharing is so general that no specific time sequence is designated. Examples are "The weather is nice here" or "The moon is full," in which no corresponding indefinite forms ("a weather" or "a moon") exist. In such cases as these, the quality of "before mentionedness" is missing; the determiners do not have what linguists call "anaphoric" function. Anaphora is repetition, but in Browning, the linguistic sense of implied repetition is most often the appropriate one. When we speak of actual repetition, we are speaking of what Paul Ricoeur calls the "self-referential feature of language" in a special way.[11] For a word or a phrase to be recognized as a repetition, it must bear a special relation to a previous word or phrase; it must "refer backward" in the semiotic chain. It is, therefore, a temporary arrest in that continual "sliding" of signifiers that Lacan has described. Some syntactic devices, like anaphoric determiners, have the force of repetitional self-reference in the absence of actual repetition: the inevitable question "What corpse?" is a phenomenological marker of this kind of arrest; it is a search for the repetition. Once we have seen that implied repetition and implied reference can be equated, it is easy to extend the analysis of linguistic self-reference to what Ricoeur calls "ostensive reference," reference to a nonlinguistic world shared by a speaker and his implied listener ("I call / *That* piece a wonder, now"). Reference to a previous word and reference to a preexisting object in the material world are, formally speaking, identical acts of diachronic "arrest," and this is why anaphoric determiners and deictics need to be classified together, along with other syntactic markers of reference.

In several places, the implications of this kind of reference through deictics and determiners are especially important for Browning's style. Here, for example, is Cleon:

> It is as thou hast heard: in one short life
> I, Cleon, have effected all *those* things
> Thou wonderingly dost enumerate.
> *That* epos on thy hundred plates of gold
> Is mine,—and also mine *the* little chant,
> So sure to rise from every fishing-bark
> When lights at prow, the seamen haul their net.
> *The* image of the sun-god on *the* phare,
> Men turn from the sun's self to see, is mine;
> *The* Poecile, o'er-storied its whole length,
> As thou didst hear, with painting, is mine too.
>
> (44-54)

The reason this poem makes the anaphoric element of Browning's mode of reference so clear is that Cleon is openly responding to a preexisting text, Protous's letter and the rumors that it, in turn, apparently refers to. The phrases "as thou hast heard" and "as thou didst hear" frame a catalogue in which the deictic ("that epos") and the definite article ("the little chant") are interchangeable. Both refer in the same way to that which has been previously mentioned or previously known by both communicants. This effect also serves to explain in part a feature of Browning's style that has always fascinated his readers, the use of extraordinarily arcane

diction, especially in the category of nouns. The questions "What
is a phare?" or "What is a Poecile?" are similar to "What corpse?"
They imply a context of reference or earlier discourse shared by
the sender and receiver of the message but not necessarily by the
eavesdropper (reader).[12] Thus, again, Browning implies a particular
time sequence, previously in progress, which the speaker of the
monologue experiences and expresses from within.

Readers often experience this aspect of style as a kind of familiarity with physical surroundings shared by a speaker and his implied
interlocutor. Andrea Del Sarto's musings to his wife provide a
typical example:

> My youth, my hope, my art, being all toned down
> To *yonder* sober pleasant Fiesole.
> There's *the* bell clinking from *the* chapel-top;
> *That* length of convent-wall across the way
> Holds *the* trees safer, huddled more inside;
> *The* last monk leaves *the* garden.
>
> (39–44)

The passage is one of gesture toward an ostensive world, a world
that has long been the context for the quarreling between Andrea
and Lucrezia. Even this somewhat static scenery makes its contribution to the implied repetitions of Andrea's life. This evening is
like others with its clinking chapel bell and the monks leaving the
garden at their regular time. These are not surprising interpretive
observations, but what so often eludes us is the fragility of the
syntactic patterns on which they depend. Merely change the
determiners, say "There's *a* bell clinking from *a* chapel-top," and
all of the prior familiarity with the surroundings that the painter
and his wife share is lost. The line as it stands in the poem entails
in its syntax a relevant past; the altered version presents a new
moment, an independent observation, a surprise.

Again I am describing an element of style that is not inherently
related to poetic form. I have focused on deictics and determiners,
but the function of implied reference back may be carried by other
features too. One other example is the genitive construction of
nouns and personal pronouns: "I'll work then for your friend's

friend," implies a known series of social relations just as "The image of the sun-god on the phare" implies a known juxtaposition of physical entities. Like the progressive modes of verb construction and modification, these vehicles for introducing an implied contiguous past may be said to exist in two ways within dramatic monologues. First, they exist as part of the general texture of the poet's language, and second, they cluster to give specific shape to poetic form.

So far in my description, I have largely focused on the way dramatic monologues begin. This is because in a poem created as a time fragment, the beginning is an especially sensitive formal nexus. But in the dramatic monologue, temporal retention and protension are not mere frontier projects of linkage; they are pervasive fields of verbal energy always being generated out of a disturbingly immanent sense of an inadequately realized present. These are poems that interpret both language and experience as an emergence of fragments that cannot be reduced to elementary discrete units nor gathered into a finished whole. To this point, I have concentrated on the syntax of clauses. In order to complete the picture of the discursive organization of whole poems, however, we need to see that in complex sentence strategies, the dramatic monologue typically makes use of an equally distinctive mode of relating clauses to one another. My example is perhaps Browning's best-known monologue.

III

The larger movement of "My Last Duchess" is a sequential and fragmentary revelation of character. In the first twenty lines, Browning offers information concerning the duke, his interlocutor, Frà Pandolf, and the duchess's portrait in an alternating pattern of suggestive but incomplete references:

> That's my last Duchess painted on the wall,
> Looking as if she were alive. I call
> That piece a wonder, now: Frà Pandolf's hands
> Worked busily a day, and there she stands.
> Will't please you sit and look at her? I said

"Frà Pandolf" by design, for never read
Strangers like you that pictured countenance,
The depth and passion of its earnest glance,
But to myself they turned (since none puts by
The curtain I have drawn for you, but I)
And seemed as they would ask me, if they durst,
How such a glance came there; so, not the first
Are you to turn and ask thus. Sir, 'twas not
Her husband's presence only, called that spot
Of joy into the Duchess' cheek: perhaps
Frà Pandolf chanced to say "Her mantle laps
Over my lady's wrist too much," or "Paint
Must never hope to reproduce the faint
Half-flush that dies along her throat:" such stuff
Was courtesy, she thought, and cause enough
For calling up that spot of joy.

(1–21)

The first two-and-a-half lines concentrate some of the devices typically used by Browning to initiate monologues. The definite article and the two deictics ("that") create at the outset the illusion of a conversation already in progress. This implication of an immediate, "dramatic" past relevant to the poem's moment is joined by reference to a more distant, narrative past. This second past appears through the adjective "last" and is confirmed in the phrase "looking as if she were alive," which implies that she is no longer living. Finally, by using the temporal adverb "now," the duke suggests a past time, "then," at which he did not esteem the painting (or the duchess) so highly. The sentence structure of the opening lines gestures, then, toward the past, but it tells us very little about that past. From an affective point of view, one important result of the formal features that characterize so many of Browning's beginnings is to raise questions: "What corpse?", "What cripple?" "What duchess?"

The technique of provoking unanswered questions, delaying the useful information that answers them as long as possible, and then, while supplying that information, raising new questions to start the process all over again constitutes one of the central rhetorical strategies of the dramatic monologue and facilitates a transition from incomplete retention to incomplete protension without establishing a "space" between them.[13] The duchess's portrait, for example, is said to be successful because it captures her passion— this we learn in line 8. Not until lines 14–15 does the duke specify that passion as "joy," and finally, in lines 20–21, we discover that he considers her joy indiscriminate and too easily stimulated. In similar fashion, the duke's visitor is told in lines 3–4 that Frà Pandolf painted the duchess's portrait in a day, creating a vague suggestion of haste and carelessness. Despite the assertion that Frà Pandolf was mentioned "by design," however, it is not until lines 20–21 that the issue of the painter's superficiality is taken up again to explain that he has been the duchess's flatterer. Thus, at all times, the poem offers an incomplete account of situation and character, along with the expectation of subsequent filling in.

This poetic strategy of delay is created and explored in part through the conscious arrangement of content and in part through sentence structure. The first four sentences of "My Last Duchess" consist mostly of simple free clauses establishing the initial series of unanswered questions about the past. As soon as the duke begins explaining himself, however, simple sentences are abandoned in favor of a complex structure that J. McH. Sinclair calls "arrest." This is a term that "indicate[s] a sentence in which the onset of a predictable α (free clause) is delayed or in which its progress is interrupted."[14] One example of this kind of interruption analyzed in Sinclair's article is the first sentence of a poem by Philip Larkin:

> Lambs that learn to walk in snow
> When their bleating clouds the air
> Meet a vast unwelcome, know
> Nothing but a sunless glare.

In Sinclair's version, the first line encompasses a nominal group that requires a verb like "meet" or "know" to complete the free clause. The second line is a bound clause that interrupts the "onset" of the free clause. Assigning the letter α to free clauses and the letter β to bound clauses, Sinclair represents the Larkin sentence in the following manner: $\alpha[\beta]\alpha$. When we turn back to the fifth sentence in "My Last Duchess," we find that Larkin's syntax, from the point of view of arrest, was child's play. If we also include the arrest of bound clauses by other bound clauses, Browning's sentence schematizes like this:

$$\alpha\alpha\beta \, [\beta \, (\beta)] \, \beta \, [\beta] \, \beta$$

This sentence is an excellent example of how the rhetorical structure of a poetic genre and the sentence structure of a poetic style can complement one another. The first free clause is the one in which the duke announces his intention to explain the mysterious name "Frà Pandolf." This clause is not in itself arrested, but the complex interruptions that follow generate an effect of arrestment with regard to the predictable semantic sequel to "I said Frà Pandolf by design." Delays appear within delays, and this is why by the time Browning's speaker has answered one of the questions he has raised, he has already raised new ones in profusion. We finally discover that the duke counts Frà Pandolf among the duchess's flatterers, but not until he has ambiguously referred to other visitors like the present one, hinted at his obsession with his own domestic power, and suggested that the appropriate attitude for others within his household is one of intimidated deference. Finally, he renews the question of the duchess's passions and responses, prolonging the reader's curiosity about his own fixation on that "spot of joy."

So far, I have mainly stressed the poem's connection with an implied past. Just as the opening lines stimulated questions about the past, however, the closing passages project our attention into the immediate future beyond the termination of the poem itself:

> Will't please you rise? We'll meet
> The company below, then. I repeat,
> The Count your master's known munificence
> Is ample warrant that no just pretence
> Of mine for dowry will be disallowed;
> Though his fair daughter's self, as I avowed
> At starting, is my object.

(47-53)

This is the first we know of the company below, the count, his daughter, and the duke's intention to remarry. All of these elements are new pieces of the past, but they are pieces of the future as well. Only here do we perceive what a small and unboundaried moment this "present" encounter has been. Twice the duke refers to statements he has made in a past beyond the limits of the poem ("I repeat" and "as I avowed at starting"). Both statements concern an arrangement that is just beginning and that is fraught with sinister uncertainty. The episode in the gallery, in other words, is not discrete; at every instant, it inextricably connects with that which has gone before and that which will come after.

To summarize then, Browning exploits language as a temporal medium in two ways. First, he heightens our awareness that individual character can be known only as process and, therefore, only incompletely at any given time. Second, he implies that the present is always being dissolved into an elusive past and future. To return to our earlier metaphor, if a whole poem could be said to have the force of progressive aspect, "My Last Duchess" is that poem.

I think it is worth asking what bearing this view of the poem has on the traditional problems critics have encountered in interpreting it. Let us look for a moment at the last four lines. The movement away from the gallery has begun when the duke makes a last gesture toward his collection and, almost incidentally, toward the past:

> Nay, we'll go
> Together down, sir. Notice Neptune, though,
> Taming a sea-horse, thought a rarity,
> Which Claus of Innsbruck cast in bronze for me!
>
> (53–56)

This is the second work of art mentioned in the poem, the first being the duchess's portrait. Both are objects, standing unchanged amid the flurry of life around them. Indeed, by their nature, they are incapable of embodying process. Time is the condition of their creation—Frà Pandolf "worked busily a day" to produce his picture—but the painter knows that his finished work will be a dead and static thing: "Paint / Must never hope to reproduce the faint / Half-flush that dies along her throat." The color of living flesh, to Frà Pandolf's eye, is a function of movement, of disappearance, but just as Claus of Innsbruck cannot reproduce the interiorly experienced process implicit in the progressive clause "[who *is*] *taming* a sea-horse," paint cannot take on life. The same is not entirely true for art that is composed in language. Language offers devices like progressive aspect ("is taming") and temporal adverbs ("worked busily *a day*"; "avowed *at starting*") that recall to mind the reality of temporal displacement. Poetry, for Browning, strives to concentrate the flux of life within speech, a principle overtly recognized as early as the preface to *Paracelsus*. There he tells his readers that "instead of having recourse to an external machinery of incidents to create and evolve the crisis I desire to produce, I have ventured to display somewhat minutely the mood itself in its rise and progress."[15] This distinction between a verbal art that can "display" life in its "rise and progress" and a plastic art that cannot "catch" that flux is crucial, I think, to the ironic strategy of "My Last Duchess."

Whereas Browning perceives an antithesis between plastic art and life itself, the duke of Ferrara projects an analogy. He considers works of art as discrete static objects to be owned and controlled, and as many readers have noticed, he thinks of persons in precisely the same way: "Though his fair daughter's self, as I avowed / At starting, is my object." People, of course, will never be very satisfactory as objects as long as they remain alive; they will embody all the fading inconsistencies that characterize life in time as Browning understands it. Hence the traits that "disgust" the duke are summarized by a verb of process, "this grew," and his remedy is murder, the stilling of the vital instability of casual, social existence.

> I gave commands
> Then all smiles stopped together. There she stands
> As if alive.
>
> (45–47)

Here the force of repetition illuminates in retrospect the opening lines. The duchess stands as if alive, not in Browning's sense of life, but as the duke would have human life exist in an art gallery of a world owned and controlled by himself. Frà Pandolf knows that this attitude demeans the living. To him, even dying is a living process, one that the duke falsifies and turns into crime with his peremptory "commands."

Many critics, even those who disagree with one another, have argued that no moral judgment inheres in the structure of the poem itself. William Cadbury believes the duke to be an ogre and contends that Browning created him "to prove a point of his own which we learn by applying the standards of an external morality."[16] Others, like Robert Langbaum, dissent, maintaining "that moral judgment does not figure importantly in our response to the duke, that we even identify ourselves with him."[17] In either case, "judgment" is something that exists only outside the poem, and the decision to apply it or not to apply it tends to be a matter of choice for the reader. But the structure of the poem seems to me to entail a serious judgment of character while simultaneously requiring our partial sympathy with the duke as a ratification of that judgment. For we are allowed to see the duke as he is incapable of seeing his fellow creatures: not as an embodiment of a changeless abstraction (his "nine-hundred-year-old name") but as a living, changing, hesitating human being who is finally knowable only in process and only in a fragmentary way. His fixed vision of his duchesses, past and future, belies the reality of his own existence, so that the final irony of the poem consists in the fact that his misconception of those around him implies a misconception of the very self he worships. The ingenuity of Browning's poem lies in the way it prevents its reader from repeating the duke's error. Both we and the duke find a vision of life in a work of art; we as easily as he might say "there *he* stands as if alive." But the meaning would be different. Browning has "made us see," as he was fond of saying the poet can do, and what we see, through poetry, is life process, while the duke in his gallery can see only the motionless dead.[18]

At this point, the realm of language intersects the realm of ideas, and we can begin to recognize familiar Victorian preoccupations, concerns in particular with the nature of experience in time. By immersing the dramatic monologue in the fragmentary unfolding of time's contours, I do not intend to deny Browning's interest in the idea of eternity or in transcendental abstraction. I would, however, insist that these notions find space in the monologue only as they function dynamically in human time. I do not find, as Shiv K. Kumar does, that it is for Browning "the function of a poet to symbolize the intersection between time and eternity."[19] This is the romanticized Browning, and Kumar, like many others, cites Browning's letter to Ruskin in which the poet speaks of "putting the infinite within the finite."[20] But there is nothing there about an epiphanic "intersection." I prefer to take Browning's use of "within" quite literally and say that in these poems, ideas of God, heaven, and eternity are human ideas being put to use in the incomplete and nonsymbolic human contexts created by the monologue form. Such inferences are perhaps closer to those of Roma A. King, who maintains that Browning's interest in the infinite notwithstanding, "the dynamic rather than the static, the state of becoming rather than of being, shapes the amorphous gestalt from which Browning viewed human experience."[21]

Browning's language and the literary form he produced represent constitutive elements in a cultural system where, in the terms of Gerald L. Bruns, "history is made to function as a formal property of thought."[22] Bruns is writing about Victorian prose writers, and his subject is their steady movement away from Romantic abstract thought:

> Indeed, it appears that for these writers the very notion of meaning itself was no longer conceivable purely in terms of abstract categories, but required for its creation or discovery the categories of process and event, sequence and development, as in a work like Newman's *An Essay on the Development of Christian Doctrine* (1845), in which the meaning of an idea is understood to be inseparable from its history.[23]

Bruns's concept of Victorian thought seems to me equally appropriate to Browning's poetry. For Browning too the meaning of an idea, a perception, or an insight is inseparable from history, this

time from a particular history, a particular "action in character."
This referral of abstraction to "mere chronos" is not, as Kumar
suggests, a trivializing gesture. It carries with it—indeed constitutes
in discourse—a large part of the Victorian period's groundwork of
social values and assumptions.

In my discussion of "Pictor Ignotus" in chapter 2, I also argued
that the dramatic monologue exposes to consciousness the contradictions intrinsic to Victorian ideology. The fundamental contradiction involved may now be stated more succinctly. Victorian
ideology appears to constitute a subject that is at once always disappearing and always consistent or nondisjunctive. This is, of course,
another way of stating the paradox of language-as-speech and
language-as-text that the dramatic monologue opens to inspection.
If the subject is constituted in language-as-speech, it is, in Lacan's
terms, "always a fading thing that runs under the chain of signifiers."[24] If, on the other hand, the subject is a text, it may be a
unity, a "character," or as Henry James would say, a "personage."
But in the dramatic monologue, the text / process of "the being
written" maintains both terms of this dyad simultaneously in view.

In most of the early monologues, the structure of this contradictory duality is the structure of irony. A speaker "speaks," but
in a "text," identifying himself in a homogeneous abstraction while
he unfolds and fades as a fragmentary speaking subject. Nevertheless, there are differences among these early poems. The Pictor
Ignotus objectifies subjectivity in his pictures just as the duke
objectifies both his duchess in her portrait and himself in his family's name. But the discourse of such poems locates the subject in
more positions than that of "the speaker." They locate both a
subject of enunciation and at least two subjects of address, called
"interlocutor" and "reader." In the language of "Pictor Ignotus,"
Browning projects, not only a heterogeneous subject of address as
the speaker speaks to his public, to God, and to the praised youth,
but also a subject of enunciation that does not either identify
with or alienate himself from his own "picture," the poem itself.
By denying the choice faced by the speaker, he withholds the consistency of moral judgment from the reader.

In these regards—and I take them to constitute the ideological goal of the poem—"My Last Duchess" only partially fulfills the potential of the genre. The interlocutor does, in fact, become split as doubt builds as to whether the duke is confiding in the envoy or sending a message to the count. But the irony of the poem, as I have argued, does entail a judgment on the duke's transpositions of people into objects. Judgments of this kind imply in themselves the existence of a unitary subject for thinking the judgments. However unstated the poem may leave its moral conclusion, the reading subject must choose either to identify with the duke or—as I believe, more correctly—to condemn him. The reader becomes the subject of a new discourse that must be monological. Such a discourse reflexively constructs the subject that initiates the poem itself in the form of an equally monological "intention," or intelligible "meaning." To me, then, "Pictor Ignotus" is by a slight measure the more successful of the two poems. Saying this, of course, means that it does what the monologue is uniquely designed to do more completely and with greater richness of application than "My Last Duchess" does.[25] For such an evaluation to carry its full force, the monologue's role in dividing the subject needs a further account. Such is the purpose of the next chapter.

The Divided Subject

I   The contradiction between per-
son-as-object and person-as-process that I discussed in the last section may be read as a single discursive dialectical movement. In the
dramatic monologue, the person-as-thing appears as an abstraction,
as someone's thought about himself or about a particular other.
Over against this abstraction stands the "real" person-as-process,
which is manifested in the material productivity of speech. The
monologue itself, as text, cannot choose between the material and
the ideal person, either morally or epistemologically. No more can
it elevate the ideal to the level of a transcendent signified. What
the monologue signifies is the contradiction itself in its discursive
unfolding. The material person is always being produced, but it
cannot be produced by any process that does not also produce a
contradictory idea of the unitary self. This process of production
leaves its traces in a kind of textual discourse that I have been
calling "The Being Written."

One needn't look far to see that this distilled and visible contradiction is one of the most powerful, though often hidden, contradictions of a more generalized ideology. Bourgeois individualism
hardly requires documentation here. But the sovereignty of the
individual never exists as a monolithic conviction, and it takes
historically specific forms in large part from its relation to the concepts that oppose it at any given time. In England, during the
magnificent expansion of industrial and scientific progress, the
antithesis to individualism arises from the inescapable sense of
progress and decay, of the unfinished nature of any moment's

achievement, and of the desire for continuity that I discussed in the last chapter.[1] The individual dissolves into the kind of movement in human time that Walter Pater describes in his conclusion to *The Renaissance*. "That clear, perpetual outline of face and limb," he says, "is but an image of ours, . . . a design in a web, the actual threads of which pass out beyond it."[2] The dramatic monologue, while presenting a "clear image," continually attempts to suggest the presence of those "actual threads" as they extend out beyond the image in both time and space. There are many ways of facing the irreducibility of the opposition, but Pater's almost wistful sadness is among the most moving:

> Analysis . . . assures us that those impressions of the individual mind to which, for each one of us, experience dwindles down, are in perpetual flight; . . . To such a tremulous wisp constantly reforming itself on the stream, to a single sharp impression, with a sense in it, a relic more or less fleeting, of such moments gone by, what is real in our life fines itself down. It is with this movement, with the passage and dissolution of impressions, images, sensations, that analysis leaves off—that continual vanishing away, that strange, perpetual weaving and unweaving of ourselves.[3]

A present that is felt to be insubstantial, "a tremulous wisp" forever fading, "dwindling down" to nearly nothing under scrutiny, needs, and must project, a past and a future that give meaning to the "perpetual weaving and unweaving of ourselves." The other side of this need is the fear that the past is alienated, has been somehow lost or severed from the present. Pater describes the past chiefly as loss in the individual's perception of his own life; writers like John Stuart Mill and Matthew Arnold expressed the plight of an entire culture. In *The Spirit of the Age*, Mill writes,

> Before men begin to think much and long on the peculiarities of their own times, they must have begun to think that those times are, or are destined to be, distinguished in a very remarkable manner from the times that preceded them. Mankind are then divided, into those who are still what they were, and those who have changed; into the men of the present age, and the men of the past. To the former, the spirit of the age is a subject of exultation; to the latter, of terror; to both, of eager and anxious interest.[4]

Mill describes with high precision the contribution made by a perceived alienation from the past to interpersonal alienation within a contemporary community. These forms of division were, I believe, a subject of "eager and anxious interest" for many Victorians. An early portrait of the self-made genius, hermetically isolated from both his contemporaries and from a meaningful past, is Carlyle's Professor Teufelsdröckh:

> Had Teufelsdröckh also a father and mother; did he at one time, wear drivel-bibs, and live on spoon-meat? Did he ever, in rapture and tears, clasp a friend's bosom to his; looks he also wistfully into the long burial-aisle of the Past, where only winds, and their low harsh moan, give inarticulate answer? [5]

Teufelsdröckh is "a Pilgrim, and Traveller from a far country," whose past, whatever it may be, bears little relevance to the knowable individual confronted by the "Editor" of *Sartor Resartus*. It is this way of perceiving the individual self as temporally, culturally, and in the end, spatially disjoined that the dramatic monologue juxtaposes against that other view in which the boundaries of the individual are a mere illusory image.

It would, however, be a mistake to read this juxtaposition as symmetrical, as an equal balance. In its ideological form, the dyad is unbalanced by the fact that the autonomy of the individual usually appears as a positive value, while the absorption of the individual into a totality beyond itself is most often seen as a dehumanization. In the dramatic monologue, Browning raises the contradiction to consciousness in part by showing how this hierarchy of values might be reversed, how the individual might become in fact more fully human in a loss of discrete unity. The logic of this reversal begins from the premise that the essence of the human is language, and language fragments the speaking subject. In the terms of *Sordello*, the subject that is whole is one constituted in homogeneous "perception," while the subject-in-language is one constituted in heterogeneous "thought." At first, Sordello attempts to resolve the contradiction by constructing language as clothing, or armor, for perception. But this fusion proves unstable:

Piece after piece that armour broke away,
Because perceptions whole, like that he sought
To clothe, reject so pure a work of thought
As language: thought may take perception's place
But hardly co-exist in any case,
Being its mere presentment—of the whole
By parts, the simultaneous and the sole
By the successive and the many.

(*Sordello*, 2.588-95)

The dramatic monologue has fairly well abandoned the project of "presenting" an underlying wholeness. It recognizes the self-destroying quality of the idea of wholeness, an idea that can only be realized in discourse. The idea of wholeness is self-destroying in Browning because the subject of its discourse—the discourse of the dramatic monologue—can never be a discrete entity.[6] As we have seen, that subject lacks discreteness because it lacks fixed boundaries, but it also lacks discreteness because it is, in itself, split. It is not only "successive"; as we began to see in "Pictor Ignotus," it is also "many."

II

In my discussion of "My Last Duchess," I raised the traditional issue of the division between the poet and the speaker in dramatic monologues. I said that the duke and his creator interpret life differently, and this implies that I can tell the difference between the "voices" of two subjects for a single discourse. This assumption about Browning has gone virtually unchallenged from the time the poet himself commented on his work to the present. As most readers know, Browning characterized his poems as "always dramatic in principle, and so many utterances of so many imaginary persons, not mine," and said, "These [idylls] of mine are called 'Dramatic' because the story is told by some actor in it, not by the poet himself."[7] Modern critics have generally followed this lead. B. W. Fuson defined the dramatic monologue in 1948 as "an isolated poem intended to stimulate the utterance not of the poet but of another individualized speaker," and more recently, in one of the best essays on the genre, Michael Mason defines a monologue in part as "a poem of which the versified part is devoted almost entirely to the imaginary utterances of some person other than the author."[8] After all of this unanimity, and after my own apparent participation in it, I wish to argue that this inferred division between poet and speaker is not in itself essential to the dramatic monologue. My argument is not a refutation but rather a complication of the traditional assumption, and for authority, I can return to Browning himself:

> Love, you saw me gather men and women,
> Live or dead or fashioned by my fancy,
> Enter each and all, and use their service,
> Speak from every mouth,—the speech, a poem.
>
> ("One Word More," 129-32)

Not all of the figures in *Men and Women* are imaginary, and Browning says that he has entered them and spoken in his own person from their mouths. I do not think that Browning is being inconsistent. The division between the voice of the poet and the voice of the imaginary speaker is based on a reader's willingness to construe them both equally as "persons." If these persons are imagined to be corporeal, then they must be discrete, mutually excluding entities. But if they are voices and merely voices, can they not in some sense be both different and the same? Lacan, among others, has suggested ways to think of being-in-language as both a selfhood and an otherness; does this not mean that the clear differentiation of individual speakers derives from an ideology that is subject to revision? This ideology is certainly a part of the dramatic monologue's repertoire of subject matter, but I think that formally, the monologue challenges the limitations of traditional Cartesian epistemology in precisely this regard. One of its effects is to divide the subjectivity of poetic discourse but not to divide it, as by mitosis, into two equally unitary subjects where before there was one. There is still only one discourse that constructs and locates its subject; all we can say is that the subject in question is bivalent, split but not multiplied. This is why the division between "speaker" and "poet" is only one version of the essential doubleness of the monologue, and an ambivalent version at that. My purpose here is to describe the monologue's doubleness in its more generalized form.[9]

One of the monologue's goals is to show how individualized or specialized language may function as an alienating force. Yet the monologue does not stop at recognizing the alienation. Its imaginative leap is to fuse these differentiating idioms into a seamless utterance, thus calling into question even the radical capacity of historical time to insist on the mutual "otherness" inherent in separate acts of speech. This chapter examines the monologue's treatment of specialized language, whether the boundaries of that specialization are those of an elite group like "poets," an idiosyncratic individual, or a particular geographical or historical location. The first step is to describe some of the formal features that lead most readers to hear two voices in dramatic monologues.

In "My Last Duchess," the differentiation of speaker from poet is not entirely dependent on the irony of the duke's equating a painted image to a living person; it may also be inferred from the fact that the duke "speaks" in rhymed couplets. Ralph Rader has described Browning's use of the couplet convention in the following terms:

> We may ask ourselves whether in reading we imaginatively hear the words of the poem as spoken by the Duke, and of course we reply that we do. We may then ask ourselves if we understand the rhymes that we hear in the poem as part of the Duke's speech, and we discover that we do not. This shows that prior to any conscious analysis our imaginations register and respond to the presence of two agents in the intuitive act of construing the poem—a created actor, the Duke, and the immanent creator Browning.[10]

These seem reasonable things to say, though in a later article, Rader appears to argue somewhat differently. Instead of identifying the couplets as a sign of the presence of Browning, he tells us "that the couplets have a very definite function—to give a sense of submerged pattern running, like the Duke's hidden purpose, through the whole."[11] I am not sure whether Rader is really revising here, but even if he is, his two statements share a common feature.

Whether we say that the structure of rhymed couplets points to a subjectivity other than that of the speaker or that it reveals a level of motive beneath the linguistic surface of a single speaker's discourse, we are observing a doubleness or bifurcation of the text.

The iambic pentameter line, even without rhyme, produces one kind of closure; syntactic periods produce another kind of closure. In a form like the Augustan couplet, these closures coincide, with the result that the relation of poetic convention to sentence structure is the relation of rhetoric to message. The couplet may generate emphasis, parallelism, or antithesis as well as a number of other modifications and effects, such as irony. "End-stopped" couplets are not, as some have imagined, a rigid convention. What they do imply, though, is a direct relationship of some kind between verse form and sentence form, leading us to read the entire discourse as an integrated whole. Between the couplet and the sentence in "My Last Duchess," however, there is no consistent relationship. Some lines are end-stopped, some are not, and the rhetorical periodicity of the duke's speech appears to draw little if anything from the verse form. This is why Rader is correct in saying that we do not hear the couplets as part of the duke's speech. Whether we wish to say that they point to the presence of the poet or to an unstated motive behind the speaker's address, we are assuming that the discourse of the poem exists for a divided subject rather than a unitary one. Rader's remarks illustrate that this doubleness can be recognized as a feature of the discourse independently of inferences we make about the separation of poet from speaker in the poem. Again, it may contribute to our inference of that separation (it usually does in the early monologues of the 1840s), but it also may have a number of other effects. My argument here is that it is discursive splitting or textual bifurcation itself, and not any of its particular effects, that helps us to recognize dramatic monologues.

Dramatic monologues call attention to the fact that language within their domain seems to operate both at a level that is consciously "poetic" in some traditional sense and at a separate syntactic, semantic, or merely "message" level. And these two levels give at least the initial impression that one is independently variable with respect to the other. This implies, for one thing, an ontological division between what language *is* as an artificial and malleable aesthetic medium and what it *says* as a constant medium of human communication. The self-conscious doubleness of the dramatic monologue points out, in other words, an alienation between poetry and discourse; between specialized usage and generalized usage; between trained language producers like poets and unspecialized language consumers like carousing monks, worldly bishops, Renaissance nobles (Browning's duke has no "skill in speech"), and, not least important, readers.[12]

The most simply articulated confrontation between poetic convention and sentence structure emerges in examples like "My Last Duchess." As a versifier, Browning was restless, constantly experimenting with different line and stanza forms, rhyme patterns, and metrical norms. He has no particular loyalty to a single prosodic or verse convention. The Spenserian stanza, the Elizabethan love sonnet, Miltonic blank verse, the heroic couplet—all of these became part of the stylistic signatures of their respective practitioners. The organizing power of balance and antithesis in Pope's couplets can be analyzed as integrally related both to the genres he writes in and his linguistic style in general. No such exercise is possible for Browning. He adapts his language to a wide variety of verse conventions, and he adapts those conventions at will to the dramatic monologue.

Nevertheless, a great many monologues seem to have some clearly definable, even obtrusive, metric, rhyme, or stanzaic scheme that relates to the poem's syntax much as the couplet did in "My Last Duchess." The discourse of "Any Wife to Any Husband," for example, is built of syntactic continuities quite independent of the stanzaic form with its complicated *a a b c c b* rhyme scheme. William Cadbury notices a similar phenomenon in "Childe Roland to the Dark Tower Came." He says that the "tone" of that poem

is created from two plaited strands. Stanza pattern and metre in "Childe Roland" support our distance, while the run-on lines which undercut the stanza pattern, and the rhythm which works against the metre, create our involvement. Stanza pattern is carefully interlocked, coming always to a full and predictable close and emphasizing by its recurrence the integrity of each stanza; but rhythmical stress is varied freely in each line and run-on lines predominate.[13]

Cadbury's remarks can alert us to the fact that poetic discourse constructs more than just a subject of its own origin. It also locates a subject for its own intelligibility, a subject for the destination of its meaning. And the monologue effectively splits or fragments the subjectivity of "the reader." On the one hand, there is the "distanced" reader, the discriminating consumer of aesthetic commodities, while on the other, there is the "involved" reader, affected and moved by the essential human identification that the poem invites. These are not projected as two different subjects; they are a single subject constituted in contradiction, a fundamental contradiction of market economies in which a product is the fruit of real human labor and meets real human needs while at the same time it is alienated from both producer and consumer. These contradictions cannot be "resolved" within the culture for which Browning wrote—the Pictor Ignotus, we may recall, could not solve his situation either by identifying with his product or by isolating himself from it and the market that brings art into being. They can only be unveiled through a splitting of the subject itself, and this is a large part of the monologue's task.

The task is in no way a narrow one, and Browning shows us how richly serious and, indeed, how playful its various executions can be. "Love Among the Ruins," for example, employs a stanza in which rhymed couplets consist of alternating long and short lines resulting in a marked pause over the short lines. Despite this coercive focus, however, a great many of the short lines could be deleted without interrupting the grammatical flow of the sentences:

Where the quiet-colored end of evening smiles,
    Miles and miles
On the solitary pastures where our sheep
    Half-asleep
Twinkle homeward thro' the twilight, stray or stop
    As they crop—
Was the site once of a city great and gay,
    (So they say)

Of our country's very capital, its prince
    Ages since
Held his court in, gathered councils, wielding far
    Peace or war.

                            (1-12)

The stanza is at once made of a language-to-make-stanzas and a language-to-make-sentences, and it is nearly possible to read them both separately but concurrently. This is not to say that the stanza would have exactly the same meaning without the short lines—this is where Browning draws back from simply multiplying or embellishing coherent discourses. The short lines emphasize the distance between the tranquil present and a turbulent past that, since its events transpired so many "ages since," is known only in the tenuousness of legend. This alternation of attention between the lost past and the present continues throughout the poem and is repeatedly reenforced in the short lines. The short lines are clearly indispensable to the sound patterns of the poem, yet often dispensable from the point of view of syntax. How much the poem's meaning relies on them is a matter of uncertainty, varying from stanza to stanza. The poem as a whole implies, without fully resolving, a fundamental question: Does poetry, in so far as it displays an ornamental artifice, communicate something that unspecialized or "ordinary" language does not?

The poem that explores this dialectical uncertainty perhaps more directly than any other is "A Toccata of Galuppi's." Generated out of the distinction between music as abstractly ordered patterns of sound and music as the medium of a message, the central question of the poem is posed at the beginning of the seventh stanza:

What? Those lesser thirds so plaintive, sixths
                  diminished sigh on sigh,
  Told them something?

Thirds and sixths describe the technical, abstract order of Galuppi's music. Do they also "mean"? Do they "tell" their listeners something?[14] Browning asks the question about music and about poetry simultaneously, not just through the poem's thematic treatment of music, but also through the function of meter in the verse itself.

The rhythmic regularity of Browning's three-line stanza form is established at the outset:

> Oh, Galuppi, Baldassaro, this is very sad to find!
> I can hardly misconceive you; it would prove me deaf
> and blind;
> But although I take your meaning, 'tis with such a
> heavy mind!

The metric form is a headless iambic line of eight feet. Traditionally, prosodic analysis moves between two levels of description. Recognizing the tendency of most English verse toward alternating lightly and heavily accented syllables, we measure the regularity of this pattern by scanning the poem's "meter." On the second level, we describe the "rhythm" as the range of variability within metrical regularity. Occasionally, however, a poem may display a pattern of accentual regularity that is not described by the metrical scansion yet is the principal source of repeating patterns of stress in the poem. This pattern is a kind of "sur-meter." It is not meter per se, since it can vary while the meter remains regular or remain regular while the meter varies. Yet the concept of rhythm must be reserved for describing variations in this sur-meter just as it does for meter itself. In the stanza from "A Toccata of Galuppi's," the most prominent stress pattern is one of four heavy beats per line, and this pattern is far more regular than that measured by the iambic meter. Hence using traditional accentual notation for the meter and the symbol x for a four-beat dominant sur-metric pattern, we get a scansion like this:

Oh, / Galup/pi, Bal/dassa/ro, this / is ver/y sad / to find!

I / can hard/ly mis/conceive / you; it / would prove / me deaf / and blind;

But / although / I take / your mea/ning, 'tis / with such / a hea/vy mind!

This double regularity of meter and sur-meter creates the repetitional effect of the lines' music, an effect that persists as long as the four heavy beats remain in the standard position, are of nearly equal weight, and are substantially heavier than any of the other metrically heavy accents. This structure breaks down, however, in stanzas like the eighth:

> "Were you happy?"—"Yes."—"and are you still as happy?"
>   "Yes. And you?"
> "Then, more kisses!"—"Did *I* stop them, when a million
>   seemed so few?"
> Hark, the dominant's persistence till it must be
>   answered to!
>
> (22-24)

To be regular, the four heavy stresses in the first line should fall evenly on the first syllable of "happy," the verb "are," the first syllable of the second "happy," and the final syllable of the line. Although echoes of this norm do remain, however, the heaviest stresses in the line fall on the two "yesses," the fifth and thirteenth syllables of the line, and both of these affirmatives are separated from the first syllables of their respective metrical feet by dialogical pauses. Moreover, though the metrically stressed "are" is regular within its own foot, it is sur-metrically unstressed, even in relation to "still." The three feet within the third set of quotation marks provide a crescendo of increasingly heavy stresses quite unlike the metronomic alternation pattern of the first stanza. Looking back at the first stanza, we can see that speech rhythms and exclamations were not absent, but they were rhythmically dominated by the verse. Conversely, in the first two lines of the eighth stanza, the sur-metrical norm is almost entirely obliterated by the irregular rise and fall, hesitation, and acceleration of natural speech. This is, of course, the familiar dialectic we have seen in other poems. Verse convention and sentence structure are fused beyond separation, but they remain discernible poles of verbal strength, as Browning reminds us by returning to the dominant both technically and thematically in the third line of the eighth stanza: "Hark, the dominant's persistence till it must be answered to!" This line is a near pun. Technically the "dominant" is a musical chord that must be "answered" by resolving to another chord later on. But the phrase "answered to" carries a connotation of moral accountability that later emerges again in the poem's thematic resolution.

The first six stanzas of "A Toccata of Galuppi's" have essentially the anaphoric function that I discussed in the last chapter. As in "My Last Duchess," however, the elements operative in deixis establish both an immediate past and a relatively distant past. The immediate past is continuous with the poem's moment in which the speaker is, and has been, listening to Galuppi's music: "Oh, Galuppi, Baldassaro, *this* is very sad to find!" The relevant distant past is the world of Baroque Venice, and it is temporally located by deictics like "thus" (l. 5) and "these" (l. 7), clusters of definite determiners (ll. 5–7), and by process forms like "once" (adverbial, l. 5) and "used to wed" (habitual aspect, l. 6). The music, then, is to the speaker both an immediate sensual experience (the rhythm of the poem might even be conditioned by that of the toccata) and a vivid conveyor of historical knowledge: "I was never out of England—it's as if I saw it all." Already implicit in this opening is a desire to repair historical discontinuity. The speaker fantasizes a verbal exchange between himself and Galuppi; his own side of the exchange is the monologue itself, while for Galuppi's part, he projects a verbal content onto music. This desire to deny the divisions of time is, of course, intimately connected with the desire to deny death. In the crudest terms, a Galuppi who could speak and answer questions through his music would, in some sense, be alive, thus sympathetically mitigating the finality of death for his interlocutor as well. A meaningless music, on the other hand, would more nearly signify the unbridgeable chasm between the dead composer and the living listener.

For music to be capable of speaking across centuries, it must first be capable of speaking to Galuppi's contemporaries. It must have said something to the Venetian court, and that "something," appropriately, is the impossible suggestion that death may be an illusion:

What? Those lesser thirds so plaintive, sixths
    diminished, sigh on sigh,
Told them something? Those suspensions, those
    solutions—"Must we die?"
Those commiserating sevenths—"Life might last!
    we can but try!"

                                 (19-21)

It is at this point that the musical structure of the stanza form begins to give way to the rhythms of speech; the conspicuous mode
of aural *being* becomes faint as the possibility of aural *saying* seeks
to predominate. And the semantic content of the projected dialogue in stanza eight is the denial of temporal displacement. The
repetition of "yes" helps accomplish this denial as it gestures toward a homogeneous and consistent condition (happiness) that is
as it was and that is signified by a virtual infinity of kisses, acts so
repetitional as to mask or abolish the sense of linear time. It has
also, as I said, temporarily abolished the sense of regular musical
rhythm, suggesting that somehow the diachronic experience of
music is a reminder of displacement and death and needs to be re-
sisted by the projection of a fixed verbal meaning, a transcendent
signification. This implication begins to explain the ominous quality of the return to the metrical norm in the third line of the eighth
stanza, of the "dominant's" disturbing "persistence" toward a
moment in time when an inevitable accounting must be made. This
is the first time in the poem that the rhythmic or technical aspect
of the music / verse becomes explicitly described as directional in
time, although the rapid tumbling quality of the verse rhythm has
perhaps suggested an energy impelled toward its own exhaustion
from the outset.

    Stanzas ten and eleven tell us what is obvious, that the life-loving
Venetians have died; and the speaker begins to lose his hold on the
fantasy that Galuppi's "old music" had generated:

But when I sit down to reason, think to take my
    stand nor swerve,
While I triumph o'er a secret wrung from nature's
    close reserve,

In you come with your cold music till I creep thro'
    every nerve.

(31–33)

The impact of the music has changed—the merely "old" has become "cold"—although it still speaks a message similar to the one
it spoke before: "Butterflies may dread extinction,—you'll not
die, / it cannot be!" Now the music is telling the speaker that he
will not die just as it had the Venetians. But the message of this
toccata has been insidious; it has spoken as much of loss as of hope
by recalling distant Venice, and this ambivalence begins to be
apparent in the relation between "message rhythm" and speech
rhythm in the later stanzas. The quotation marks reappear; Galuppi
is speaking again, but now the speech rhythms fail to overcome
the dark verse rhythms as radically as they did in stanza eight.
Hark the dominant's persistance—

Dust and ashes, dead and done with, Venice spent
    what Venice earned.
The soul, doubtless, is immortal—where a soul can
    be discerned.

Yours for instance: you know physics, something
    of geology,
Mathematics are your pastime; souls shall rise in
    their degree;
Butterflies may dread extinction,—you'll not die,
    it cannot be!

(35–39)

—till it must be answered to. In the phrases "Dust and ashes, dead
and done with" are resolved the dialectic between music that says
something and music that does not. The projected "argument" of
the toccata tries to justify itself by a feeble appeal to the deathless-
ness of soul, a metaphysical commodity that the Venetians must
not have had, since they died, but that the speaker of the monologue surely does have. But by this time, the message has irrevocably become one with the implied displacement of the on-rushing
rhythm. The speaker knows it. The saying and the being of both

music and poetry point toward only one kind of stasis or completeness beyond the end of the present dramatic moment: death itself. Lines 20–23 may be read almost as a miniature dramatic monologue within the larger one called "A Toccata of Galuppi's":

> . . . "Must we die?"
> . . . "Life might last! we can but try!"
>
> "Were you happy?"—"Yes."—"And are you still as
>   happy?"—"Yes. And you?"
> —"Then, more kisses!"—"Did *I* stop them, when a million
>   seemed so few?"

We hear, to be sure, more than one voice, but the passage has all the necessary features of the monologue: reference to an indefinite past and future, the doubling of speech and poetic elements, and structures of [social] exchange. That "monologue" was a fragment in a pair of lives that ended, a projection of meaning onto music for two people who found their timelessness only in "dust and ashes." The meaning of such a discourse is always double, although it cannot be factored out into two irreducible elements. And it is also always fused. Similarly, all of the subjects for this kind of discourse are at once double and unfactorable. It is both the Venetians and Galuppi who speak, and it is both Galuppi and the "speaker" of the poem for whom the intelligibility of meaning is in question. In the terms of Bakhtin and Kristeva, then, the Venetian fragment, like citation in the novel, is fully "dialogical."[15]

The enclosing dramatic monologue is similar in a way that characterizes the genre, though at times, the monologue's subject of utterance so overshadows the implicit subject of enunciation that the possibility of dialogical or ambivalent meaning seems endangered. These are the poems that often seem doctrinal or programmatic or "optimistic" to Browning's readers. The monologue so attractively invokes the ideology of the unified individual that by also invoking the possibility of discourse as dialogical or ambivalent, it only displays a contradiction rather than resolving or naturalizing it in a consistent convention, as realist fiction naturalizes the split between monological narrative and dialogical citation.

"A Toccata of Galuppi's" is a classic dramatic monologue. Nevertheless, there is one major difference between the function of the traditional poetic artifice in this poem and in a poem like "My Last Duchess." In the duke of Ferrara's monologue, the bifurcation of discourse contributed to the implication of a speaker's identity separate from the poet's identity. This was necessary to the irony of that particular poem. In "A Toccata of Galuppi's," though the subject is still divided, no such function appears. Is the speaker Robert Browning or someone else? We learn that whoever he is, he has an interest in physics, geology, and mathematics. Are we to search Browning's biography to solve the formal problems posed by the poem and the genre? I think this would contribute little to the interpretation of either. Just as the narrator in fiction may, in some cases, also be the character whose speech is cited, so the poet may or may not be the same person as the speaker of the poem. In the case of fiction, a distinction still exists between a subject of utterance and a subject of enunciation, the latter being the one who creates a second meaning (even for his own reported speech) in dialogue with an implied reader. In the same way, the subject of enunciation in "A Toccata of Galuppi's" offers a meaning for the speaker's words that is different from the speaker's meaning if only by virtue of the fact that the speaker addresses his words to someone other than the reader of the poem. Whether that speaker (subject of utterance) and the subject of enunciation are the "same person" is irrelevant; all that matters is that the discourse itself formally locates two different centers of intelligibility through its own bivalent structure.

One of the persistent mysteries of Browning's style lies in the distinctness with which it is both always the same and always different, always Browning's very Victorian English and always capable of particularizing speakers as different as Bishop Blougram and Caliban. To observe this is different from observing the linguistic range of Shakespeare creating Prospero and Caliban or Hyppolita and Bottom. Style in the Renaissance is neatly ordered in different levels, levels that may easily be used to signify different social groups. Movement from one level to another within a single play tells us something about the relative sophistication of different characters and about how seriously we are to take them and their dilemmas. The poet who is a master of style can move thoroughly from one level to another as a means of creating interactions among the characters within the single work. Indeed, as T. S. Eliot pointed out long ago, one measure of an Elizabethan writer's genius is his ability to make his own linguistic idiosyncrasies disappear as he moves among the different voices of his fictional world.

As the Elizabethan habit of thinking in hierarchies of plateaus disappeared, so too did the skills appropriate to that organization. This is one reason why after the seventeenth century, Shakespeare's range of characterization is not to be found in English drama. The conceptual and philosophical framework within which a poet learns several distinctly different styles has lost too much of its former influence. From the eighteenth century until the middle of the nineteenth, no comparable force of linguistic diversification is to be found. Among major poets, only Wordsworth attempted sustained experiments in the imitation of unfamiliar voices, and neither his reasons for doing so nor his results clearly foreshadow the innovations of Browning and Tennyson.

If the Elizabethan playwright leaves the fewest possible traces of his own speech in the speech of his characters, a Victorian poet like Browning carefully leaves his mark on each of his fictional "men and women." Robert Langbaum has discussed the dramatic monologue as a "piece" of an Elizabethan-type drama with its context of action stripped away.[16] This allows him to write persuasively about the illusion of fragmentariness generated by the genre, but it prevents him from investigating the continuity among different monologues. Dramatic action or interaction among the speakers of different styles creates continuity in a Shakespearean play. Often it takes a character like Prince Hal, who can speak both the language of drawers and the language of kings, to effect the social resolutions that the play requires. This kind of continuity is unavailable to the Victorian poet (witness Browning's disastrous career as a dramatist), but Browning found another kind of continuity among his speakers, one that makes the dramatic monologue *collection* as important to the history of genres as the structure of the individual monologue itself. Browning's speakers cannot speak to one another; they would be wholly isolated voices were it not for the insistent markers of a familiar Victorian language that at once translates and integrates the several voices of several times and places. Browning says in "One Word More" that he has "gathered" disparate men and women in order to "speak from each mouth," and this formal act of gathering has been too little emphasized in Browning studies. In time, he discovered a fictional framework within which he could "gather" and relate dramatic monologues without returning to the futile attempt at writing plays. This resolution was *The Ring and the Book*. Indeed, it is useful to consider the outline of Browning's poetic career as a movement from the failure to write successful plays to the invention of a short form that could gesture toward dramatic continuity without recovering it, and finally to a gathering of the shorter forms in artificially integrated collections, a process that culminated with the invention, in *The Ring and the Book*, of a governing fiction for the collection itself.

The key formal device in this evolution is, I think, the doubleness of language that so emphatically keeps the Victorian poet's own style before us even as each successive speaker reveals the extremities of his own specialized voice. The enclosing fiction of *The Ring and the Book* provided thematic means for the manifestation of such idiosyncracies; we call them different "perspectives" on the murder case. Accordingly, Browning's stylistic variations are less necessary and less radical there than in the earlier monologues.

One does not, of course, in reading the monologues, consciously separate familiar contemporary traits of speech from those that give a particular speaker his memorable individuality. It is not just two voices but the fusion of two voices that Browning's poems force us to entertain. This fusion may recognize and resist the discontinuity between the present and the remote past, between the clergy and the lay public, between the well-educated and the common man, between the poet and his audience, or even between two different aspects of a single personality. In general, the isolated and the special production or consumption of language is acknowledged and then absorbed into the gathering of the monologues in Browning's collections.

III

The issue of the poet / specialist's alienation from the speaker as ordinary man is a special case of a problem that haunted many Victorians. In poetics, we have seen it emerge in the distinction between a potentially ornamental artifice in language and the "useful" capacity of language to convey messages. Antitheses between style and utility are, of course, old in literary tradition by the nineteenth century; indeed, they were very old when Ben Jonson justified the Elizabethan plain style as representing "language such as men do use." But in the nineteenth century, the association of ornamental style with the oppressive power of great wealth gained in force and thus intensified the social and economic alienation of style and use. In a recent book on Victorian design, for example, Herwin Schaefer has ably demonstrated what he calls a "two-track" tradition in the production of everything from fine instruments and great machines to the most common consumer goods: "the one [track] utilitarian, functional, matter-of-fact, the other a matter of prestige, of aesthetic, and social differentiation." Schaefer cites Rousseau and, later, Thorstein Veblen among those who deplored the separation of beauty from function. On the other side, he calls our attention to commentators who celebrate it and lament the opportunity for "persons to assume a semblance of decoration far beyond either their means or their station."[17] In this disagreement, both the egalitarian and the aristocratic sides assume the polarization of beauty and function, and Schaefer goes on to discuss numerous examples of designers in the nineteenth century, like Horatio Greenough, who attempt to resolve the antithesis. The most common model for the reconciliation was, not surprisingly, nature itself, in which form and function seemed ideally indistinguishable. This simple association can, of course, alert us to less obvious manifestations of the problem of aesthetic specialization. Darwin comes immediately to mind, in those often tortured passages in which he tries to reconcile the fine plumage of birds to the essentially utilitarian premise underlying the concept of natural selection. Or we may well think of the lifelong desire of John Stuart Mill to accommodate the strict Benthamite training of his mind to his undeniable spiritual response to natural beauty.

Many more examples might be cited, but these few can at least indicate how frequently the alienation of aesthetic values vexes the various departments of Victorian thought. For Browning, as we have seen, the nearest analog to poetry in this regard is music, and he returns to the relationship between music and communication in a number of poems about poets, singers, and musicians. One of the most interesting cases is "Saul." Like "A Toccata of Galuppi's," "Saul" is a poem in which music says something. David recounts how he sang to Saul and revived the great king, and the language displays the doubleness I have been describing. The regular periodicity of the anapestic rhymed couplets contrasts with the irregular accelerations and hesitations of the speech rhythms:

> Then I played the help-tune of our reapers, their
>   wine-song, when hand
> Grasps at hand, eye lights eye in good friendship,
>   and great hearts expand
> And grow one in the sense of this world's life.—
>   And then, the last song
> When the dead man is praised on his journey—
>   "Bear, bear him along
> With his few faults shut up like dead flowerets!
>   Are balm-seeds not here
> To console us? The land has none left such as
>   he on the bier.
> Oh, would we might keep thee, my brother!"
>
>   (49–55)

As in so many other poems, the verse units may or may not coincide with syntactic and rhetorical units; the relationship appears to be random. If we ask, as Ralph Rader asks about the duke of Ferrara, whether we hear the structure of the verse as part of the speaker's voice, we shall be bound to answer, as Rader does, that we do not. But this poem contains a complication that is not found in the earlier poem. After eight verse paragraphs of narration, David repeats the actual song that he sang to Saul, and this song too is rendered in anapestic rhymed couplets. This time, however, it is not at all certain that the regularity of the verse is a thing apart from the act of speech attributed to David. As easily as we can ask whether verse conventions constitute a part of David's speech or a part of Browning's poetry, we can also ask whether they constitute a part of David's speech or of David's own poetry. Browning is careful to frustrate the attempt to answer the latter question. The transition from speech to music in the poem is marked and yet seamless:

> And I bent once again to my playing, pursued it unchecked,
> As I sang,—
>
> ix
>
> "Oh, our manhood's prime vigor! No spirit
> feels waste,
> Not a muscle is stopped in its playing nor sinew unbraced."
>
> (67–69)

There is not any doubt that David's description of what happened occurs in stanza eight, while his reenactment of the song is wholly contained in stanza nine. Nevertheless, this division is not observed when it comes to the verse line. The final line fragment of stanza eight, "As I sang," is completed by the first line of the song in stanza nine. If we ask, therefore, whether the narrative and the song are discrete or continuous with one another, we shall get conflicting answers depending on whether our frame of reference is the verse stanza or the verse line. We cannot answer the question categorically for the poem as a whole. Accordingly, if we ask whether a given feature, such as anapestic meter, is a part of poetry or a part of speech, we will also be denied a conclusive answer, and this latter condition will also draw to our attention the impossibility of finally attributing some features to Browning's voice and some to David's.

In poem after poem, Browning's magic lies in his ability to offer an illusion of an idiosyncratic voice dividing men from men and to make that illusion waver before our eyes as the voice of each of his men and women is, however ambivalently, "gathered" into that one voice that rings most clearly when all the poems have been read. It would be misleading merely to raise this final voice to a higher level of idiosyncracy by calling it Browning's voice. It is the voice of a hypothetical language, one that displays the dialectic between the idiosyncratic and the generally shared. Thus the central contradiction of the dramatic monologue sets, as it did in "Pictor Ignotus," the private interest of the coherent individual against the general interest of the entire community. These interests are mutually exclusive, but in Browning they appear dialectically as a single ideological necessity.

Of course, ideology is also designed to obscure or veil something that is not itself, and Marx has shown in *The German Ideology* how the antithesis between private interest and general interest veils the reality of class interest. Browning brings contradiction to consciousness in the monologue in two forms, but it is in the slight nonalignment of these two forms that we can see the class interest that supports and perpetuates the contradictions. The two forms may be represented by two oppositions: *specialized discourse / unspecialized discourse* and *idiosyncratic voice / the language of the community*. The latter is perhaps most familiar as the distinction between speech production (*parole*) and language as an abstract system or code (*langue*), but it is distinctly not identical to the first antithesis. This inequality stems precisely from the fact that, while the idiosyncratic voice represents the mythical individual, specialized discourse represents a class interest.

In Victorian England, an individual's ability to improve his competitive posture toward his fellows increasingly became linked to the class credential of his education. One marker of a person's education was his speech, including his command of prestige uses of language like the poetic. The roots of social differentiation according to cultivated speech characteristics reach back to well before the nineteenth century; the relation of "prescriptive grammar" to social change in the eighteenth century has been described by Elizabeth Traugott in the following terms: "Perhaps the main social factor in the development of prescriptive grammars was the rise of the middle class. In urban communities the gentry felt threatened and sought ways to keep themselves apart from the middle class. They looked for overt behavioral tokens by which to single themselves out from others, tokens which would create barriers between themselves and the middle class. Language was an obvious vehicle for such an aim."[18] From this beginning, and within the middle class itself, a more complex system of specialized language grouping developed in the nineteenth century. The organization of these groups was not always clearly hierarchical, but fine distinctions, especially in the region of vocabulary, served increasingly to differentiate a plurality of competing elites: scientific, literary, diplomatic, financial, and so on. This development away from a simple gentry / commoner division toward a more complex and compartmentalized social structure derives in part from the division of labor and knowledge in the industrial world and in part from a concept of progress according to which certain collectives can attain or strive for a status superior to that of their predecessors. One result of these distinctions and ambitions is the formulation of interest groups with characteristic voices in the system of political thought that produced the parliamentary reform of 1832. That act may be seen as simply the most visible marker of a number of social transformations designed to elevate the status of a given class (e.g., industrial workers) or a given region (e.g., the cities). In the case of parliamentary reform, the new status directly entailed the right to present a new class-determined voice in adversary debate with established ruling interests.

The elitism of interest groups and the specialization of their languages are also allied with both nationalistic and racial pride. In particular, historically and geographically distant cultures, once revered for aesthetic or intellectual sophistication, could now become the objects of condescension based on England's scientific and industrial prowess. Charles Morazé has pointed out that Chinese culture, such a paragon of achievement to the eighteenth century, "revealed" to the nineteenth its inadequacy to compete with Western scientific progress due to its lack of a specialized language of logical reasoning.[19]

All of these distinct vocabularies—of interest groups, of aristocracies, of scientific and aesthetic elites, of distant cultures, both primitive and exotic, of the educated in rhetoric or in logical processes—all of these idioms appear in one form or another in Browning's monologues. Nearly every speaker projected by these poems can be identified according to his or her inclusion in or exclusion from a particular elite with its own hierarchy of values.

The dialectic of discourses in the dramatic monologue is thus a complex one. Literature itself had become, as Raymond Williams tells us, "a specialized and selective category," consciously distinguished both from other specialized discourses like the scientific and from general or "popular" discourse even in printed books.[20] In the monologue, therefore, we find the opposition of poetic discourse to other specialized discourses; the opposition of specialized discourse itself to generalized, popular, or even colloquial Victorian speech; and the opposition of generalized discourse to idiosyncratic discourse. This profoundly dialogical language, along with the fragmentation of the subject that it entails, raises, as we have seen, complex and difficult questions about the nature of communication. The model of communication questioned by the monologue is that of reciprocity or exchange. "Exchange" in a market system implies the existence of discrete and coherent subjects or private interests. The question addressed in the next chapter is what happens to communication as exchange when the subject of the monologue's discourse is paradoxically both individual and, at the same time, unboundaried and divided.

The Cooperating Fancy

I   One of the most commonly observed features of dramatic monologues is the implied listener. In most monologues (though not all) the speaker appears to be speaking to someone rather than soliloquizing and in many cases acknowledges a response.[1] Some critics, like Robert Langbaum, attribute this characteristic to the monologue's intermediate status between the drama and the lyric. For Langbaum, monologues are fragments of hypothetical plays that have shed most of the connective tissue of action and circumstance to become introspective, confessional lyrics. The poems have a peculiar intensity of expressive force, "more words, ingenuity and argument than seem necessary for the purpose," where "purpose" is defined in terms of the possible function of such a speech in a play.[2] According to this analysis, the implied listener serves as an index to the implied context, which is inadequate to explain the intensity or elaborateness of the monologue itself.

The simplest problem with this approach is the fact that Browning also wrote plays and other poems to which the same generalization might apply. *Paracelsus*, for example, is a full dramatic sequence, encompassing most of the adult life of its protagonist. Yet the speeches and actions of Festus, Paracelsus's friend and interlocutor, fail to account for the intensity and complexity of Paracelsus's confessions in precisely the way described by Langbaum as a defining feature of the fragmentary monologue. Nevertheless, if Langbaum's remarks fall short of defining the genre, they do address an affective truth about many monologues: the implied listener does seem an uneasy visitor from the world of dramatic or conversational exchange in the world of lyric expression. Browning might have written (and sometimes did write) dramatic dialogues, perhaps on the model of Landor's *Imaginary Conversations,* giving the second party an active participation, without writing full plays. But his preferred practice was to make the listener one of those "extensions of the web" beyond the speaker's moment, and the mode of direct address is, in one sense, another instance of the kind of deixis that I described in chapter 3. Indeed, all of the linguistic devices that indicate the presence of a listener can be analyzed in exactly the same way that I analyzed deictics and definite determiners earlier. Now I hope to show what issues are raised by the dramatic monologue when the object of deictic reference is a human listener.

There is an important difference between this listener and the rest of the ostensive world: the statue of Neptune and the duchess's portrait cannot respond; the count's emissary can. Reference to a person capable of responding is an important feature of the dramatic monologue, and yet the genre contains a built-in ambivalence toward the responding listener. The listener's ability to respond is always "there" in the consciousness of the speaker, either as potential or as realized fact, but it cannot be "there" in the dramatic monologue. From the reader's perspective, the interlocutor as agent is always a tenuous force because he is required by the genre to be silent or unheard. The dramatic monologue, in other words, presents a delicate antithesis between the speaking subject as isolated and that same subject as constituted only by language in the process of communication and exchange.

We can easily recognize this opposition as a generalized form of the impossible choice of the Pictor Ignotus, which I discussed at length in chapter 2. Does the painter submit himself in "each new picture" to the discussions and commercial exchanges of the marketplace or does he withdraw to those "endless cloisters and eternal aisles" to molder " 'mid echoes the light footstep never woke"? But in the balanced antithesis generated by the monologue itself, there is a difference. In "Pictor Ignotus," the choice between isolation and communication was a choice made entirely within the ideology of the homogeneous individual subject. I have shown, in the last two chapters, how the monologue reveals the contradictions of this ideology; it remains to show that when the subject-in-communication is the subject of a dramatic monologue, we have a discourse that at least raises the possibility of the choice of "Pictor Ignotus" being reconstituted as a viable choice between quite different epistemologies. We might call these two epistemologies (1) a Cartesian epistemology in which the self is unitary and ontologically exclusive of all that is not the self; and (2) a "cybernetic" epistemology in which the self is only constituted as part of a larger system of relationships and interactions. I shall have more to say about these epistemologies, and I shall argue that the dramatic monologue instantiates the struggle between them. But unlike the other dialectical poises that Browning simply unveils or brings to consciousness, this antithesis opens the question of value. For Browning, in the structure of the dramatic monologue, isolation represents a fear while coherent interaction represents a desire; and the particular poems examine subjects who either succeed or fail to "realize" their listeners in meaningful reciprocity and exchange. This is true even when an actual listener is not implied but only projected or desired by the speaker. All dramatic monologues at least fantasize a listener, and this is chiefly what differentiates them from lyrics or extracted soliloquies.

The simplest and most frequent context for the implied listener is conversation. Browning uses other devices like the epistle in "Cleon" and "Karshish" or the imagined discourse of music in "A Toccata of Galuppi's" or "Master Hugues of Saxe Gotha," but these will be seen on examination to employ the patterns of conversation in the same way as the more straightforward examples. Recent studies of the structure and logic of conversation by sociolinguists and ethnomethodologists can suggest several reasons why some of the conventions of conversation are especially suited to the functions of the dramatic monologue. Malcolm Coulthard, for example, points out how deeply the rules of conversational discourse (as opposed to intrinsic grammatical rules) depend on preexisting shared knowledge, "not simply shared rules for the interpretation of linguistic items, but shared knowledge of the world, to which a speaker can allude or appeal."[3] We have already seen in chapter 3 how the assumption of a shared context preceding the moment of the poem is crucial to the strategies of the monologue. Perhaps even more important, researchers like Harvey Sacks, Emanuel Schegloff, Gail Jefferson, and Starkey Duncan have begun analyzing conversational exchange itself in ways that can help specify the ambivalence behind the monologue's structure.[4]

Conversational analysis, a branch of sociolinguistics, concerns the rules governing the taking of turns among participants in conversation. Sacks, Schegloff, and Jefferson reason that turn-taking occurs so efficiently that a set of operating rules must be shared by all speakers within a given culture. Since there is value attached to "having one's say," they call the organization of conversation an "economy," a system of exchange, ordered by what Duncan terms a "grammar."[5] The crucial moments of action within this economy are those in which speaking rights are transferred from one speaker to another. The transfer of speaking rights may be effected by the current speaker, who selects the next speaker, or by a nonspeaker who selects himself as the next speaker. These acts of selection can occur, moreover, only at certain places in the discourse called "turn-relevance-places." Clearly, these turn-relevance-places may be indicated in numerous nonlinguistic ways that cannot easily be carried over into a literary text. They may be marked by intonation, hand gestures, slight movements of the head and body, or even, in some cases, by external circumstances. There are, however, linguistic markers of turn relevance as well. These most often consist of what Sacks and Duncan call "adjacency pairs," a locution (first pair part) uttered by one speaker that virtually assures a conventional reciprocal locution (second pair part) on the part of a selected next speaker: "There is a class of first pair parts which includes Questions, Greetings, Challenges, Threats, Warnings, Offers, Requests, Complaints, Invitations, Announcements. For some first pair parts the second pair part is reciprocal, Greeting-Greeting. For some there is only one appropriate second, Question-Answer, for some more than one, Complaint-Apology / Justification."[6]

When dramatic monologues imply a particular addressee, they are often punctuated by these turn-relevance pair parts. Considering for the moment only interrogatives, we can distinguish several different types, and these imply different degrees of expected or desired reciprocity. By far the most demanding are "content questions," questions, usually beginning with "wh," that require a semantically substantial or complex reply. Less demanding are the so-called truth questions, which call for only "existential" responses: "yes," "no," "maybe," "probably," and the like. Confirmative questions like "It's raining, isn't it?" are essentially truth questions but may be considered separately since they invite no more than "back channel" responses, slight verbal gestures that do not fully qualify as a speaking turn. Beyond these, there are various kinds of pseudoquestions, sentences that appear interrogative but that are really other kinds of speech acts. Exclamations like "What could I do?" are frequently of this type, as are commands or requests like "Can you water the roses?" or invitations like "Will you sit down?" In the latter case, the listener is not being asked to answer the question but to sit down.

As we might expect, the type of interrogative that appears most often in the Romantic lyric is the pseudoquestion. This is true even when the poem is ostensibly addressed to someone in particular. Thus in "Epipsychidion," for example, questions like the following actually have the force of exclamatory statements. They do not mark turn-relevance-places and accordingly do not identify the poem as part of a projected verbal exchange:

> Art thou not void of guile,
> A lovely soul formed to be blessed and bless?
> A well of sealed and secret happiness,
> Whose waters like blithe light and music are,
> Vanquishing dissonance and gloom? A Star
> Which moves not in the moving heavens, alone?
> A Smile amid dark frowns? a gentle tone
> Amid rude voices? a beloved light?
> A Solitude, a Refuge, a Delight?
>
> (56–64)

Shelley is not asking Emily whether she is a refuge and a delight; he is discovering a passionate way of cataloguing subjectively "all that thou are" in the context of his own life.

By contrast, in Victorian monologues structured on the conversation model, interrogatives most often mark genuine turn-relevance-places:

> Do you feel thankful, ay or no,
> For this fair town's face, yonder river's line,
> The mountain round it and the sky above,
> Much more the figures of man, woman, child,
> These are the frame to? What's it all about?
> To be passed over, despised? or dwelt upon,
> Wondered at? oh, this last of course!—you say.
> But why not do as well as say,—paint these
> Just as they are, careless what comes of it?
>
> ("Fra Lippo Lippi," 286–94)

In this example, we can see that it is not crucial to the function of the interrogative whether the available turn is actually taken. In line 292, we know that the officer has probably spoken because Lippo acknowledges the fact, but any of the other interrogatives are adequate to the function of selecting a next speaker. It is important to make this distinction between a turn-relevance marker, or first pair part, and an actual turn transfer. A turn-relevance-place only signifies the potential for exchange, and a great many of these potential moments of reciprocity in dramatic monologues are in fact examples of failed reciprocity or impossible reciprocity. The latter is true, for example, in Tennyson's "Tithonus":

> Can thy love,
> Thy beauty, make amends, tho' even now
> Close over us, the silver star, thy guide,
> Shines in those tremulous eyes that fill with tears
> To hear me? Let me go; take back thy gift.
> Why should a man desire in any way
> To vary from the kindly race of men,
> Or pass beyond the goal of ordinance
> Where all should pause, as is most meet for all?
>
> (23–31)

Here there is no possibility or expectation that Eos will reply. The verbal exchange between Tithonus and the goddess has been terminated for all eternity, and the "gift" that resulted from it is irrevocable. Tithonus knows this, but the poem is about the fruitless desire for an impossible reversal of time, and Tennyson conceives this desire in terms of Tithonus's vain wish to be answered once again. The dramatic monologue may represent a tenuous but actual exchange, as in "Fra Lippo Lippi," or it may represent the desire for an impossible exchange. In between these poles, we shall find a great variety of partially received and returned communications. What is essential to the form is that it always confronts the problem of the fragility of communicative reciprocity. The most common way of fulfilling this function is through the presentation of conversational turn-places in a poetic form where the next speaker's response, if there is one, cannot be directly represented.

Because intonational and kinesic markers of turn relevance are, along with the interlocutors' utterances, excluded from textual representation in the monologue, Browning often indicates his speaker's assumption of a new turn through an acknowledgment of a previous turn taken by the implied interlocutor. Thus when Fra Lippo Lippi says "Who am I? / Why, one, sir, who is lodging with a friend," he repeats (acknowledges) a content question that has been addressed to him and takes his turn by answering it. The same technique appears in "By the Fireside":

> What did I say?—that a small bird sings
>   All day long, save when a brown pair
> Of hawks from the wood float with wide wings
>   Strained to a bell: 'gainst noon-day glare
> You count the streaks and rings.
>
> (151–55)

This method, which is incidental here and in many other monologues, becomes the ordering principle of whole poems in examples like "Cleon" and "Karshish." The epistolary monologue is entirely constructed of acknowledgment and response; the channels of reciprocal communication between Cleon and Protus would appear to be unobstructed as a precondition of the poem's fiction.

If verbal conversation is the principal mode of reciprocal exchange directly signified in dramatic monologues, still it is not the only one. The two poles of preselection and acknowledgment may apply to action as well as to discourse. When Andrea del Sarto says to his wife "You turn your face, but does it bring your heart?" he is acknowledging a physical action that may be a gesture or communication directed at himself. The turning of Lucrezia's head is as much a part of the implied system of meaningful exchange as anything she might say. The same is true when the speaker selects a next *actant* instead of a next speaker. Dramatic monologues are dense with commands, invitations, and requests with implications of reciprocity, such as Tithonus's "take back thy gift" or Lippo's "Let's sit and set things straight now, hip to haunch." I would include all such speech acts aimed at producing reciprocity in the form of action as among the rhetorical devices that generate dramatic monologues.

These linguistic markers of potential or actual exchange in no way bear the entire burden of directing the dramatic monologue toward the problem of social interaction and its fragility. Rather, they provide a kind of skeleton on which the poet can organize a wealth of metaphors, images, thematic developments, and other conventional elements for the purpose of exploring the subtleties and nuances of individual cases. In a few instances, the skeleton is all but missing, but in these we are made, through the arrangement of other kinds of deictic reference and of poetic conventions, to feel its absence acutely; these are the poems that deal most directly with hopelessly unfulfilled desire. I shall discuss what I consider the most compelling of this relatively small group of poems in my interpretation of "Childe Roland to the Dark Tower Came," but for the purpose of detailing the function of the skeleton itself, I shall turn now to one of Browning's best-known monologues, "Andrea del Sarto."

II

The success of communication and exchange in Browning's monologues may be gauged in part by the degree to which acknowledged responses are interpretable by the speaker. Fra Lippo

Lippi has no difficulty interpreting the constable's responses, and thus, when Lippo says late in the poem "You understand me," we can easily credit his confidence that the exchange has been successful. In addition, the frequency of interpretable turns in the conversation suggests that when Lippo says of the prior's condemnation "Now is this sense, I ask?" the channels are open for the constable to speak, despite the absence of any overt acknowledgment of an answer. The degree of interpretability in no way depends on whether the implied response is verbal. Gestures and actions will do as well as words, as in "A Light Woman," where the speaker observes "you look away, and your lip is curled." This acknowledgment of a wholly unambiguous gesture may usefully be contrasted with the first acknowledgment in "Andrea del Sarto": "You turn your face, but does it bring your heart?" Lucrezia's turn of the head, like her smiles later on, is beyond Andrea's power of interpretation. The gestures fail to form part of a reciprocal interaction between the painter and his wife; and looking further, we can see that Andrea's interrogatives are equally stillborn messengers. They do seem to emanate from a desire for some kind of reply, but their context is always the impossibility of a meaningful break in Lucrezia's silence:

>   Had the mouth there urged
> "God and the glory! never care for gain.
> The present by the future, what is that?
> Live for fame, side by side with Agnolo!
> Rafael is waiting: up to God, all three!"
> I might have done it for you. So it seems:
> Perhaps not. All is as God over-rules.
> Beside, incentives come from the soul's self;
> The rest avail not. Why do I need you?
> What wife had Rafael, or has Agnolo?
>
>   (127–36)

These questions she cannot answer. Andrea has already said that she has been inadequate in speech and that had she been more responsive, it would have made no difference anyway, since all incentives come from within the self. He has isolated her "mouth" beyond the boundaries of his own consciousness and pronounced it irrelevant even as he ostensibly directs questions to her. His questions are content questions in form only. This poem, in contrast with "Fra Lippo Lippi," is full of questions like "What of that?" or "What does the mountain care?" or "What is lost?" These are not merely exclamations of the kind we saw in Shelley; they clearly represent a speaker in search of answers. But this speaker does not seem to know what kind of answers he needs, and he does not direct his questions to anyone from whom he expects a reply. In our earlier terms, he cannot select a next speaker, even when he signifies a turn-relevance-place in the poem's discourse. Lucrezia remains an enigma to him, but we will not discover why by searching Vasari for clues to her historical character. Our understanding of this poem will be an understanding of Andrea's own communicational disability, a disability of which Lucrezia's patient and vacuous smile is only a reflection.

Andrea can only love Lucrezia as part of a picture. She serves as his model, her smile becomes his "picture ready made," and even his physical attraction to her finds expression in the painter's technical vocabulary: "My serpentining beauty, rounds on rounds." He chides her because she fails to "understand [or] care to understand about [his] art," and yet, like the duke of Ferrara, he understands her only in terms of painting. Painting, as Andrea practices the art, is characterized by its flawlessness, its perfection: "All is silver-gray / Placid and perfect with my art." This concept of perfection becomes the term he applies to his love for Lucrezia:

—How could you ever prick those perfect ears,
Even to put the pearl there!

(27–28)

        oh, with the same perfect brow,
And perfect eyes, and more than perfect mouth,

(122–23)

and, again, in order to express his resignation to failure and to empty dreams of greatness for himself:

Only let me sit
The gray remainder of the evening out,
Idle, you call it, and muse perfectly
How I could paint, were I but back in France.

(226–29)

"Perfection," of course, has become an empty mark of value, especially in the second quotation where the comparative "more than perfect" renders "perfect" as somewhat less than ultimate perfection and thus meaningless. Furthermore, "perfection" and "grayness" are often associated in Andrea's musings. "Gray" emerges as the antithesis of "gold," and this antithesis symbolizes the distinction between a life of idle isolation and one of vital social interchange and personal sympathy. The implications of goldness become perhaps most clear in Andrea's reflection on better days in the French court: [7]

I surely then could sometimes leave the ground,
Put on the glory, Rafael's daily wear,
In that humane great monarch's golden look,
One finger in his beard or twisted curl
Over his mouth's good mark that made the smile,
One arm about my shoulder, round my neck,
The jingle of his gold chain in my ear.

(151–57)

The two phrases in which gold appears are those that mark Andrea's memory of the gestures of love and esteem proffered by Francis toward himself. He well knows, however, that something was, and is, lacking in his own nature that is needed to reciprocate such feelings:

Too live the life grew, golden and not gray,
And I'm the weak-eyed bat no sun should tempt
Out of the grange whose four walls make his world.

(168–70)

Andrea is enclosed within the prison of himself and cannot "reach," as other painters do, whether toward others or toward God. This much at least he knows about himself, but his antithesis between gray and gold in fact proves inadequate as a paradigm of self-knowledge.

What Andrea cannot see is that both visions, the gray life and the gold, depend on the security signified by images of enclosure.[8] He imagines his gray four walls as the antithesis of the court's vitality as well as a protection against the "Paris lords" with whom conversation would be unthinkable. But the terms in which he values the golden friendship of Francis are those of encirclement too: the arm around his shoulders and neck. It was not the vital interactions of court society that inspired Andrea with the ability to "leave the ground"; it was the protective boundaries of patronage. A connection between the embrace and the four walls is neither arbitrary nor unprepared at this point in the monologue. Andrea has revealed his obsession with enclosure from the beginning, and in terms that further explain his aesthetic objectification of his wife. He wishes to constrain his wife's freedom, either with love or with money, and he focuses on her hand, which he holds. He first promises to "shut the money into this small hand" and later makes her hand a synecdoche for herself:

> Your soft hand is a woman of itself,
> And mine the man's bared breast she curls inside.
>
> (21–22)

This relation, characterized by enclosure, protection, and inviolable possession, foreshadows the embrace of Francis, who both shelters and, in a sense, "owns" Andrea. Possession has, of course, become more and more difficult for Andrea to sustain as his wife has become more restless, a problem he reveals in a series of progressively weaker genitives:

> My face, my moon, my everybody's moon,
> Which everybody looks on and calls his,
> And, I suppose, is looked on by in turn,
> While she looks—no one's: very dear, no less.
>
> (29–32)

In the phrase "my everybody's moon," the two genitives, both being of the possessive variety, cancel each other out, making Lucrezia "no one's." But Andrea, apparently without realizing it, articulates the kind of human relationship that represents the alternative to possession: a kind of economy of reciprocity (persons "looking on" one another "in turn") that is not limiting in the way that he would wish to constrain Lucrezia's freedom.

Of course, Andrea knows from experience that Lucrezia cannot be incarcerated. His response, however, is not to give up thinking of her in that way but to expand the enclosure:

> Love, we are in God's hand.
> How strange now, looks the life he makes us lead:
> So free we seem, so fettered fast we are!
>
> (49–51)

This passage is important, because here Andrea moves from speaking only of a woman's containment within the limiting enclosure of an embrace to the formulation of an enclosure that includes himself: "*we* are in God's hand." At this point, the penetration of Browning's psychology begins to emerge; he sees that one's attempts to discover predetermined limitations on the freedom of another often reflect the fear that one's own limitations are self-imposed. Thus Andrea, in attempting to persuade his wife that her search for freedom is fruitless, asserts that both she and he are inevitably "fettered fast," an assertion that introduces a soothingly deterministic element into his own failure. This prefigures most of the rhetoric of the poem from this point onward, a rhetoric that finally returns to the image of physical enclosure in the "grange whose four walls make [Andrea's] world." Andrea's sense of his own incarceration explains (to him) his failures, and the inadequacy of his analysis lies in its passive conception of the relation between persons and their circumstances as well as the relation between persons and other persons. For interaction and social exchange, he substitutes confinement and patronage. He was forced to leave Francis's court because he belonged to Lucrezia, because she held power over him. That power, the power of her beauty, is expressed in yet another metaphor of enclosure:

> oh, with the same perfect brow,
> And perfect eyes, and more than perfect mouth
> And the low voice my soul hears, as a bird
> The fowler's pipe, and *follows to the snare*—
>
> (122-25; emphasis mine)

In leaving Francis, he moves from one protective enclosure to another, but he cannot be owned by both the king and his wife; capitulation to one means betrayal of the other. This is the disability that ruins Andrea's life: the limits of his conception of human relations preclude a genuinely social or loving reciprocity with others. Even near the end of the poem, when Andrea tries to make gestures of affection toward his wife, they remain gestures of circumscription and possession:

> Let my hands frame your face in your hair's gold
> You beautiful Lucrezia that are mine!
>
> (175-76)

He misuses Lucrezia's "gold" to symbolize possessive enclosure just as he has misused and perverted the gold of Francis's court to house and constrain Lucrezia in reality. The result of this passion to possess and imprison is ultimately Andrea's own imprisonment, with the possessed gold symbolically enclosing the possessor:

> oft at nights
> When I look up from painting, eyes tired out,
> The walls become illumined, brick from brick
> Distinct, instead of mortar, fierce bright gold,
> That gold of his I did cement them with!
>
> (214-18)

Some readers have felt that Andrea comes to understand himself better at the end of his monologue, but it seems to me that this is true only in the most superficial sense. Certainly, he resigns himself, as he has undoubtedly done many times before, to Lucrezia's departure, but his own isolationist values remain unchanged. He responds to the momentary loss of Lucrezia by constructing a dream of heaven:

In heaven, perhaps, new chances, one more chance—
Four great walls in the New Jerusalem
Meted on each side by the angel's reed,
For Leonard, Rafael, Agnolo and me
To cover—the three first without a wife,
While I have mine!

(260-65)

Andrea understands his wife's infidelities as restlessness, a suscepti-
bility to change, which, in heaven, would cease. She would finally
become his secure possession, just as he would be secure and pro-
tected within these four celestial walls.

Andrea del Sarto's consistent recourse to images of enclosure
and possession reveals a hermetic mind incapable of meaningful intercourse. This is why questions—conventionally "open moments"
of access between speakers—seem for him so aimless. His view of
himself as an isolated cell precludes his indulgence in the normal
verbal structure of conversation, and this implication is embedded
in the linguistic texture of the monologue. In short, while other
monologues organize deictic gestures to imply an unbounded ostensive world, Andrea is capable of these verbal gestures only
within his fixed enclosures. Kept "inside," his reality is immediate
and definite. He can observe Lucrezia, among the other objects in
his chamber, in technical detail, and even in his fantasy, the gold
mortar between each brick is startlingly "distinct." Shortly after he
has offered Lucrezia the metaphor of her hand as the whole woman,
he perceives his other surroundings in the same terms.

There's the bell clinking from the chapel-top;
That length of convent-wall across the way
Holds the trees safer, huddled more inside;
The last monk leaves the garden; days decrease
And autumn grows, autumn in everything.

(41-45)

Huddled safely inside a cloister, details are definite and concrete,
specified by deictics and definite determiners and placed in clear
spatial relations to one another. But when Andrea is forced to project his imagination indefinitely outward, either spatially into the

social world beyond his walls or temporally into desires and regrets, reality becomes less distinct. Ironically, his greatest vagueness concerns his paintings, especially as they compete with those of other painters. When Raphael's picture is safely within Andrea's chamber, he can see it in detail: "That arm is wrongly put." But when he speaks of his own painting in general, the deictic mode gives way to a kind of "empty" deixis that is directly related to the "empty" interrogatives I mentioned earlier:

> I can do with my pencil *what I know*
> *What I see, what* at bottom of my heart
> *I wish for,* if I ever wish so deep—
>
> (60–62)

The italicized noun phrases, complements of the verb "do," mark the absence of answers to the questions, "What do I know?" "What do I see?" and "What do I wish for?" If the subject-verb-complement structure of a sentence conventionally relates the self in some way to that which is outside the self, Andrea's sentences never reach the outside—they merely turn an answerless question vaguely back upon the self-contained subject, "I." This failure of contact with a definite reality outside the subjective enclosure is, in "Andrea del Sarto," repeatedly represented as a failure to consummate his exchanges with others. The structure of reciprocity exists in Andrea's language, but the implied assignment and exchange of agent and patient roles between two speakers cannot take place, because Andrea himself is both agent and patient:

> I, painting *from myself and to myself,*
> Know *what I do,* am unmoved by men's blame
> Or their praise either. Somebody remarks
> Morello's outline there is wrongly traced,
> His hue mistaken; *what* of that? or else,
> Rightly traced and well ordered; *what of that?*
> Speak as they please, *what does the mountain care?*
> Ah, but a man's reach should exceed his grasp,
> Or *what's a heaven for?* All is silver-gray
> Placid and perfect with my art: the worse!

I know both *what I want* and *what might gain,*
And yet how profitless to know, to sigh
"Had I been two, another and myself,
Our head would have o'erlooked the world!" No doubt.

(90–103; emphasis mine)

Andrea conceives of his painting only as "speaking" to himself. If the reception of works of art has any meaning, it is closed to Andrea; he can only ask, "What of that?" Even when he becomes assertive, attempts to believe in "reaching" beyond his enclosing "grasp," his concept of the reaching's goal is expressed in those indefinite interrogatives again: "what I want and what might gain." Does he know what he might reach for? If he does, he cannot communicate that ambition concretely, and the alternative to ambition is just another question: "What's a heaven for?" Beyond the boundaries of Andrea's subjectivity, the human world is absent or indistinct, and interrelations within that world are therefore meaningless. In social roles like the criticism and exchange of art, no person has a definite identity for him. It is only "somebody" who criticizes Morello's outline, Lucrezia's "friend's friend" is a distant abstraction, and Andrea has no idea what that friend's own subject, his own way, his own time, or his own price might be. The practical transaction of which he agrees to be a part is, in other words, one he cannot make concrete in his own imagination. Later, when he boasts "I do what many dream of all their lives," he not only leaves his enviable deed indefinite, he also does not fix on who these "many" actually are:

I do what many dream of, all their lives,
—Dream? strive to do, and agonize to do,
And fail in doing. I could count twenty such
On twice your fingers, and not leave this town,
Who strive—you don't know how the others strive
To paint a little thing like that you smeared
Carelessly passing with your robes afloat—
Yet do much less, so much less, Someone says,
(I know his name, no matter)—so much less!

(69–77)

The object of imitation becomes no more definite than "a little thing," and the imitators themselves are not identified in his discourse. As living, interacting agents, human beings have no real presence for Andrea. The only human plurality he can conceive is that of repetition or replication: "Had I been two, another and myself, / Our head would have o'erlooked the world!" Similarly he can value his painting only as it might have made him "another" Raphael or Michelangelo, and his wife must be endlessly replicated in the form of successive painted Virgins.

Interrogatives, as functional modes of conversation, effect a displacement, the transfer of speaking rights. For Andrea del Sarto, they produce only a repetition, the repetition of an indefinite question that can produce only silence or an uninterpretable smile as answer. The world beyond his self-imposed walls cannot reply because it is only a confusing "what" instead of the deictic "that" which releases the speakers of other dramatic monologues to make connection with their worlds. The ostensive world of the dramatic monologue is never immediate; it is never indisputably "there" as the speaker himself is "there" in the poem's discourse. The speaker's vitality alone can reconstruct an ostensive world for a reader and successfully imply its concrete extension in time and space. The necessary ingredient in this vitality, moreover, is the capacity for human reciprocity, social or individual, and this is the ingredient Andrea so tragically lacks. As long as he cannot ask meaningful questions that demand substantive replies, he cannot clearly realize an external reality, even his own "two hundred pictures." The mind that helplessly asks of his painting, "What's it worth?" is the same mind that asks of Lucrezia, "The Cousin! what does he to please you more?" Whether the relevant economy is the valuation and exchange of property or the social exchange among friends, lovers, and friends of friends, its functional principle is inaccessible to Andrea's understanding. Hence four walls inevitably enclose his own heaven, his own prison, and the uninterrupted drone of his own isolated voice.

Once again, as he had done a decade earlier in "Pictor Ignotus," Browning shows us a painter who conceives of his own identity as homogeneous and self-contained. Once again, the choice is the same. Submit the whole self to the marketplace and a social system in which all exchange is subject to the alienations of a market economy or withdraw, betray the contracts of social life and the laws of economic life in order to be self-sufficient. Andrea vacillates between these two poles and cannot finally resign himself to either. As a dramatic monologue, however, "Andrea del Sarto" opens the question of whether all human reciprocity need inevitably be governed by the ideology of exchange-value. The poem suggests that Andrea specifically chooses to think of his wife's value in monetary / aesthetic terms and that if he thought of her less as a possession, he might learn to effect the reciprocity that she presently finds elsewhere. While we encounter here the same contradictions that Browning represented in "Pictor Ignotus," we are left with an additional question: What would have to be different for exchange-as-communication to be separated from exchange-as-commerce or -exploitation? The implicit answer of the monologue as a genre would seem to be that the speaker's understanding of the nature of his or her own subjectivity would have to change.

A considerable number of these poems explore the ways communication can dysfunction. The speaker of "Two in the Campagna" confronts a lover who is fully as unresponsive as Lucrezia. In this case, however, the speaker displays none of the complex disabilities that cripple Andrea. He asks questions about the lady's feelings and about his own fate that are fully answerable, unobstructed turn-relevance-places, should the lady choose to answer. The fact that she does not seems merely to illustrate the fact that love's intimacies are short lived, and we have encountered this particular pair at a time when the economy of life, and thus of conversation, has become asymmetrical. In a more complex case, one that once again raises an explicit economic alienation between speaker and interlocutor, Bishop Blougram asks Gigadibs, "In truth's name, don't you want my bishopric, / My daily bread, my influence and my state?" or later, "What's your reward, self-abnegating friend?" Here interrogatives are used as goads, reminding Gigadibs that real communication with the bishop depends on shared economic and ideological values. Because Blougram asks questions that have meaning only within a market ideology, a potential next speaker who doubts that ideology cannot complete the communicative circuit by returning intelligible answers to the questions.

III

Since the dramatic monologue requires one party in a conversation to speak unrecorded, if at all, successful verbal exchange is more difficult to embody in the genre than interactional dysfunction. This formal resistance contributes to the sense that when two people genuinely understand each other, they do so despite a world that thwarts communication at every turn. Hence an important part of Browning's poetic task is to specify the features of various social contexts or values that so deeply threaten the pathways of reciprocal understanding.

When Browning confronts questions of value, he does so, not from a socialist point of view, but from a democratic one. He holds out the hope that the values of communication and free exchange can be preserved independent of their involvement in the alienation and exploitation of the marketplace. This Browning, the Browning who poses middle-class moral and religious questions, may seem to be at odds with the Browning who so profoundly questions the very intelligibility of the middle-class unitary subject. It is certainly true that these poems acknowledge the contradictions of ideology selectively. They have no alternative coherent ideology within which to locate their own discourse, and they must at times adopt the perspective of relatively progressive democratic assumptions in order to challenge antidemocratic constraints on communication. Once a social system of communication has been established, the subject can be represented as having no identity independent of that system. And Browning is concerned to reveal the conservative counterforces that deny value to communicative exchange itself.

He recognizes these forces in the form of a stratified social organization and the hierarchic method of value determination that derives historically from that organization. Throughout his poems, Browning identifies faith in the authority of a fixed social hierarchy with a value code that is in itself hierarchical. The speaker who accepts or defends his place in an ascending scale of classes or ranks usually generates metaphors, images, and formulas in which the good is placed "above" the bad in some kind of vertical space. This method of determining value virtually always turns out to be ineffective. The duke in "My Last Duchess," for example, tells the count's envoy that he chooses "never to stoop," and his gallery, containing works that symbolize his power, is located above the part of his villa in which he receives visitors. Yet when he suggests "Let's go together down sir," he includes the envoy as an equal partner in the "descent." Thus, although he asserts his superiority, he undercuts the system that would give it meaning by placing a mere envoy "above" the count, his master, both physically and in terms of communicational privilege. In simpler terms, by confiding "I choose never to stoop," the duke does, in fact, stoop.

Value-laden discriminations of upward and downward are everywhere in Browning's monologues, and in more straightforward cases, the speaker himself may successfully challenge the vertical code and reveal an alternative. "Fra Lippo Lippi" abounds in the language of altitudes. The house of the Cosimo of the Medici "caps" the corner, signifying to the officer the status of his "betters." The aesthetic opinions of the rank-and-file monks are preempted by their "betters," who proceed to advise Lippo in vertical terms:

> Your business is not to catch men with show,
> With homage to the perishable clay,
> But lift them over it, ignore it all,
> Make them forget there's such a thing as flesh.
>
> (178–81)

And Lippo, when he leaves his patron's house to join common carousers in the street, descends:

> There was a ladder! Down I let myself,
> Hands and feet, scrambling somehow, and so dropped,
> And after them . . .
>
> (64–66)

The syntactic inversion of "Down I let myself," the gentle alliteration with "dropped," and the suggestion of irrevocable consequence in "and so dropped" all serve to emphasize a vague sense of degradation implicit in Lippo's indiscretion. Provisionally, in other words, Browning invokes the language of up and down as a normative structure. Piety, obedience, social rank, and a certain kind of art come to be defined by the vertical code. This is true even in common locutions that use vertical language in the most casual way:

> And so as I was stealing back again
> To get to bed and have a bit of sleep
> Ere I rise up to-morrow and go work
> On Jerome knocking at his poor old breast
> With his great round stone to subdue the flesh.
>
> (70–74)

From the low life of the street, Lippo ascends into a patron's house, after which he "rises up" (yet further on the moral scale) to paint pious pictures of saints "subduing" the very flesh that he himself has so scandalously indulged below. For the irreverent, "rise up" means only "get out of bed," but in the too-pervasive parlance of Lippo's community, he also elevates himself in painting those tedious saints.

The movement from elements of the street life, mischievous indiscretion, and living by wit and impulse rather than by rules of conduct to acts of conformity and conventional piety repeatedly brings forth the vertical code, as in the young Lippo's last action before being "raised" to the comfort and discipline of the convent: "The wind doubled me up and down I went" (87). And when he begins to paint ordinary people, the same kind of language appears, as my emphasis shows.

> From good old gossips waiting to confess
> Their cribs of *barrel-droppings*, candle-ends,—
> To the breathless fellow at the *altar-foot*
>
> (148–50)

Look at the boy who *stoops* to pat the dog!

(169)

Like the Italian nobleman in "Up in the Villa, Down in the City,"
Lippo, of course, values precisely that living manifold of the low
life, the "uncontrollable mystery on the bestial floor," as Yeats
was to put it. Accordingly, in his self-defense, Lippo uses vertical
relationships neutrally if at all; for him they are emptied of their
reference to an absolute value hierarchy. Hence he asks scornfully,

> Do you feel thankful, ay or no,
> For this fair town's face, yonder river's line,
> The mountain round it and the sky above,
> Much more the figures of man, woman, child,
> These are the frame to? What's it all about?
> To be passed over, despised? or dwelt upon,
> Wondered at?

(285-91)

Lippo, of course, prefers to "wonder at" the created universe rather
than subordinate it. When he describes the painting he will paint,
he does not abandon religious subjects but arranges them in a kind
of horizontal extension or social gathering. Saint John, Saint Am-
brose, the Madonna with babe, and naturalistic angels—all are there
along with Job and "God in the midst," just as Lippo himself prefers to be in the midst of human society rather than aloof in a
convent or patron's house. Indeed, Lippo will paint himself into
that exalted company:

> Well, all these
> Secured at their devotion, up shall come
> Out of a corner when you least expect,
> As one by a dark stair into a great light,
> Music and talking, who but Lippo! I!—

(359-63)

The painter, by including himself, raises himself, but instead of
raising himself to something above the realm of human, or "fleshly,"
intercourse, he comes into "a great light, / Music and talking." Thus

his "blushing face / Under the cover of a hundred wings" comes as an image of inclusion in company, an inclusion that has been justified by an inversion of heirarchical order:

> Then steps a sweet angelic slip of a thing
> Forward, puts out a soft palm—"Not so fast!"
> —Addresses the celestial presence, "nay—
> He made you and devised you, after all,
> Though he's none of you! Could Saint John there draw—
> His camel-hair makes up a painting brush?
> We come to brother Lippo for all that."
>
> (370–76)

Lippo, the lover of low life, flesh and blood, becomes the "creator" of the celelstial presence, reversing the principle on which the vertical relation between God and his creatures is based. This reversal does not, of course, turn "high" into "low" on the scale of value. Rather it calls into question the scale itself by imputing to it a confusing or misleading structure:

> As it is,
> You tell too many lies and hurt yourself:
> You don't like what you only like too much,
> You do like what, if given you at your word,
> You find abundantly detestable.
> For me, I think I speak as I was taught;
> I always see the garden and God there
> A-making man's wife: and, my lesson learned,
> The value and significance of flesh,
> I can't unlearn ten minutes afterwards.
>
> (260–69)

The vertical division of imperatives leads to what modern psychoanalysis calls "double binds," undeniable commands at different levels that appear to contradict one another.[9] If God and the flesh are conceived as discretely separated on a vertical scale of values, this kind of schizogenic paralysis is inevitable: we are "born under one law, to another bound." But Lippo recommends dis-

carding the digital Neoplatonic ladder in favor of a convivial continuity in which God, angels, saints, and men can interact in time
and space, learning through communication the "value and significance of flesh." Value, in such a model, derives from communal
acts of signification and not from fixed symbols of status or power.
This is why it is important, as I pointed out in chapter 3, that Lippo's relation to the constable must shift from its initial foundation
of power balanced against status to one of solidarity. By effecting
the shift convincingly, Browning wrote a successful dramatic
monologue, and by creating the fiction for a successful dramatic
monologue, he created the opportunity for a critique of values
organized by vertical scales.

"Fra Lippo Lippi" illustrates the limitations of the vertical code
through a speaker who is conscious of those limitations. In "Cleon,"
Browning accomplishes the same thing ironically, by displaying
the inflexibilities of his speaker's reasoning. Cleon's articulation of
values unfolds in strictly hierarchical terms, as he reveals in his
opening praise of Protus:

> Thou, in the daily building of thy tower,—
> Whether in fierce and sudden spasms of toil,
> Or through dim lulls of unapparent growth,
> Or when the general work 'mid good acclaim
> Climbed with the eye to cheer the architect,—
> Didst ne'er engage in work for mere work's sake—
> Hadst ever in thy heart the luring hope
> Of some eventual rest a-top of it,
> Whence all the tumult of the building hushed,
> Thou first of men mightst look out to the East:
> The vulgar saw thy tower, thou sawest the sun.
>
> (26–36)

Serially, "the vulgar," Protus (his tower), and "the sun" (presumably Zeus) rise from the low to the high in order to assert Protus's
status and his corresponding virtue. It is not surprising, therefore,
that Cleon and Protus prove unable to resolve the confusion brought
on by experience that resists the determination of human "progress" in these same terms:

In man there's failure, only since he left
The lower and inconscious forms of life.
We called it an advance, the rendering plain
Man's spirit might grow conscious of man's life,
And, by new lore so added to the old,
Take each step higher over the brute's head.
This grew the only life, the pleasure-house,
Watch-tower and treasure-fortress of the soul,
Which whole surrounding flats of natural life
Seemed only fit to yield subsistence to;
A tower that crowns a country. But alas,
The soul now climbs it just to perish there!

(225–36)

Cleon's exposition makes full use of the vertical code, defining progress with the tower image as he has done before and including even the oblique reference to royalty in "A tower that crowns a country." This code, however, proves inadequate to affirm value in human life: "Most progress is most failure: thou sayest well" (272). As many readers have realized, "Cleon" is a poem about the frustration that could have been relieved by the recognition of Christ's significance, a significance that Cleon describes in longing for it but that he cannot discover in its real manifestation. The frustration itself is twofold. Cleon cannot find value in human action and striving, and he cannot discover God's purpose. Furthermore, he conceives both of these in vertical language:

Long since, I imaged, wrote the fiction out,
That he or other god descended here
And, once for all, showed simultaneously
What, in its nature, never can be shown,
Piecemeal or in succession.

(115–19)

Unlike Lippo's God, who lives "in the midst" of creation, Cleon's God must be "above," for he is looked for to "descend." The futile search for transcending value on a hierarchic scale continues in this vein with the single exception of Cleon's fascination with Protus's female slave. He recognizes her and the youthful rower "with the moulded muscles there" as enjoying a vitality closed to himself. Though she is no more than a slave, she is young, and youth has a value that neither status nor art can reproduce. Cleon gives only brief attention to this casual observation, but its implications, unperceived by him, supply the basis of Browning's irony through the remainder of the poem. Hence, in the final paragraph, when Cleon replies to Protus's inquiries concerning Saint Paul, the attribution of value to the activities of "slaves" appears unthinkable:

> Thou canst not think a mere barbarian Jew,
> As Paulus proves to be, one circumcised,
> Hath access to a secret shut from us?
> Thou wrongest our philosophy, O king,
> In stooping to inquire of such an one,
> As if his answer could impose at all!
> He writeth, doth he? well, and he may write.
> Oh, the Jew findeth scholars! certain slaves
> Who touched on this same isle, preached him and Christ;
> And (as I gathered from a bystander)
> Their doctrine could be held by no sane man.
>
> (343-53)

Cleon's rejection of Saint Paul takes its form from the assumption that the hierarchic structure of aristocratic and intellectual "rank" corresponds to the structure of absolute truth. A "mere barbarian Jew" could not have access to secrets that are unavailable to philosophers and kings. To give such a person any but the most indirect notice would be to "stoop" and would accomplish nothing. Serious consideration of Christian doctrine might call into question the authority of philosophers and kings, but these matters are beyond Cleon's imagining. Christian doctrine might answer all of his questions and relieve him of his despair, but Cleon cannot know this for the same reason that has produced his confusion in the first place: he proves unable, for the purpose of affirming value, to understand human action and speech in any way not determined by the boundaries of a predetermined hierarchy. In the end, however, he, like the duke of Ferrara, reveals his own immersion in the common humanity he scorns. Just as the duke confides in a mere servant, Cleon cites as authoritative the philosophic opinion of an anonymous "bystander."

IV

The dramatic monologue represents a speaking subject as one element in a more or less functional circuit or system. Throughout the last three chapters, I have been pointing out features of the genre that implicitly offer a radical critique of nineteenth-century concepts of the self. I would call the self of the monologue a "cybernetic" self, chiefly because the framework of cybernetics so effectively calls into question the boundaries of any individual element within a systemic reality. Browning's speakers always operate as parts of open systems, whether the system is defined as an endlessly interrelated series of temporal fragments, as a commonality of language, or as a social economy of exchange and reciprocity. The individual for Browning is never complete. His very individuality can only be recognized "piecemeal and in succession" as he is transformed in time, as he participates in a transindividual style of speech, and as he interacts with other individuals through response and acknowledgment. The self, in other words, is not the container of the mind that the dramatic monologue represents. That mind, as Gregory Bateson has said in another context, "is immanent in the larger system, man *plus* environment."[10] This extension affects, not only Browning's social vision, but his vision of nature as well. If truth and knowledge do not admit of the kind of closure that Cleon desires, boundaries between the natural and the human are correspondingly difficult to enforce. The philosopher who would conquer nature, who sees it as "only fit to yield subsistence to" himself, does so at the cost of forgetting that he is himself part of that nature. Browning's poems, in other words, continually challenge the Cartesian separation of matter and spirit by recognizing all substance and all mind as parts of an open-ended, nonstatic system in time and space.

Browning has often been taken to task for his Christianity; it has been called facile or sentimental. However this may be, Browning's religious impulse consistently arises from the desire to recognize a power greater than (not "higher than") the self. This religious orientation, according to Bateson, lies at the heart of the cybernetic vision of reality:

> There is a Power greater than the self. Cybernetics would . . . recognize that the "self" as ordinarily understood is only a small part of a much larger trial-and-error system which does the thinking, acting, and deciding. . . . The "self" is a false reification of an improperly delimited part of this much larger field of interlocking processes. Cybernetics also recognizes that two or more persons—any group of persons—may together form such a thinking-and-acting system.
>
> This Power is felt to be personal and to be intimately linked with each person. It is "God as *you* understand him to be."[11]

This is the theology of Fra Lippo Lippi. Lippo's God is always "in the midst" of his creation, even as he encompasses it all, and Lippo himself is not a discrete selfhood contrasted with the collective of heaven. He is a shy and insignificant part of the scene, a lowly creature of God, and yet he is simultaneously the creator of the entire heaven, including that God. In this vision, there is no reification of the self, the environment, or even of God. Lippo is a part of every corner of the system, and the whole system in which he interacts is a part of him. The fact that the system is "greater than the self" does not mean that it is alien from the self. The cybernetic self denies the boundaries of individuality, and it is no contradiction that the true God of the Creation is also "God as Lippo understands him to be."

V

Fra Lippo Lippi is also an artist, and his monologue offers a theology within which Browning projects, by analogy, a "power greater than the poetic self" through his community of *Men and Women*. If every monologue is a speech act functioning within an ostensive fictional system, so too is it an element of interaction in the system of social reality that Browning called the British public.

When we think about the interactions of a monologue's speaker with his listener and with a shared world, we cannot forget that the selfhood of that speaker is also indissolubly integrated into the poetic self that created him. That self too has a listener, and for the poem to achieve its full being, that listener, the reader, must also participate in an active, creative interaction. Earlier I said that Browning's language and the genre he invented challenge the elitism of specialized language, poetic language in particular. Accordingly, the indefinite extensions in time and space implied by the monologue invite and even require the reader to fill in the continuum with his own imaginative participation in the making of the fiction. The poet, in other words, is no longer the Romantic oracle, the disembodying ventriloquist, the teacher and unacknowledged legislator of the world. He is the body becoming transubjective in a language that must be completed by an act of response. Browning saw the need for such a language as early as the famous introduction to *Paracelsus:*

> It is certain, . . . that a work like mine depends more immediately on the intelligence and sympathy of the reader for its success: indeed were my scenes stars, it must be his co-operating fancy which, supplying all chasms, should connect the scattered lights into one constellation—a Lyre or a Crown.[12]

The language that demands this "co-operating fancy" from real readers in the cybernetic time and space of Browning's audience does not employ the transcendent "cosmic syntax" that critics like Earl Wasserman and Edward Bostetter attribute to all Romantic and post-Romantic poetry.[13] Poets since the Enlightenment, in Wasserman's words, "shape the autonomous poetic reality that the cosmic syntax permits."[14] But Browning's poetic reality is not "autonomous," and neither, for that matter, is his syntax. Especially when Browning seems to court obscurity, the reader must stop the comfortable flow of his reading and either reconstruct complicated sentence structures or supply the missing elements in fragmented ones. In the case of fragmentation, however, the sentence fragment can almost always be read as a complete sentence by the "co-operating fancy." The following typical passage is an example of a kind of narrative shorthand, leaving out main verbs that are nevertheless easily supplied by the reader:

> And so along the wall, over the bridge,
> By the straight cut to the convent [we went]. Six
>   words [were spoken] there,
> While I stood munching my first bread that month.
>
> ("Fra Lippo Lippi," 90–92)

This kind of abbreviated clause structure demands a high degree of complementarity between the language competence of the author and that of the reader. Indeed, so much willing cooperation is demanded by Browning's style that the effect at large is to demystify the Romantic "autonomous poetic reality," replacing it with a concept of poetry as an occasion for both poet and reader to express their interdependence.[15] Furthermore, the growth of this kind of poetic economy has a strong diachronic dimension. Each new poem is not a new reality for the actively creative reader. The act of completing the message of previous poems conditions the reader's readiness for the poet's style, and thus the strong continuity of style from monologue to monologue is a continuity in the whole system of author, society, and reader.

In such a system, to return to cybernetic terms, the author acts as a "governor" who alters his own behavior in response to the conditioned creativity of cooperating fancies. When the conditioning fails, or when the subsequent poetic input is insufficiently familiar, the governor has misfunctioned and so too does the entire communicative system. In literary terms, this means that the economy of exchange between poet and reader may be very fragile and vulnerable to potential processes of reisolation. Indeed, Browning's contemporary critics often seem acutely aware of the threat posed by a thoroughgoing individualism to the literary economy. In 1856, for example, one G. Brimley complained in *Fraser's Magazine* that Browning sometimes frustrates the participating reader, thus becoming "a law and idol to himself." But Brimley also recognized the responsibility of all members of the system to make poetry succeed:

It may fairly be questioned whether the pains by which such a poet as Mr. Tennyson, for instance, makes his poems as good and perfect as he can, before offering them to the public, ever meets with general appreciation, inasmuch as such painstaking in a writer demands a corresponding painstaking in the reader.[16]

Maisie Ward cites a comment made by Ruskin on the difficulties of contemporary writing that she believes accurately defines the problems posed by Browning's style:

The worst of it is this kind of concentrated writing needs so much solution before the reader can fully see the good of it, that people's patience fails them and they give up the thing as insoluble, though truly it ought to be the current of common thought like Saladin's talisman, dipped in clear water, not soluble altogether, but making the element medicinal.[17]

The failure of patience cited by Ruskin was common enough among Browning's readers, but the striking feature of the reviews is the degree to which hostile and friendly critics alike adopted Browning's own terms of author / reader reciprocity.[18] I have mentioned Brimley among Browning's harsher detractors; others might as easily have served, like the anonymous reviewer in *The Athenaeum* of November 1855 who wonders "why [Browning] should turn away from themes in which every one can answer to his sympathies, and from modes of the lyre which find their echoes wherever hearts and ears know aught of music."[19]

Readers more favorable to Browning's eccentric style and, one hopes, more intelligent in executing the poetic contract, seize precisely on the active role of the reader in effecting this necessary echo. For George Eliot, the value of great poetry lies in effects on the reader that derive from the labor of understanding, and she condemns those who expect the poet to be the sole "active" agent:

To read poems is often a substitute for thought: fine-sounding conventional phrases and the sing-song of verse demand no co-operation in the reader; they glide over his mind with the agreeable unmeaningness of "the compliments of the season," or a speaker's exordium of "feelings too deep for expression." *But let him expect no such drowsy passivity in reading*

Browning. Here he will find no conventionality, no melodious commonplace, but freshness, originality, sometimes eccentricity of expression; no
didactic laying-out of a subject, but dramatic indication, *which requires
the reader to trace by his own mental activity the underground stream of
thought that jets out in elliptical and pithy verse.* To read Browning he
must exert himself, but he will exert himself to some purpose. If he finds
the meaning difficult of access, it is always worth his effort—if he has to
dive deep "he rises with his pearl." Indeed, in Browning's best poems he
makes us feel that what we took for obscurity in him was superficiality in
ourselves. [20]

George Eliot disagrees with Browning's critics about the value of
the "commonplace" as opposed to that of "eccentricity." Both
parties argue, however, on the basis of an assumed reciprocity between the poet and reader. This structure informs the entire controversy concerning Browning's "obscurity" during his lifetime
and, in its most articulate manifestations, enlists the reader as
something like a collaborative creator of the poem. It is worth
mentioning in passing that this kind of demand is implicit, not
only in Victorian poetic practice, but in revisions of conventional
narrative conventions as well. George Eliot's own addresses to the
reader in her novels come immediately to mind. Most often, they
too invite an active filling in of details from the reader's own
cooperating fancy:

If you want to know more particularly how Mary looked, ten to one you
will see a face like hers in the crowded street to-morrow, if you are there
on the watch: she will not be among those daughters of Zion who are
haughty, and walk with stretched-out necks and wanton eyes, mincing as
they go: let all those pass, and fix your eyes on some small plump brown-
ish person of firm but quiet carriage, who looks about her, but does not
suppose that anybody is looking at her. If she has a broad face and square
brow, well-marked eyebrows and curly dark hair, a certain expression of
amusement in her glance which her mouth keeps the secret of, and for the
rest features entirely insignificant—take that ordinary but not disagreeable
person for a portrait of Mary Garth. [21]

This is not a description; it is a recognition that every Mary Garth
for every reader will be a different one, that the language of description can be no more than a meeting place where sender and

receiver of the literary message collaborate in creating the fiction. Such an approach, reflected in George Eliot's comments on Browning, demystifies the author as absolute creator or seer and makes of the literary work an occasion for reciprocity and fictive interplay. This interplay is a social system, a cybernetic circuit, an economy of exchange. It figures incidentally in several Victorian literary genres, but only in the dramatic monologue does it organize both the fictional plane of the poem's content and the "real" plane of the text in the world.

VI

In this chapter, and the two that precede it, I have attempted a generic description of the dramatic monologue. I have argued that the typical formal features of the monologue's discourse construct and locate an ambivalent or contradictory subject. Though this subject at first appears the epitome of forceful and coherent Cartesian selfhood, close inspection reveals that it also lacks the clear temporal boundaries necessary to discrete homogeneity, that the source of its discourse is divided, and that the subject itself only exists in its dynamic and interactive relations within a system of social codes and messages. In chapter 2, I said that a full account of the monologue's production would require a careful scrutiny of the intersection of social forces with the constraints of literary history. Much of my analysis has been intended to show how the monologue both revises Romantic poetic conventions and brings before the conscious eye the contradictions inherent in nineteenth-century middle-class ideology. The latter might be summarized, as Marx did it, in the opposition of private interest and general interest. For Marx, the concept necessary to resolve this dialectical pair was the concept of social class. For Browning, the situation appears more complex and less theoretically clear.

In a dramatic monologue like "Pictor Ignotus," the subject-as-homogeneous-entity faces the untenable choice of investing or hoarding the self and its "talents." As long as the speaker is a "true person," he must either embody his entire identity in "each new picture"—submit himself to the whole public marketplace—or he must withdraw entirely. But the subject on which this opposition of public vulnerability and private obscurity depends is radically called into question by the form of the monologue itself. No monologue presents the subject as a complete identity that can be wholly invested or withheld. The self, always losing a fading past and gaining an uncertain future, is always in the process of being alienated from its products or from any particular "present" in which it would be possible to say "I chose my portion." Moreover, the "I" in that sentence is not unitary in the monologue. In Browning's new contradiction, the source or author of the discourse is always double, leading us to say paradoxically that the text of the "monologue" is always "dialogical." By this we mean that it has two meanings and that these two meanings not only come from a divided origin but are destined *for* two different respondents simultaneously. And a discourse that depends on a reciprocating subject of address for the completion of its meaning further demystifies the unitary subject who "intends" a unitary meaning for the discourse that he or she authors.

Thus the "contradiction" faced by the Pictor Ignotus resolves dialectically into the single term of the homogeneous and discrete subject, a concept that in turn produces its own antithesis, the heterogeneous and fragmented dialogical subject. It is this last opposition that all dramatic monologues present without resolving. By doing do, they step beyond the more apparent contradictions of middle-class ideology, and they advance the struggle with literary form that Browning found most acutely revealed in Shelley.

My analysis has indicated the intersection of ideological and literary historical axes that I began by positing in chapter 2. But it has also left some important questions unresolved that seem germane to the production of dramatic monologues. First, I have described typical features of the monologue and how their recognition can help us interpret typical poems. This does not tell us how elastic the concept of the genre is, how much of the formal apparatus of the monologue can be deleted or displaced while still leaving the poem at the ideological / literary coordinates that locate the genre. Second, my account so far says nothing of how a particular poet produces such poems, how Robert Browning's own

intellectual or psychic processes—taken in themselves as material—
interact with the constraints already encoded in the monologue's
conventions. And third, my discussion of social forces and ideology
thus far has remained generalized. I have invoked the market
system, the specialization of discourse, the alienation of labor, and
the ideology of individualism, but I have said little about the relation of Browning's poetry to actual historical events and conditions. But the problem of concrete history is, in Browning's case,
most difficult. Browning's most immediate social context is, of
course, Victorian England, but because after his marriage he spent
so much of his time in Italy and France, and because he concerned
himself so intently with the affairs of those countries, we may
need, at least in theory, to take into account the full range of nineteenth-century European history. The latter is, of course, far
beyond the scope of this book. For me, the following chapters
raise more questions than they answer. They suggest how psychoanalytic and specific historical factors enter into the production
of individual poems, but much more needs to be done. Because
this book deals with the production of the monologue as a class of
poems, many of the most interesting specific questions must, for
the time being, be deferred.

Browning, Childe Roland, and the Speech of Dreams

I   *M*y account of the dramatic monologue uses different formal criteria from those of most existing definitions of the genre, while it preserves the intention to include most of the poems traditionally called dramatic monologues by informed readers. Until we move beyond the Victorian period into the twentieth century, I doubt that my description would exclude any important poems that are generally accepted as being in the class of monologues. In the Victorian period, that class is rather small, however, and I should like to include within it a few poems that have not been considered monologues in the past. I have argued that the distinction between the poet and the monologue's speaker is not criterial for the form, and I have avoided saying that a particular interlocutor must be implied. The doubleness of the monologue's language and its structures of reciprocity and exchange made it convenient to employ these conventions in a large number of poems, but a few of the best dramatic monologues omit them. In this chapter, I want to examine two of Browning's poems—"One Word More," where the speaker is explicitly Browning himself, and "Childe Roland to the Dark Tower Came," where there is no listener. I hope to show that recognizing these, along with Elizabeth Barrett's *Sonnets from the Portuguese,* as dramatic monologues can help us to understand the psychological, social, and semiotic processes by which all monologues come into being and interpret their world.

II

To Browning, poetic discourse is transactional. He uses it to map exchanges in the fictional world of the dramatic monologue, and he invites real readers into colloquy with his own imagination. The most important colloquy of his own life, indeed one of the truly grand continuing "conversations" of the nineteenth century, was his marriage to Elizabeth Barrett, and I want to show now the peculiar suitability of the monologue in projecting communication between the Brownings.

Neither "One Word More" nor *Sonnets from the Portuguese* are spoken by personae other than the poet, and yet I believe that both display all of the features I have attributed to the monologue or, in the latter case, to the monologue collection. In writing *Sonnets from the Portuguese,* Elizabeth Barrett revived a venerable English genre: not just the sonnet, but the sonnet sequence. We cannot adequately describe the genre of the English love sonnet in the sixteenth century by attending to individual poems. In most cases, an important narrative continuity linked poem to poem, establishing a literary kind that, as J. L. Lever has said of *Astrophel and Stella,* "told the story of a modern love affair in all its phases."[1] Later, in the seventeenth century, as the love of woman and the love of God became ever more intricately intervolved, the sonnet sequence was increasingly turned to serious religious purposes. Fulke Greville, for example, abandoned the fourteen-line sonnet form in many of the poems in his *Caelica* but retained the narrative sequence for the purpose of chronicling his gradual substitution of spiritual for corporeal love. Donne, on the other hand, found in the mystical image of the circle a nontemporal principle of continuity between regular sonnets in his *La Corona* sequence: the last line of each poem is identical to the first line of the next, and the last line of the final poem is the first line of the initial one. In manifestations like these, the genre of the sonnet sequence appears to have reached its maximum in self-conscious ingenuity, and soon thereafter the form virtually disappeared from English poetry. Indeed the sonnet itself virtually disappeared after Milton and did not again become a fruitful convention until the nineteenth century.

In the hands of the Romantics, Wordsworth and Keats in particular, the sonnet found a new lyric purpose. But the lyric outpouring of reconsidered emotion makes no demands on the relations between poems. Like Shelley's images in the similes of "To a Skylark," each Romantic sonnet is self-contained in its subject and its moment in time. Hence, with the arguable early exception of Wordsworth's "River Duddon" sonnets, the sonnet sequence as a distinct genre was not to be revived in modern times—except in the work of a few Victorian experimenters like Rossetti in *The House of Life,* Meredith in *Modern Love,* and Elizabeth Barrett in *Sonnets from the Portuguese.*[2]

Elizabeth Barrett's sonnet sequence provides a fine example of how an emerging new literary form gains in prestige by masquerading as a venerable old genre. If I am correct about the dramatic monologue collection, one of its irreducible requirements is some principle of continuity between individual poems in the form of an enclosing fiction. In *The Ring and the Book,* the enclosing fiction is the Roman murder story and the possibility of varying fragmentary perspectives on it. In *Men and Women,* the enclosing fiction is the more subtle gathering of individual voices from disparate historical periods and places to speak the common language of Victorian England. For Elizabeth Barrett, the enclosing fiction is much simpler. In 1845, the role of a lover was hardly "reality" to her, and she found in the English sonnet sequence an enclosing fiction for the day-to-day vacillations of her feelings for Robert Browning. She wrote sonnets to him without intending them to be actually received by him. The continuities of her fiction are temporal and conversational, and this requirement accounts for the apparent formal suitability of the sonnet sequence. But with a few exceptions, the poems she wrote are not Sidneyan or Shakespearean sonnets; they are dramatic monologues.

The temporal context of *Sonnets from the Portuguese* is the succession of visits paid by Browning to the cloistered Elizabeth during their courtship. The poems are full of deictic reference to those meetings, and as often as not, the reference is made by way of adding to a conversational exchange already in progress. The thirty-third and thirty-fourth sonnets, for example, must be read together and in the context of issues raised in actual discussions between Elizabeth and Robert:

XXXIII

Yes, call me by my pet name! let me hear
The name I used to run at, when a child,
From innocent play, and leave the cowslips piled,
To glance up in some face that proved me dear
With the look of its eyes. I miss the clear
Fond voices which, being drawn and reconciled
Into the music of Heaven's undefiled,
Call me no longer. Silence on the bier,
While I call God—call God!—So let thy mouth
Be heir to those who are now exanimate.
Gather the north flowers to complete the south,
And catch the early love up in the late.
Yes, call me by that name,—and I, in truth,
With the same heart, will answer and not wait.

XXXIV

With the same heart, I said, I'll answer thee
As those, when thou shalt call me by my name—
Lo, the vain promise! is the same, the same,
Perplexed and ruffled by life's strategy?
When called before, I told how hastily
I dropped my flowers or brake off from a game,
To run and answer with a smile that came
At play's last moment, and went on with me
Through my obedience. When I answer now,
I drop a grave thought, break from solitude;
Yet still my heart goes to thee—ponder how—
Not as to a single good, but all my good!
Lay thy hand on it, best one, and allow
That no child's foot could run fast as this blood.

Like so many of Browning's monologues, sonnet 33 locates the moment of speech as a fragment of two separate strands of temporal experience. The main body of the poem articulates a continuum from childhood to adulthood in which those who were early entrusted with Elizabeth's love—those who called her by her pet name ("Ba")—have died and can now be replaced by someone bringing and offering a new kind of love. The beginning and ending at the same time gesture toward a different temporal scale in which a conversation with Robert himself is continuously unfolding. Both continua are shaped by the complementary exchange of call and answer, with the difference that the poem, as part of the conversational dimension, actually precipitates the exchange by answering an implied previous question: "Yes, call me by my pet name!" The sonnet, in fact, refers to Browning's hesitant "call" in his letter of December 19, 1845:

> (But I *have* a new thing to say or sing—you never before heard me love and bless and send my heart after . . . "Ba"—did you?) Ba . . . and that is you! I TRIED . . . (more than *wanted*) to call you that, on Wednesday![3]

and her "answer" of two days later:

> I think of you always. May God bless you. "Love me forever," as
> Your
> Ba[4]

Not only is sonnet 33 an open-ended fragment within the long process of Elizabeth's growing older and within the shorter process of her unfolding conversation with Robert, it is also a fragment in relation to the other sonnets in the sequence. Sonnet 34 could not be read in the absence of sonnet 33; it refers obliquely back to the events introduced there, and references like "when thou shalt call me by my name" make sense only when we know that "my name" is really "my pet name." The Renaissance sonnet is remarkable for its resources of internal symmetry and closure, resources that Romantic poets continued to explore and exploit. But although Elizabeth Barrett retains an elaborate traditional rhyme scheme, each poem is an open-ended continuation of multiple contexts of speech. Hence she creates the same doubleness of discourse—a discourse for making conventional sonnets and a language for calling and answering—that we have observed in Browning's monologues. Moreover, the subject for this discourse is divided and deeply ambivalent. The ambivalence here is especially graphic, since the poems are intimately addressed to Robert while, at the same time, they are withheld from him. The ambivalence of the *Sonnets from the Portuguese* as communication is also matched by a complementary ambivalence of the poems *as poems.* They are written in a conventional poetic form, implying an address to a public audience familiar with that form. But Elizabeth Barrett did not publish the poems until five years later and only with Robert's persistent urging. Because the subject of the poems is not consistently either Elizabeth-as-poet or Elizabeth-as-lover, the text of *Sonnets from the Portuguese,* though so obviously directed outward, remains for a time paralyzed, private. Like Andrea del Sarto, Elizabeth writes "from myself and to myself," perhaps remaining hesitant to present a heterogeneous text to an audience conditioned to demand sharp separation between private communication and public (poetic) discourse.

Rhetorical and structural devices like the ones used in sonnets 33 and 34 appear throughout the sequence to create, with a few interruptions, an intricate emerging record of love's process. This modification of the older sonnet sequence is based on the same linguistic groundwork that supports Browning's poems of the same period and later. The two poems I have cited abound in anaphoric reference, and especially in the thirty-fourth sonnet, we can observe the elaborate modification of active verbs by temporal adverbial phrases that I discussed in chapter 3. The opening of sonnet 22 offers another excellent example of typical progressive constructions as well as a highly arrested sentence structure:

> When our two souls stand up erect and strong,
> Face to face, silent, drawing nigh and nigher,
> Until the lengthening wings break into fire
> At either curved point,—what bitter wrong
> Can the earth do to us, that we should not long
> Be here contented? Think. In mounting higher,
> The angels would press on us and aspire
> To drop some golden orb of perfect song
> Into our deep, dear silence.

As we have so often seen in Browning's poems, participles generated from verbs of progressive aspect ("drawing" and "mounting") modify perfective verbs to establish an interior perspective on an unbounded process. Moreover, the initial stative verb ("stand") is further modified by a bound clause introduced by a temporal connective ("until") and a containing subject ("wings") that is modified by yet another participle derived from a progressive verb ("lengthening").

This is the language spoken by Robert Browning and Elizabeth Barrett, a language they did not learn from one another. Neither did they learn from one another how to write rudimentary dramatic monologues. I do not believe that the *Sonnets from the Portuguese* were written in conscious imitation of Browning, and yet Elizabeth's confrontation with a past genre, the love sonnet sequence, generated a new form that is strikingly similar to the genre that arose from Browning's much more complicated relation to his Romantic predecessors. Each sonnet implies those retentions and protensions in time and space that are typical of Browning's poems but that neither the Elizabethan nor the Romantic sonnet anticipate. Each poem despecializes poetic utterance in the particularity of everyday speech and the unbroken continuity between the poem and actual conversations between Elizabeth and Robert. The sonnets, therefore, implicitly challenge the division between the imaginative world of the poet as poet and the real world of the poet as human being. Literary language and ordinary language have been made one, and the age-old separation in dramatic literature between actor and auditor has been suspended as well. Finally, the *Sonnets from the Portugese* create a world organized by reciprocal exchange and, at least hypothetically, demand a collaborative response from their "audience." These, as I hope to show, are equally the implications of Browning's most direct poetic address to Elizabeth in "One Word More," composed a decade after the *Sonnets from the Portuguese.*

Perhaps it is only heuristically valid to read "One Word More" as the loving response implicitly requested in Elizabeth Barrett's sonnets, but DeVane, for one, speculated early that Browning "was especially eager [to dedicate a volume of his poems to his wife] after the publication of the *Sonnets from the Portuguese* in 1850."[5] As I have described the form, "One Word More" is fully as much a dramatic monologue as any other poem in *Men and Women.* Indeed, in one regard, the fusion of a formal language-for-poetry and a more rough-hewn language-for-speech, this poem presents one of the more striking examples in the collection.

Browning is openly addressing his wife in his own voice, and yet here he chooses the droning trochaic pentameter meter, one of the most restrictive prosodic conventions in the poet's technical repertoire. At times, the meter forces him into locutions and word orders he would never use in speech:

> While he mused on love and Beatrice,
> While he softened *o'er* his outlined angel,
> *In they broke,* those "people of importance."
>
> (54–56; emphasis mine)

On other occasions, the meter and the uneven rhythms of direct address seem perfectly integrated. The voice we hear in "One Word More" is that same two-in-one voice that we hear in all of the monologues. The difference is that in, for example, "Andrea Del Sarto," we can assign "identities" to the two voices—we can call them "the speaker" and "the poet." Here the relation has been distilled down to its generalized essentials: the voice of the poet as public artist and the voice of the poet as private man. It is not surprising that in the dedicatory poem of his greatest collection, Browning should treat directly the problematic bifurcation of the poet's medium that had been an implicit issue in so many other monologues.

Addressing Elizabeth, Browning first affirms the value of private communication and, in the famous examples of Raphael and Dante, suggests that the loving artist must occasionally find a medium other than the one with which he addresses the public at large. Even here, though, he declines to invoke a hypothetical "natural language of men" as his Romantic predecessors might have done; instead he posits an exchange of arts in which the intimate language of the painter become poetry and vice versa. By this method, Browning has already subtly denied the ontological distinction between art and nature. Either poetry or painting can be either artificial or natural, depending on its use in a particular context. And every artist longs

> to find his love a language
> Fit and fair and simple and sufficient—
> Using nature that's an art to others,
> Not, this one time, art that's turned his nature.

$$\text{(61-64)}$$

The idea that art "turns" or corrupts the "natural" man is not a new one, but Browning gives it an oddly Victorian twist. He says that the artist seeks a singular loving communication in order to "gain the man's joy, miss the artist's sorrow," and he explains that the artist's "sorrow" derives from the failure of the collective to reciprocate appropriately when the artist offers his gift. Moses struck the rock and broke the drought only to bring forth, in response, the scorn of the people. Hence, like all artists working within their public "calling," he must ever preserve a mask, a persona: "Never dares the man put off the prophet." This persona, this protective role of the public specialist, does more than lead to the artist's own sorrow; it alienates him forever in historical time by allowing his own personal communication to be literally consumed by a public in search of commodities to possess. As the insensitivity of the French "rap-and-rending nation" would later be blamed for the loss of the historical truth behind the Old Yellow Book, so Bologna and Florence have obliterated all traces of Raphael's and Dante's merely human selves. Raphael's volume of sonnets was guarded by a single person, Guido Reni, but in time,

> Guido Reni dying, all Bologna
> Cried, and the world cried too, "Ours the treasure!"
> Suddenly, as rare things will, it vanished.

$$\text{(29-31)}$$

Moses, wrapped in his role as prophet, leaves no trace of himself as a man, and the poet groping for lost human continuities can only speculate, create a fiction in which the man behind the prophetic mask loves "one face from out the thousands." Perhaps like Cleon, but more honest with himself, he loved a slave. Browning suggests a fantasy in which Moses, so far "above" the slave and so near to God's will, can envy the simple reciprocal exchange of sustenance enjoyed by the slave and her camel.

The scenarios and metaphors of the first eleven stanzas of "One Word More" are fictions, born of that historical absence of human continuity that we have seen shaping Browning's poetry from *Pauline* to *The Ring and the Book*. But "One Word More" returns, in stanza 12, to the real present and acknowledges the fact that fluent communication in an alien medium is, for the Victorian poet, at best a lost ideal. His world is a world of specialization, and the specialist cannot presume to appropriate the language of another speciality:

> I shall never, in the years remaining,
> Paint you pictures, no, nor carve you statues,
> Make you music that should all-express me.
>
> (109–11)

Browning, though his experience with the British public has been as alienating as any artist's, cannot despecialize some other art to produce "nature that's an art to others"; his gift to Elizabeth can be "verse and nothing else." Nevertheless, "a semblance of resource avails us— / Shade so finely touched, love's sense must seize it." Constrained as he is, Browning can alter his verse ever so slightly. Technically, he does so by turning to the odd trochaic meter that he was never to use again. But this is merely one variation among all those other variations of metric and stanzaic forms; it is not larger in degree than any of the others. I would argue that the same is true of the fact that he speaks "this once in my true person." The way Browning makes the distinction is to reintroduce the dichotomy between the public and private by saying "I am mine and yours—the rest be all men's." "The rest" are the fifty men and women of his book of monologues, and yet as soon as he divides the voices that are "all men's" from the one that belongs to Elizabeth, it becomes clear that, like the division between nature and art, this division is bound to collapse. Browning will publish "One Word More"; it too will become "all men's." And however public the rest of the monologues may be, they are also especially for Elizabeth:

> Let me speak this once in my true person,
> Not as Lippo, Roland or Andrea,
> Though the fruit of speech be just this sentence:
> Pray you, look on these my men and women,
> Take [you] and keep my fifty poems finished;
> Where my heart lies, let my brain lie also!
> Poor the speech; be how I speak, for all things.
>
> (137–43)

That revisionary "though" is the turning point of the poem. He will give his private poem to the public and his fifty other poems to Elizabeth. They are all made of his own speech, and that speech, however "poor," is meant "for all things." The gap between nature and art, between the work of the heart and that of the brain, has finally been narrowed until the two lie superimposed in the same imaginative space.

Browning has been denied the expedient imputed to Raphael and Dante of choosing another medium, and yet he cannot forget the lover's yearning for an intimate mode of communicating. His poem has not abolished the reality of public and private messages, it has merely fused them in the continuity of speech. Browning needs a final image for this fusion, and he provides it in the famous metaphor of the moon. The "public" side of the moon, seen by the world from London to Florence, and the "private" side, reserved for that one "mortal" the moon loves, are nevertheless two parts of a single sphere. That sphere, from either side, is only seen in partial and shifting manifestations, like the souls of those speakers who make Browning's poems. For the onlooker, the two sides cannot be seen at once, but they can be seen by turns. Browning realizes that for Elizabeth—his "moon of poets"—he is neither exclusively part of her audience nor simply her "one mortal":

> This I say of me, but think of you, Love!
> This to you—yourself my moon of poets!

Ah, but that's the world's side, there's the wonder,
Thus they see you, praise you, think they know you!
There, in turn I stand with them and praise you—
Out of my own self, I dare to phrase it.
But the best is when I glide from out them,
Cross a step or two of dubious twilight,
Come out on the other side, the novel
Silent silver lights and darks undreamed of,
Where I hush and bless myself with silence.

(187–97)

This penultimate stanza reveals the symmetrical reciprocity Browning perceives in his relation to Elizabeth. As Moses imagines that he will exchange sustenance with his wife, Browning projects an exchange of praise. Through the seventeenth stanza, the image of the moon has stood as a figure for Browning as poet with Elizabeth the onlooker. He has been trying to explain that all of *his* poetry "boasts two soul-sides." But in the eighteenth stanza, the figurative roles are reversed, with Elizabeth becoming the poet / moon and Browning the praising auditor who moves through a continuous twilight space between "the world" and her singular love.

The metaphor of the moon expresses all of the generic features of Browning's dramatic monologues: the fact that they never present a static image but rather a moment of fragmentary process (the moon is "dying now impoverished here in London"); their manifestations of human communication as a reciprocal exchange; and their fusion of the specialized and the unspecialized voice. The latter, throughout the monologues, requires the most delicately tuned attention to read—it has the fewest explicit markers—but in the last four lines of his greatest book, it is this upon which Browning insists. The lover's message, specialized or not, is one message for poet or painter. The speech of the heart and the speech of the brain are finally only one speech "for all things":

Oh, their Rafael of the dear Madonnas,
Oh, their Dante of the dread Inferno,
Wrote one song—and in my brain I sing it,
Drew one angel—[borne], see, on my bosom!

(198–201)

Speaking in his own voice, "R.B." is realized poetically just as Lippo, Roland, or Andrea are realized. Indeed, if anything, the conversational "One Word More" is a less idiosyncratic monologue than some of the others that, like "Childe Roland to the Dark Tower Came," he explicitly offers to Elizabeth as representative of the gathering. At the end of this chapter, I will argue that Childe Roland can be, in a special sense, identified with Browning, but Roland, unlike the "R.B." of the final poem, has no one to talk to.

III

Many years after he wrote "Childe Roland to the Dark Tower Came," Browning recalled the circumstances of its composition:

> Childe Roland came upon me as a kind of dream. I had to write it, then and there, and I finished it the same day, I believe. But it was simply that I had to do it. I did not know then what I meant beyond that, and I'm sure I don't know now.[6]

This famous comment, along with the curious twists and turns of the poem itself, has served for years to vex readers in search of symbolic or allegorical content. The poem seems to have a symbolic quality, yet it steadfastly refuses to yield a satisfactory and coherent symbolic meaning. On the other hand, what seems anomalous from the point of view of the literary critic would surely seem perfectly ordinary from the point of view of the psychoanalyst or interpreter of dreams. A man has a dream, and his forced attention to this dream leads him to retell it to himself in progressively coherent redactions. If he has a gift for writing, he may manage to record the dream at some stage of its waking normalization. For the psychoanalyst, the dream does have a symbolic content, and the process of interpretation is the process of revealing that content. Presumably then, the literary critic might adopt the methods of the psychoanalyst to interpret the poem correctly.

Would it were so simple. Unfortunately, the psychoanalytic interpretation of a poem like "Childe Roland" is initially precluded by two of the simplest and most fundamental principles of the discipline, at least according to Freud. In explaining the method of revealing the latent content hidden beneath the manifest content of dreams, Freud says, "I must begin with the assertion that in every dream it is possible to find a point of contact with the experience of the previous day."[7] In addition, he reports after giving a patient the correct interpretation of her dream, "I was able to do so because I was familiar with the whole of the dreamer's previous history."[8] Freud stresses that no recorded dream contains its own intrinsic interpretations independent of a context; the analyst must be able to question the dreamer regarding relevant details in both the previous day's events and the dreamer's past life. We cannot do this with Browning, which explains in part why "Childe Roland" seems to have the properties of a symbolic text but refuses to yield symbolic meanings.

W. C. DeVane said that in "Childe Roland to the Dark Tower Came," Browning expressed the innermost pattern of his mind.[9] Jacques Lacan, along with Freud, insists that the inner, to become patterned, must become one with the other, the otherness that is language. In *The Interpretation of Dreams,* Freud writes, "The dream-thoughts and the dream-content are presented to us like two versions of the same subject-matter in two different languages. Or, more properly, the dream-content seems like a transcript of the dream-thoughts into another mode of expression, whose characters and syntactic laws it is our business to discover by comparing the original and the translation."[10] When the matter is stated this way, polarizing the private and public worlds of dream-thoughts and dream-content, the interpreter of Browning's text will remain unable to proceed from one to the other. It appears, however, that this two-text model is too simple. In the first place, it is never the case that only one "dream-content" is being interpreted. In the process of memory itself, the dreamer always tells and retells the dream to himself, constantly creating an endless succession of texts in which each new version further rationalizes the dream while retaining traces of its immediate predecessors in the chain of dream-works. This constant process of waking revision can be explained in terms of Freud's concept of memory itself. In a 1916 letter, he writes:

> As you know, I am working on the assumption that our psychical mechanism has come about by a process of stratification: the material present-at-hand as memory traces is from time to time subjected to a restructuring in accordance with fresh circumstances—it undergoes, as it were, a re-transcription. Thus what is essentially new in my theory is the thesis that memory is present-at-hand not once, but several times over, that is registered or deposited in various species of signs.[11]

The word here translated "re-transcription" is *Umschrift,* which can also mean something like "paraphrase" or "another kind of writing." Similarly, the dream-thoughts themselves, however unconscious, probably represent a sequence of textual revisions of a memory reaching back to an experience in early life. Hence it is at least possible that the terms "dream-thoughts" and "dream-content" represent no more than a methodological classification of an indefinite series of texts into two genres, what Freud calls "modes of expression."

This particular division of genres is clearly useful to the psychoanalyst, and it is clearly not useful to the literary critic. But this does not mean that the underlying principle of psychoanalytic interpretation has been invalidated for literary criticism. That principle, as I read it, is that interpretation is the process of articulating and explaining the relationship between a text at some point in the sequence and certain of its predecessors. The psychoanalyst's purpose is served when the object-text is consciously known by the dreamer while the predecessor text is not available to consciousness. By explaining the relation between the two texts, the analyst brings the predecessor to consciousness for the patient, and this is the essence of his therapy. I would argue that the literary critic who wishes to make communicable meanings available to his reader also engages in explaining the relation between two or more texts in a sequence; the difference is that the distinction between conscious and unconscious is not relevant to the critic's purpose, and the predecessor text must be discoverable through its traces in the object text.

To return to Browning's account of "Childe Roland," I think we can say that he records two distinct moments in a temporal sequence of dream-texts. First he says that "Childe Roland" came upon him as a kind of dream, and this episodic "coming upon" suggests that at the moment of recalling the dream, he had already encoded it in language, or in one "mode of expression." Then, he says, he "had to write it then and there," thus creating a second text in an altered mode of expression. If I am correct in thinking that interpretation is explaining the relation between these two texts (and not somehow "recovering" the earlier text in toto), then an essential part of that interpretation will be explaining the relation between their two modes of expression. I think these modes can be distinguished, with traces of the first abundantly present in the second; I shall call the precedent text (following Freud) a "dream-work" and the final text a "dramatic monologue." The final problem is to describe the pathways of transcription that made this particular sequence possible. I wish to show that clear markers of the initial dream-work remain in "Childe Roland" and that they prove compatible with the structure of the dramatic monologue. I also wish to demonstrate the dramatic monologue's power to organize, interpret, and transform experience, in this case an experience already encoded in Browning's dream.

To rehearse at length the well-known dreamlike qualities of the poem would be pointless; they are easily recognizable, especially in the details of Roland's landscape and the visionary omission of logical transitions between moments of perception. Freud points out that dreams juxtapose discrete dream-thoughts and "have no means at their disposal" for representing logical relationships among them. In this, he says, dreams are like painting or sculpture and not like poetry. He goes on to furnish several examples of the types of logical connection missing in dreams. Dreams lack representations of " 'if,' 'because,' 'just as,' 'although,' 'either-or,' and all the other conjunctions without which we cannot understand sentences or speeches." These connections do, of course, appear in the recorded text of the dream, but they are not to be read at face value:

If, however, in reproducing a dream, its narrator feels inclined to make use of an 'either-or'—e.g. 'it was either a garden or a sitting-room'—what was present in the dream-thoughts was not an alternative but an 'and,' a simple addition. An 'either-or' is mostly used to describe a dream-element that has a quality of vagueness—which, however, is capable of being resolved. In such cases the rule for interpretation is: treat the two apparent alternatives as of equal validity and link them together with an 'and.'[12]

Freud saw a connection between linkages like "either-or" and explicit similitudes like "just as." In "Childe Roland" similitudes appear as uncertain alternatives, while indefinite connections of either-or are usually based on confusing similitude:

> —It may have been a water-rat I speared,
> But, ugh! it sounded like a baby's shriek.
>
> (125–26)

This is both a similitude and a sign of Roland's doubt. That doubt can be generalized as a repeated assertion that the poem's landscape is either inhuman/inanimate or human/animate. At times the juxtaposition of "either-or" and "just as" is explicit:

> Now blotches rankling, colored gay and grim,
>   Now patches where some leanness of the soil's
>   Broke into moss or substances like boils.
>
> (151–53)

Roland is saying that the nonhuman moss on the ground looks like boils on human skin, but he expresses the likeness grammatically as an either-or relation. If this poem does indeed bear traces of a dream-text, Freud would have us read this relation as additive, substituting "and" for "either-or." The language of the poem itself lends some credence to the experiment, since, conversely, the antithetical alternatives "gay" and "grim" (normally something can be gay or grim but not both) are linked by the additive conjunction "and."

In short, I wish to argue that the transformation of the formula "either inhuman or human" into "both inhuman and human" as a projection or wish fulfillment is essential to the interpretation of this poem. I wish to read "Childe Roland," not as a dream-text, but as a first interpretation of a dream-text, a first awareness of the logic by which the dream's images are to be linked. This logic involves the projection of human nature onto Nature in general out of an unfulfilled desire for reciprocal communication. The verbal manifestation of (or desire for) human reciprocity is what the dramatic monologue formally projects in its orthodox forms, and it is precisely what Roland lacks. In poetic terms, Roland speaks through a literary form that ordinarily implies an inter-locutor, but for Roland, the interlocutor is missing.

✕ The formal requirements of the dream-text meet those of the dramatic monologue in this poem because the former entails techniques of projecting the human other as a desire and thus creating the text itself as a dream-fulfilled wish for the conditions of the dramatic monologue's implied world. The dramatic mono-logue itself can technically represent no more than a desire for exchange, since direct presentation of the exchange itself is ex-cluded by the form. Hence the dream-text and the dramatic mono-logue can find a common ground, but only when the literary form has transformed and interpreted the recorded dream. One of the methods of this transformation is to depict Nature in such a way that "either-or" implies "and" and, in so doing, helps define Roland's predicament. ✕

Nature herself is generalized in her relation to Roland through one such either-or construction: " 'See / Or shut your eyes,' said Nature peevishly." Roland's experience is predominantly visual and auditory, and the distinction between the immediate detail and its metaphoric alternative can be reformulated as the distinc-tion between what he sees and what he does not see. Dreams do not contain negations, though, so that if we are to read "or" as "and," we should expect the imperative to "see or shut your eyes" to be a false imperative, a nonchoice. What we find, in fact, is just this: when Roland most consciously looks, he sees least. Once having entered "the ominous tract," he turns to look back whence he has come only "a pace or two" only to see "nothing but plain to the horizon's bound." Similarly, when he later peers forward along his path, he can descry "no sight as far as eye could strain." When sight comes upon him, it is not through some willed act of

seeing but precisely at the moment when he is caught visually un-
awares, the moment when his eyes are shut. Roland, since he cannot induce or control seeing by opening his eyes, invalidates the
apparent alternative, "see or shut your eyes." He is like the old
horse on the plain, whose eyes are shut but whose every bone is
"a-stare." He does not even attempt to honor Nature's proffered
choice, since he both strains to see and shuts his eyes:

> I shut my eyes and turned them on my heart
>> As a man calls for wine before he fights,
>> I asked one draught of earlier, happier sights,
> Ere fitly I could hope to play my part.
>
> (85–88)

Roland, by shutting his eyes, does not exclude sight; he merely
seeks internally for "happier sights," a vision of that band of knights
among whom the quest for the Dark Tower began. He seeks an
alternative vision, but again, the alternative is denied, since his
inward "sights" are no happier than his outward ones. In short,
keeping Roland's eyes open does not guarantee seeing, and shutting
them does not preclude seeing. Roland is not only incapable of
treating seeing and not seeing as real alternatives, he is also incapable of choosing to obey or disobey Nature's command, since he
appears destined both to see and fail to see independently of his
own volition. The only way, therefore, to make sense of Nature's
command is to read it as a dream-text distortion and to correct it
to read "Shut your eyes *and* see."

Performing this simple operation opens up the poem's other
either-or structure in an interesting way, since Roland's inward
sight is of a human world, while his outward sight is of a nonhuman
one. It becomes possible, in other words, to take Browning's
dream as, in Freud's terms, a "displacement" of the human world
into the nonhuman landscape and to read the poem as a partial
analysis of that displacement. I have argued that the dramatic
monologue is a form centrally concerned with projected human
interaction, and I believe that by acknowledging the role of displacement in Browning's precedent dream-text, we can recognize
"Childe Roland to the Dark Tower Came" as a dramatic monologue

in this sense. Most critics, like Phelps and Langbaum, have read the poem as a struggle either with the self or with a hostile environment and have concluded that Roland achieves an existential "triumph" at the end.[13] Because I see the poem as an interpretation of a dream about the loss of human communication and exchange, Roland appears to me to be exploring the terror of loneliness, a terror-in-contradiction over which he does not triumph and that remains unrelieved at the end. Hence, in my view, Roland's final blast on the slug-horn carries with it none of the exhilarations perceived by idealist critics; it is rather his ultimate, inarticulate expression of isolated despair.

Roland's separation from the world of human communication is signaled in the poem's opening lines. Like so many of Browning's monologues, "Childe Roland" begins with a reference to a precedent action, in this case something said by an unidentified person whom the speaker distrusts. Instead of clarifying the speaker's relation to the old cripple, however, the first two stanzas merely elaborate ambiguities. The traveler cannot make out the real intentions behind the directions he is given; language cannot be trusted as a reliable gesture of guidance or sympathy. Thus the "hoary cripple," with his projected "skull-like laugh," is like a dead man to one who would reach out for assistance on an uncertain road. So Childe Roland "turns aside" from this last and most inadequate contact with the human world in a gesture that forms a simile for death itself:

> As when a sick man very near to death
> >   Seems dead indeed, and feels begin and end
> >   The tears and takes the farewell of each friend,
> And hears one bid the other go, draw breath
> Freelier outside, ("since all is o'er," he saith,
> >   "And the blow fallen no grieving can amend;")
>
> While some discuss if near the other graves
> >   Be room enough for this, and when a day
> >   Suits best for carrying the corpse away,
> With care about the banners scarves and staves:

And still the man hears all, and only craves
He may not shame such tender love and stay.

(25-36)

Critics have ignored this remarkable passage almost unanimously; in most major treatments of the poem, it is not so much as mentioned. I suspect that such an extended simile seems gratuitous and finally unintelligible, since it is difficult to see just how Roland's situation resembles that of the dying man. If, however, we speculate that these two stanzas record part of Browning's original dream-work, their relation to the rest of the poem makes surprisingly good sense.

Freud tells us that an extended dream is often accompanied by a "secondary dream" that appears not to be logically or causally connected to the main dream. This secondary dream is often related to the main dream by the relation of " 'just as' assisted by the tendency of the dream-work towards condensation."[14] But the ground of the similitude may not be apparent without decoding a particular transformation. One such transformation common to dream-thoughts represents the "just as" relation as "just the reverse," and this, I believe, is what has happened in "Childe Roland." Both the poem as a whole and the dying man simile concern the separation of an individual from his intimate associates through death. The main dream presents Roland as the last of "the Band" to die, and this condition is the basis of Roland's despair. For the dream to be intelligible as a wish-fulfillment, however, it must be read "just [as] the reverse" of a desired condition in which Roland is the first to die. The key to the logic of the wish-fulfillment is therefore to be found in the two stanzas about the dying man. There the protagonist lives even his last few moments in the ebb and flow of verbal exchange among friends. He "takes the farewell of each friend" individually, after which he lingers for a time as the friends continue to interact among themselves, perpetuating the society he is leaving. His formal leave-taking, quite properly, concerns each separate friend, but his last perception, and the one through which he credits their love, is the perception of conventional cooperation among them in preparation for his burial.

For Roland, the situation is exactly the opposite. His quest has been undertaken in concert with others—"the Band"—the knights who have sought the Dark Tower. But Roland is the last of that company. Instead of taking leave of his friends, like the dying man, he has been left alone by them. Each knight has acted alone, disregarding the others, and the result is the dissolution of the Band and isolation for the only remaining member. Browning marks this isolation here, as he does in "Andrea Del Sarto," by creating a gray and nondescript landscape, cut off from the familiar human world:

> For mark! no sooner was I finally found
>   Pledged to the plain, after a pace or two,
>   Than, pausing to throw backward a last view
> O'er the safe road, 'twas gone; gray plain all round.
>
> (51–54)

The antithesis to this gray world, again as in "Andrea," is the "golden" warmth of human friendship. The similarity to Andrea's memory of King Francis is striking:

> Not it! I fancied Cuthbert's reddening face
>   Beneath its garniture of curly gold,
>   Dear fellow, till I almost felt him fold
> An arm in mine to fix me to the place.
>
> (91–94)

This is what Roland sees when he shuts his eyes, but in the poem, he soon recognizes the solidarity of the Band as a delusion; Cuthbert, Giles, and all the rest have been secret traitors, destroying themselves and their community with their betrayals.

Enduring human connection, such as that enjoyed even by the dying man, has proved unattainable for Roland, and he displaces onto the landscape both this disjunctiveness and his remaining desire for interaction and reciprocity. Details in the landscape seem to rise up suddenly without relation to one another or to their surroundings. Suppressing his terror, Roland attempts to supply imaginary relations where none apparently exist, and it is important to notice that, even in recognizing the landscape's desolation, he projects human actions, gestures, and characteristics:

No! penury, inertness, and *grimace,*
  In some strange sort, were the land's portion.

                                              (61–62)

If there pushed any ragged thistle-stalk
  Above its *mates,* the *head was chopped;* the bents
Were *jealous* else.

                                              (67–69)

As for the grass, it grew as scant as *hair*
  In leprosy.

                                  (73–74; emphasis mine)

It is not only in explicit either-or relations or stated similitudes that Roland personifies the inhuman plain. His desire is manifested everywhere in the objective world, and yet his projections offer no relief. For human qualities, Roland's external environment, like his internal memory, offers only images of deterioration, alienation, privation. Roland, confirmed in his isolation, can only "turn away," as he did from the mysterious cripple, to confront his lonely future.[15]

However inevitable and uncompromising his fate may be, the need to reach outward beyond the self into a sympathetic human world informs Roland's monologue to the end. In this, he is like all of Browning's men and women. They succeed and fail to different degrees and for different reasons, but all recognize in the structure of the human communal world, and more especially in the communicatory power of language, at least an ideal vehicle of self-definition through the achievement of "sympathy." In most cases the relative satisfaction of these needs depends on the speaker's capacity to understand and use the social conventions of language and gesture. But a few poems relate situations that are already hopeless for reasons that are unapparent or unavoidable. "Childe Roland" is one of these and as such is closer in its implications to poems like "A Light Woman" and "A Serenade at the Villa" than to other monologues. In "A Light Woman," the speaker's sympathy for his friend leads him to feign gestures of intimacy toward the friend's lover. He is successful by normal standards, since she reciprocates; like Lucrezia, she "turns away" from an earlier lover toward a new one:

> So, I gave her eyes my own eyes to take,
>   My hand sought hers as in earnest need,
> And round she turned for my noble sake,
>   And gave me herself indeed.
>
> (17–20)

Normal standards, however, do not apply. The need to affirm the relation of friendship has led him to an action as false on one level as it is true on the deeper level of genuine human sympathy for his friend's entrapment. The result is hostility all round. The friend comes to despise the speaker, who, in turn, must sever his link with the "light woman." This kind of situational futility is characteristic of all of Browning's poems about inescapable alienation and loneliness.

"A Serenade at the Villa" is a simpler case, but it indicates more clearly the affinity of these pessimistic poems with "Childe Roland." A lover sings to a woman who fails to respond to his overtures, and that failure is reflected in his depiction of the landscape, the atmosphere of which bears a remarkable resemblance to that of "Childe Roland":

> So wore night; the East was gray,
>   White the broad-faced hemlock flowers:
> There would be another day;
>   Ere its first of heavy hours
> Found me, I had passed away.
>
> (21–25)

> When no moon succeeds the sun,
>   Nor can pierce the midnight's tent
> Any star, the smallest one,
>   While some drops, where lightning rent,
> Show the final storm begun—
>
> (41–45)

The landscape, dark, gray, and serene, symbolizes a situation in which one man's attempts to establish sympathetic contact with another person have failed. His language of love, in song, has been flung outward to find no reciprocation, and this failure is figured in his perception of the garden:

> When the fire-fly hides its spot,
>   When the garden-voices fail
> In the darkness thick and hot,—
>   Shall another voice avail,
> That shape be where these are not?
>
> (46–50)

This conformity of Nature to the darkness and alienation brought about by the failure of human voices only serves to emphasize a desperate need for the response that never comes, for it illustrates the degree to which a man's perceptual and conceptual life derives from external human relations. In Browning, the use of personification, even to depict a hostile world, is a measure of the speaker's attempt to find human intercourse where none exists, and this is a measure of the loss inherent in the severance or inadequacy of human sympathy:

> Oh how dark your villa was,
>   Windows fast and obdurate!
> How the garden grudged me grass
>   Where I stood—the iron gate
> Ground its teeth to let me pass!
>
> (56–60)

The singer's disappointment has been unequivocal, and yet it continues to occur as an ongoing condition of his life. The poem itself, addressing as it does a woman whom he knows he cannot reach with song, reenacts the cause of the despair it expresses. It is a cry in a vacuum, a communication with someone who is not there.[16]

Like the speaker in "A Serenade at the Villa," Childe Roland imputes human gestures, emotions, and exchanges to the grayest and most lifeless of Nature's grotesques. Alders kneel, willows fling themselves "headlong in a fit / Of mute despair, a suicidal throng,"

and the river "does wrong" to the trees along its banks. When he
tries to imagine real human endeavor in such an environment, however, he can only think of brute struggle:

> Who were the strugglers, what war did they wage,
> Whose savage trample thus could pad the dank
> Soil to a plash? Toads in a poisoned tank,
>   Or wild cats in a red-hot iron cage—
>
> The fight must so have seemed in that fell cirque.
>   What penned them there, with all the plain to choose?
>   No foot-print leading to that horrid mews,
> None out of it. Mad brewage set to work
> Their brains, no doubt, like galley-slaves the Turk
>   Pits for his pastime, Christians against Jews.
>
> (129-38)

No footprint, no sign of human commerce, remains on the land.
However Roland might try to imagine the history of the place, he
can project human lives on it only in the form of insane or meaningless strife. He is lost in a realm that lacks continuities, and no
detail illustrates this fragmentation better than the Dark Tower
itself:

> What in the midst lay but the Tower itself?
>   The round squat turret, blind as the fool's heart,
>   Built of brown stone, without a counterpart
> In the whole world. The tempest's mocking elf
> Points to the shipman thus the unseen shelf
>   He strikes on, only when the timbers start.
>
> (181-86)

The tower stands without connection to the known world; it has
no counterpart. In this stanza, Browning directly equates Roland's
inability to see according to Nature's earlier imperative with the
futility of imagining human continuities in the dream landscape.
Childe Roland's desire from the beginning is to find guidance. He
has quested in the path of others only to find the others lost. He
has sought direction from an old cripple who proves to be sinister

and who guides him into a country of nightmarish disorientation. Going forth on that landscape, he finally projects the function of guidance on a dark bird that seems to come from nowhere:

> Naught in the distance but the evening, naught
>   To point my footstep further! At the thought,
>   A great black bird, Apollyon's bosom-friend,
> Sailed past, nor beat his wide wing dragon-penned
>   That brushed my cap—perchance the guide I sought.
>
> (158–62)

Yet just before he sees the Tower itself, his sense is of being tricked, being led into a trap that has closed. Guidance, throughout the poem, proves empty, unreliable, false. The analogy for Roland's coming on the Tower is one of guidance given too late, of gesture and communication to the shipman from the mocking elf that do not avail.

I said before that "Childe Roland" is a poem about the terror of loneliness. In this, it truly represents the dark side of a contradictory world. For a poet whose very language embodies the vital, shifting relations among men and women and infuses into nature the patterns of those relations, the definition of a disordered and nonsensical universe naturally arises from the nonexistence of viable human contact. Thus "Childe Roland" chronicles a man's vain attempt to anchor the self externally, to find his bearings. In Browning's terms, to turn inward to confront only the self is not to triumph. Andrea does so, only to find his own sterility. But Roland is a true knight of the Band, always seeking to rediscover the comradeship that has given his life its order and direction. His quest is finally not to find the meaningless Dark Tower but to recover contact with those other knights who have been lost in seeking it. Hence the Tower is not the last discovery he makes. After the Tower comes light and noise, and the noise becomes the "Names in my ears / Of all the lost adventurers my peers." The thought of them comes back to him in the pattern prefigured by the simile of the dying man: one individual after another, with the group subsumed at the end by an inclusive, communal idea:

How such a one was strong, and such was bold,
And such was fortunate, yet each of old
    Lost, lost! one moment knelled the woe of years.

(196-98)

The only attribute that makes Roland's peers a coherent group is their destruction; "each" had his own merits, but "all" are lost.

By this route do we come to the last stanza, Childe Roland's final vision, not of the Tower, but of the knightly company:

There they stood, ranged along the hill-sides, met
    To view the last of me, a living frame
    For one more picture! in a sheet of flame
I saw them and I knew them all. And yet
Dauntless the slug-horn to my lips I set,
    And blew. *"Childe Roland to the Dark Tower Came."*

(199-204)

Suddenly, he can see his lost peers gathered together as before, but the vision only intensifies the tragedy of his quest. For they stand silently apart along the hillsides, unapproachable in a sheet of flame. Roland can see them, and he can recognize them, "and yet . . . " If I am correct in saying that Roland's monologue records a futile reaching out for human contact, these words, "and yet," provide the key to interpreting the poem's final lines. The vision of his comrades stands there to taunt him with the thought of former commerce, "and yet" no communication is possible. The company as a community is dead, and Roland in his final act registers the full realization that he too is therefore irrevocably lost. That act is a single, inarticulate blast on the slug-horn, a relinquishing of language, a desperate, if nobly "dauntless," acknowledgment of Childe Roland's total isolation and severance from human society. As long as he continues speaking, even though he has no listener, an expressed hope remains that the exchange between persons that is implied by language can be reestablished. But the monologue ends with that last chilling pair of words, "and blew," set off in a line by themselves, putting an end to speech and to Roland's monologue. The repetition of the title, "Childe

Roland to the Dark Tower Came," added in italics and enclosed in quotation marks, is not part of the monologue itself; it is not something Roland says. The title circumscribes speech within the boundaries of its own vacuity of meaning in *King Lear:* Edgar says it to no one, and it means nothing. The poem, like the line in Edgar's song, and like the dream-thoughts from which it sprang, stands disconnected from ordinary human commerce, an unacknowledged cry in a wilderness of separation. In most of his monologues, Browning exploits techniques of implying the continuation of action into a projected future. "Childe Roland," along with a few other poems like "A Serenade at the Villa," defines a smaller category of monologues spoken in situations that have no future. These poems are not "optimistic," and they are not "triumphant"; they explore the extremes of possible human deprivation within the patterns of Browning's thought, and nowhere is that deprivation more eloquently expressed than in the single, undifferentiated note of Childe Roland's horn.

IV

According to Freud, when "some extraneous person" is represented as the protagonist of a dream, it is safe to assume that this figure is really identical with the dreamer himself.[17] I read "Childe Roland to the Dark Tower Came" as a kind of inverted image of "One Word More": they represent the extremes of isolation and intimacy in Browning's world. Each poem is rich because it includes the spectre of its antitype; Roland can still articulate the desire for a reforged human linkage, and the Browning of "One Word More" acknowledges public alienation as the context of his love for Elizabeth. From this viewpoint, Roland himself becomes almost a Yeatsian mask for "R.B.," an always-present mask that ought to forestall simplistic generalizations about Browning's "optimism." Indeed, the pathways of exchange and trust that Browning so lovingly affirms in London in 1855 had already been called deeply into question in Paris during the last days of 1851. Certainly, Browning felt deeply his isolation during that period, living in his "little nest . . . at the far-end of a twig in this wind-shaken tree of Paris" where Louis Napoleon was consolidating the demise of communal government.[18] He could hear death outside in the roar of cannon, and he attributed the debacle in part to weaknesses in the members of a "Band" who could not act in concert: "the stupid, selfish & suicidal Assembly."[19] He also felt a disturbing estrangement from Elizabeth at that time, and he felt his estrangement from England. As Elizabeth shrewdly observed, "I always think that England influences him just in proportion to his removal from England."[20]

I wish at once to oppose and unite these two poems less as a biographical exercise than as an illustration of the formal flexibility of the dramatic monologue in representing the different points of view a poet may occupy at different times. In refusing to allow the dreamer to dissociate himself from the protagonist of his dream, Freud appears to be resisting a false division quite analogous to the division between the speaker and the poet in the dramatic monologue. He is saying that the voice recorded in the memory of a dream with an "extraneous" protagonist is a bifurcated voice. It is both the voice of the dreamer and the voice of "someone else," and yet, in the telling, these two voices are inevitably fused into one. I have argued that one constitutive feature of the dramatic monologue is just such a fusion of a divided subject into a single voice. There seems to be more than just a fortuitous similarity between the structure of dreams and that of dramatic monologues.[21]

In short, the contradictions inherent in the homogeneous subject, contradictions obscured by ideology, reappear in the dream-text. They reappear in the opposition of the dreamer's conscious perception of the dream's protagonist as "another" to his or her unconscious representation of the self in the same protagonist. Following Lacan, Coward and Ellis propose to historicize Freud by recognizing that his "discovery" of the unconscious was the discovery of the splitting of the subject that only occurred within the material social conditions of nineteenth-century Europe.[22] In my interpretation of Browning's dream-text, I suggested an internal contradiction in which Roland is both the first to die and the last to die. In addition, I have said that Roland is both Browning and not-Browning. All of this we can say about the dream itself. About the monologue, we can say that Roland despairs of speech because there is no longer an other to respond, while "Browning" has, at the same time, written the text "Childe Roland to the Dark Tower Came," an act that implies a dialogical relation with some audience. The monologue, in other words, translates contradictions, which have been freed from the ideological sphere through the expression of the unconscious in a dream, into "another mode of expression," a literary genre whose own structure already accommodates the contradictions in question. From this I think we can conclude that "the dramatic monologue" is a concept classifying poems that are all produced in a similar way; "Childe Roland to the Dark Tower Came" merely makes the process explicit because it derives so immediately from an actual dream.

To say that a certain psychic structure (the division of conscious from unconscious thought) is characteristic of the material and ideological conditions of a particular period is to imply that this structure is produced through the socializing processes of infant self-differentiation and language acquisition during early childhood. To say further that similar structures find expression among writers in literary genres characteristic of the same period is to explain partially how these genres "are produced." But the psychic structures remain continuous while literary production is intermittent. Just as Freud required the discovery of some concrete event of the preceding day to explain why a particular dream occurred on a particular night, we also need to view individual poems as particular events prompted by immediate circumstances that focus with a special intensity the anxieties and unresolved contradictions that are constant in the poet's psyche. In the case of "Childe Roland to the Dark Tower Came" I find it useful to locate the production of the poem itself—on the second or third of January 1852—as the convergence of disparate forces generated by an overdetermining and mutually reenforcing group of occurrences. These occurrences are political (the coup d'état of Louis Napoleon), social (Browning's temporary isolation from England and from his friends in Italy), familiar (his passionate democratic arguments against Elizabeth's continuing defense of the "strong individual" as the proper center of governmental power), intellectual (his confrontations with his friend Carlyle's theories of hero-worship), psychological (the dream itself), and literary (his New Year's resolution to resume the intensive composition of dramatic monologues).

If we now return to the initial question of this book—how and why the dramatic monologue was produced at a particular conjuncture in English literary history—we shall need, again, to posit a dialectical answer. We shall need to say that each work a writer composes is determined by a confluence of particular material and ideological circumstances such as the ones I have been describing, but that the consistency of a genre implies a structural and temporal continuity of the social and economic forces that produce those particular circumstances. Over the duration of this continuity, the poems themselves become more and more consistent, or classifiable, until the habit of writing dramatic monologues becomes, in itself, as in Browning's New Year's resolution, a determining force that alters and shapes all of the others. Thus the production of the individual poem and the production of "the dramatic monologue" come to require one another in a genuine dialectical interaction.

In previous chapters, I have argued for an intersection of literary history and the social whole as a condition for what Althusser calls the "relative autonomy" of literary production. We have now seen that literary production must be understood simultaneously on two levels, that of classes of works or genres and that of the concrete product, the poem or book. To the more generalized level of genre corresponds the more abstract formulations of social forces: alienation, the specialized division of labor and discourse, the opposition of private and general interests, and so on. To the individual act of production corresponds the actual experience of these social forces in the events of the writer's own life. Marx himself insisted repeatedly that the relation between concept and practice be understood as dialectical, and it is thus not surprising that the relation between the genre and the work should be found to be dialectical as well.

In the first five chapters of this book, I have treated individual poems chiefly as "examples" of the genre of dramatic monologues.

In this chapter, I have offered an interpretation of "Childe Roland to the Dark Tower Came" that derives in large part from the immediate and concrete circumstances of that poem's unique production. The combination of these two types of analysis should encourage us to see the process of literary production as neither singular nor wholly generalized. One of the material conditions of the individual poem's composition is precisely the existence of a concept of genre that is simultaneously generated on the plane of higher abstraction. This simultaneity of the particular and the abstract in any activity of production was acknowledged by Marx, we may recall, through the example of the architect whose imaginative conception of his building is inseparable from the process of producing the building itself. Similarly, the abstract conception of the dramatic monologue (derived from a dialectic of social and literary abstractions) is inseparable from the material process of writing. Thus, the writing of poems is, in the dialectical sense, a "relatively autonomous" activity, neither entirely determined by social and economic circumstances nor hermetically contained within the independent history of writing. This means that when more than one writer experiments with a new form, the autonomy or "freedom" of each is also always "relatively" constrained. In the next chapter, I shall indicate something of the range achieved by the dramatic monologue in hands other than Browning's.

SEVEN

Others: Using and Losing Connection

I   In earlier chapters, I have shown
how Browning's monologues depart from Romantic precedent.
Now it remains to indicate something of the range of the genre's
potential in the hands of other Victorian poets. As we look toward
the end of the nineteenth century, however, we shall find it necessary to consider more than just English uses of the form. American
poets experimented with single dramatic personae, and it is in the
American tradition that we can most clearly observe how the
monologue slowly became something not itself. The last part of
this chapter will deal with the poetry of Pound and Eliot as they
first embrace and finally abandon the monologue's special opportunities and limitations.

One cannot really say that the dramatic monologue was a dominant literary form in the nineteenth century. Much of its prestige
derives from its later influence; in the mid nineteenth century, it
was the central mode of expression for only one poet, Robert
Browning. Nevertheless, Browning did not "invent" the genre in
isolation. Tennyson wrote a small number of monologues before
Browning did and continued to write new ones and tinker with the
old ones throughout his career. The two greatest Victorian poets,
in other words, seem to have developed the form more or less
simultaneously and without apparent exchange of direct influence,
at least until the 1880s, when Tennyson occasionally imitates
Browning.

Nevertheless, the student of any period must somehow give full
credence to the stylistic diversity among the writers of that period.

For this there could hardly be a better opportunity than a comparison of the poetry of Browning and Tennyson. Listening to the music of Tennyson, who could mistake the author for Browning?

> Cold and clear-cut face, why come you so cruelly meek,
> Breaking a slumber in which all spleenful folly was drown'd?
> Pale with the golden beam of an eyelash dead on the cheek,
> Passionless, pale, cold face, star-sweet on a gloom profound;
> Womanlike, taking revenge too deep for a transient wrong
> Done but in thought to your beauty, and ever as pale as before
> Growing and fading and growing, till I could bear it no more,
> But arose, and all by myself in my own dark garden ground,
> Listening now to the tide in its broad-flung shipwrecking roar,
> Now to the scream of a madden'd beach dragg'd down by the wave,
> Walk'd in a wintry wind by a ghastly glimmer, and found
> The shining daffodil dead, and Orion low in his grave.
>
> *(Maud, 1.88–101)*

In the subtle play of alliteration and assonance, the passage is a miracle of sonorous complexity. It presents the moment when the speaker has completed his journey from indifference to captivation by Maud's beauty, a moment both conceptually and stylistically alien to the unsentimental and convivial Browning. Yet for all its individuality of mood, tone, and subject, the linguistic fabric of Tennyson's writing displays a remarkable affinity with that of Browning.

Much of the ringing quality of the verse music that seems so recognizably Tennyson's is focused in the high density of adverbial present participles, which as I pointed out in chapter 3, in large portion impart the open-ended progressivity to Browning's syntax as well. In fourteen lines, the "ing" verb form occurs ten times. Not at all an epiphanic discrete moment of revelation, the speaker's change of heart takes place in a virtual liquid medium of "growing and fading and growing": process without boundary, change without articulation. Within this medium, events and even states become an indissoluble part of that same, seemingly inexorable, fluidity. Like Browning, Tennyson also imparts the quality of open-ended progressivity to his moment of speech with temporal adverbial phrases like "half the night long" and "till I could bear it no more," but his emphasis is decidedly different. Where Browning's characteristic voice leans heavily on the more mundane and conversational effects of common temporal adverbs and the various forms of verbal gesture and anaphoric deixis, Tennyson looks to the progressive form of the verb itself and its various adjectival and adverbial transformations. Stylistically, the two poets remain as distinct as one could wish, but their styles are not built from an infinitely wide selection of linguistic material. The limitations they share, when classified, seem narrow, but in fact, Browning and Tennyson amply demonstrate what a striking range of poetic flexibility the language habits of a particular period can offer.

The language of Tennyson's poetry is chosen in part for its qualities of sound, and the musicality of verse serves a purpose quite analogous to that served by arbitrary stanzaic or rhyme patterns and conspicuous meters in Browning. On the one hand, the purely abstract sound-artifice seems a thing in itself, with its own propelling energy and its own logic of variation and modulation. As pure style it flows on, independent of the communicational or conceptual dimension of the language as sense and syntax. Yet as soon as we say this, we have said too much. Even contemporary commentators like Robert James Mann perceived that Tennyson's own craft, "the absolute originality and the surpassing skill of the Laureate" is one with the "power of language to symbolize in sound [a particular speaker's] mental states and perceptions."[1] Dr. Mann, in other words, raises exactly the question raised in Browning's case: is the texture of sentences-to-make-poetry the independent medium of the poet's special craft or does it "symbolize" the mental states and perceptions communicated by a particular unspecialized speaker under particular life circumstances?

The speech of the speaker in *Maud,* like that of Browning's Childe Roland, is at once pure sound and a celebration of soundlessness. The gradual "growing and fading and growing" of his love for Maud comes upon him "without a sound," and the passage of time is marked by a continuous "listening" to the sounds of an inhuman sea. This protagonist is alone in very much the same way Roland is alone, and again like Roland, he projects human traits and human scenarios onto an emptied Nature. For Browning, the predominant sense is the visual as he grotesquely humanizes the landscape. The emphasis for Tennyson is on sound, as the beach becomes a screaming victim pulled under the sea. For the lover of Maud, abstract sound becomes human sound in the imagination, and we are invited to share both the need and the poetic project of fulfillment by turning the abstract music of the verse into a human story. Such a project, like fiction itself, can only raise the issue of human interaction, however, and the speaker of this poem must remain alone—indeed exiled—until he can exchange the abstract psychic violence of his pure and musical love of Maud for the material violence of war and social purpose.

Very little actual speech passes between the speaker and Maud, and in the poem itself, language is apparently directed outward without hope of return. Like Andrea del Sarto, this speaker can formulate a variety of questions that would constitute turn-relevance-places in his discourse, but to his own isolated and melancholic ear, his speech sounds much like the speech of the sea:

Who knows the ways of the world, how God will bring them about?
Our planet is one, the suns are many, the world is wide.
Shall I weep if a Poland fall? shall I shriek if a Hungary fail?
Or an infant civilization be ruled with rod or with knout?
I have not made the world, and He that made it will guide.

(1.145–49)

He asks questions that do not call for answers. He speaks of his love but not to his love. His speech, whether music or shriek, is only sound, matched against the soundlessness of his loving Maud. In the end, in a pattern that Tennyson had explored before in "Locksley Hall," he abandons love and its alienated medium, the music of poetry, for communal action in "a cause that I felt to be pure and true."[2]

In the passage describing the slow growth of the speaker's love for Maud's beauty, he signifies the felt loss of his youth in an image of thwarted spring. He says that he "Walk'd in a wintry wind by a ghastly glimmer, and found / The shining daffodil dead, and Orion

low in his grave." In part 3, after the madness of murder, estrangement, and exile, he returns to that image as an emblem of hope:

My mood is changed, for it fell at a time of year
When the face of night is fair on the dewy downs,
And the shining daffodil dies, and the Charioteer
And starry Gemini hang like glorious crowns
Over Orion's grave low down in the west,
That like a silent lightning under the stars
She seem'd to divide in a dream from a band of the blest,
And spoke of a hope for the world in the coming wars—
"And in that hope, dear soul, let trouble have rest,
Knowing I tarry for thee," and pointed to Mars
As he glow'd like a ruddy shield on the Lion's breast.

                                                    (3.4–14)

The imagination now is focused, not on Maud's abstract and silent
and singular beauty, but on a dream of her speaking out of a company, a "band." The vision was, as the speaker says, "but a dream,"
yet it marks the beginning of a movement away from the madness
of the isolated ego and toward a "mixing" of the self-in-speech
with a community unwilling merely to "shriek" and leave the world
as God made it:

And I stood on a giant deck and mixt my breath
With a loyal people shouting a battlecry,
Till I saw the dreary phantom arise and fly   /
Far into the North, and battle, and seas of death.

                                                    (3.34–37)

In these and the lines that follow, the poetic music of the poem's
earlier passages remains a presence, but a presence diminished. The
progressive constructions are still there (coming, knowing, shouting), but they resonate less aggressively as pure sound; they have
become absorbed into the record of real human action and real
human speech.

Tennyson's mixing of the self with a community ("I am one
with my kind") is not the discovery of a Romantic unity or wholeness. The speaker learns how to integrate himself with a particular

fragment of a historical world in the unfolding, and in doing so, he integrates poetic speech and sound with the purposeful "breath" of his compatriots. As a dramatic monologue, *Maud* addresses problems that are, on examination, remarkably contiguous with the issues treated in poems like "A Toccata of Galuppi's" or "Childe Roland to the Dark Tower Came." Yet to say this is not to imagine that the intellectual commitments, political views, or poetic styles of Tennyson and Browning are in any way identical.

By calling *Maud* a dramatic monologue, I do not mean to ignore either its subtitle or the impressive exposition of scholars like A. Dwight Culler, who has so carefully distinguished between the monologue and the monodrama.[3] Viewed statically, *Maud* is a kind of hybrid of the Romantic monodrama as we find it in French and German literature and the Victorian dramatic monologue. Certainly, the poem does more than present a series of emotional tableaux; it penetrates the psychic horrors of the isolated ego as well as potential alternatives in collective action, and it chronicles its speaker's emergence from the one to the other. Examining the poem as a moment in literary history, however, we can say that Tennyson appropriates a Romantic genre, the monodrama, to the needs of an emerging Victorian genre, the dramatic monologue. The poem is not just part one kind and part another; it is one kind—indeed one literary era—becoming another.

The most available formal objection to calling *Maud* a monologue is that the speaker does not address anyone in particular. At times, he appears to address Maud herself, but by far the bulk of the poem is more of a meditation than a conversation. To me, this feature merely renders the poem similar to "Childe Roland to the Dark Tower Came" or "A Serenade at the Villa," but fixed categorical boundaries are not my real concern. The concept of literary genre is useful because it gives us a way to see our deceptively static texts as moments in change, and the characteristics that I have attributed to the dramatic monologue provide terms for understanding why *Maud* makes sense as a Victorian-not-Romantic-not-yet-modern poem.[4] Indeed many of Tennyson's monologues make less insistent use of the devices of reciprocity than Browning's do, but those devices are not merely innocently absent. They are at

times invoked and then abandoned to draw attention to the isolation of the speaker, as in *Maud* or in "Locksley Hall."

The latter poem begins as an address to the speaker's "comrades," a request and acknowledgment of compliance. Gaining his
privacy, the speaker indulges his love fury until he is called back to
his "band" by the anticipated "sound upon the bugle-horn." As in
Maud, he abandons his abstract and self-destructive reverie for collective political and military action by responding to the signal and
following the wind seaward. This movement out to sea becomes an
emblematic gesture for Tennyson, signifying a transformation of
discourse out of introspective soliloquy toward comradeship. In
"Ulysses," to cite a well-known example, the direct address implicit
in the conventions of personal introduction ("This is my son,
mine own Telemachus") only fully materializes near the end of
the monologue when Ulysses specifically exhorts his mariners to
push on seaward. Such a late revelation of what kind of poem we
are reading is closely related to the delay of crucial information
that characterizes so many of Browning's rhetorical strategies. In
"Ulysses," I believe the purpose is to question the boundaries
between thought and speech, between introspective self-knowledge
and other-dependent communication. Ulysses' assertion "I am a
part of all that I have met" might well be a perfectly orthodox
Romantic statement of transcendence, similar to Emerson's "Every
thing is kin of mine" in "Mithridates" or Wallace Stevens's "one
says that one is part of everything" in "The Course of a Particular."
But neither of these poems has any of the features of the dramatic
monologue (despite Mithridates' being someone "other than"
Emerson), and we need to ask what the relation "part of" means
in a poem of the kind Tennyson wrote. The dramatic monologue
does not posit ideal totalities, and hence, Ulysses' "all" is local-
ized: "all that I have met" (up until now), and the subject of the
poem's ending is its speaker's fantasy about what he may subse-
quently meet: old friends and present comrades. The relation "part
of," in other words, is social and temporally fragmentary.[5] Indeed,
its nature is made perfectly clear in Ulysses' own qualification of
the claim that he is part of all that he has met:

Yet all experience is an arch wherethro'
Gleams that untravell'd world whose margin fades
For ever and for ever when I move.

(19–21)

These lines describe perfectly the world of the dramatic monologue. Ulysses is the archetypal monologist, precisely because, of all literary forms, this one most exactly scrutinizes and gives substance to the blurred border between the traveled and the as yet untraveled world.

Tennyson continued to experiment with the monologue from early in his career ("Oenone") to quite late ("Tiresias," "The Ancient Sage"). His range includes the cutely comic ("Will Waterproof His Lyrical Monologue") along with the melodramatically pessimistic ("Rizpah"). He is, if anything, more experimental in the form than Browning is, more self-conscious in his manipulation of its conventions. The impression of unbroken discursive continuity, for example, is created in the Northern Farmer poems, not only by the familiar deictics and progressives ("Wheer 'asta bean saw long and mea liggin' 'ere aloan?"), but by the very attempt to render dialect. This continuity is a particular line of events and speech in a particular linguistic community, and yet, because the language is superficially difficult for the cosmopolitan reader to construe, it requires that collaborative effort to create the poem that I discussed in chapter 5. Any reader who makes sense of these poems must translate the marks on the page into sound and then wed that unfamiliar sound pattern to intelligible meaning. The sound that must be fused with sense is not just the sound of dialect; it is also the sound of poetic convention. The "new style" northern farmer employs rhyme, a sophisticated poetic meter, and the poet's specialized gimmick of onomotopoeia, but what we first take simply as abstract syllables imitating the sound of a horse's canter turn out not to be pure sound at all. "Proputty, proputty, proputty" is really "property, property, property" in the farmer's ear, and its obsessional repetition points to the central theme of the poem: loving an abstraction, the old man can neither recognize nor participate in a love based on concrete interaction with his son.

Among Tennyson's most subtle and complex dramatic monologues, in my view, is "Tithonus." The concept of earthly immortality becomes, in this poem, a paradoxical violation of possible earthly values, since the subject of such immortality would necessarily be a transcendent one. Immortality is "cruel" because the immortal man has not only lost the Romantic sense of participation in a metaphysical wholeness, he has also lost the framework within which to feel the fragmentary quality of his temporal experience. The contradictory power of the dramatic monologue's vision comes from the uncertainty of the moment and its delicate connections between past and future along with the dialogical ambivalence of its subject.

Tithonus, though he moves sequentially through time, has exhausted the desires, fears, suspenseful anticipations, and anxieties that articulate time for less afflicted men. He is

> Here at the quiet limit of the world,
> A white-hair'd shadow roaming like a dream
> The ever-silent spaces of the East,
> Far-folded mists, and gleaming halls of morn.

> (7–10)

These lines follow the poem's initial image of the rhythmic cycles of natural and human life and death. They contrast with it a progressive action, "roaming," which not only lacks arbitrary or perfective boundaries in the linguistic sense, it also lacks the possibility of ordinary natural boundaries.

It may be useful to recall that when in "Childe Roland to the Dark Tower Came," the speaker abandons the last projection of some kind of closure to his experience of isolation, he also abandons speech; his monologue ends. That poem chiefly probed the psychology of being truly alone as a prelude to silence. In "Tithonus," Tennyson begins by positing a state of silence as a prelude to exposing the implications of isolation hidden in the idea of immortality. Tithonus begins his monologue in a particular but soundless place, "the quiet limit of the world," "the ever-silent spaces of the East." Tennyson creates, in other words, a kind of paradox that we have seen him experiment with before: a speaker who is speaking to someone but who is simultaneously establishing himself in a realm of silence. This paradox immediately calls into question the status of speech, but it does more; it calls into question the status of the poetic text as a medium of exchange.

Confronting a text in the case of the Northern Farmer poems, a reader must first painstakingly create for himself a pattern of sound, then self-consciously criticize his own attribution of meaning to that pattern. These requirements produce a state of involvement or commitment out of which to criticize the relation between the sounds of speech and its meanings in the discourse of the fictional speaker, thus once again challenging or confusing the borders between the text's fictional and the reader's nonfictional world-in-language. In poems like "Childe Roland" or "Tithonus," the reader is similarly made overtly conscious of his translation of text into speech by being denied that pathway by the poem itself. Roland's is the speech that, by the terms of his exile-quest, can be heard by no one; the "pure text" of Tithonus occurs in a world that is "ever-silent."

Yet Tithonus does speak, and he speaks to someone, the goddess Eos, who has granted his wish for immortality. He recalls an initial exchange: "I ask'd thee, 'Give me immortality.' / Then didst thou grant mine asking with a smile"; and he regards the exchange as economic, for he likens the goddess's carelessness in giving with that of "wealthy men who care not how they give." Tithonus then tells how time, though it cannot kill him, has wasted him and made him old. It is not, however, the physical discomfort or disfigurement that he chiefly laments; it is the paradox of a man wishing to be immortal "like" a god. This paradox lies in the fact that the initial exchange that was designed to bring Tithonus nearer to Eos, who loved him, has only immortalized one of the world's great distances, that between youth and age. Both man and goddess are immortal, but they are not "like" one another; they are, Tithonus repeats, "Immortal age beside immortal youth." Tithonus's error, really a semantic one arising from his mystification

of the word "immortal," must be read against the traditional
Christian precept that death really brings man nearer to God. But
it must also be read, I think, against a careful interpretation of the
concept "nearer." If nearness is metaphorical, if to be "near"
another is to be "like" that other, then man's coming "nearer" a
god will necessarily be paradoxical. If, however, nearness is an
interactional concept, it becomes possible to say that the richness
of the interaction between man and god depends on the difference
between them. This, I think, is the point of Tennyson's poem. The
exchange, asking and giving, is based on the difference between an
immortal goddess and a mortal man. When that difference is removed, the pathway of exchange is removed also, and the world
becomes a world of silence. It is speech as communicational "nearness" that has been terminated, and the remainder of the poem
explores the implications of such a loss.

As soon as Tithonus acknowledges the distance between immortal age and immortal youth, he attempts to reconstitute the
circuit of exchange with Eos by asking a question, making a request,
and then asking another question:

> Can thy love,
> Thy beauty, make amends, tho' even now,
> Close over us, the silver star, thy guide,
> Shines in those tremulous eyes that fill with tears
> To hear me? Let me go; take back thy gift.
> Why should a man desire in any way
> To vary from the kindly race of men,
> Or pass beyond the goal of ordinance
> Where all should pause, as is most meet for all?

(23-31)

I pointed out in chapter 5 that the dramatic monologue imposes a
special sensitivity to the status of interrogatives as devices of reciprocity. The first of Tithonus's questions potentially marks a
genuine turn-relevance-place in his projected conversation with the
goddess, but he receives for answer only the ambiguous tears of
pity. Next he implores her to reverse the earlier exchange—"take
back thy gift"—and finally he asks a question that is unanswerable

in the same sense that, for example, Andrea del Sarto's "What does the mountain care?" is unanswerable. To all of this, the goddess does not reply. Tithonus can see her, but there can be no discourse between them. For him, the goddess can be only an image in that misty, gleaming, glimmering tableau that Tennyson has already identified with silence in the opening verse paragraph. It is worth noticing that in the passages that create this optical atmosphere, Tennyson invariably returns to mild excesses of alliteration and assonance, identifying, in other words, the pure sound patterns of the Beautiful Poem with the "silencing" of Tithonus's speech-as-communication. The vision of Eos is an extravagance of progressive constructions and resonance. She is sensually very much alive and in process, but though she is "close" to Tithonus, she does not respond. The combination of this endless change combined with inability to answer the pleas and questions addressed to her is summarized in a separate verse paragraph:

> Lo! ever thus thou growest beautiful
> In silence, then before thine answer given
> Departest, and thy tears are on my cheek.
>
> (43-45)

As the poem itself is always heavy with the meaningless beauty of sound, Tithonus's own awareness can never be free of the immediacy, whether palpable, imagined, or remembered, of Eos's sensuous presence. That presence prevents him from accepting his irreversible separation, and the remainder of the poem is a celebration of that gradual change that leads to death for men but not for gods. At the end, he fantasizes his own death in a paradox that is really a counterparadox to his original tragedy. He implores the goddess, who has already departed without answering:

> Release me, and restore me to the ground.
> Thou seest all things, thou wilt see my grave;
> Thou wilt renew thy beauty morn by morn,
> I earth in earth forget these empty courts,
> And thee returning on thy silver wheels.
>
> (72-76)

Thithonus's desire for Eos is a desire for death, his memory of her a memory of mortality. Process for her is not movement toward death; it is only a renewal of beauty. In seeking vainly to reopen the exchange of gift giving and returning, Tithonus would reestablish the distance between man and goddess that he initially sought to abolish, and in doing so he would forget her very beauty-in-process, her endless "returning on [her] silver wheels." The paradox this time lies in the fact that his desire for growth and change is directed at those qualities of beauty in the goddess and depends on his progressive memory of her. But it is also a desire to "forget." When he is immortal, in other words, he is bound by time through memory, while to regain his mortality, to reassume the burden of death in time, would be to relinquish memory.

"Tithonus" is a poem about the desire to escape death in earthly terms, it is a poem about erotic fantasy, and it is a poem about poetic beauty. The fantasy of sexual blending into a perfect unity of being with the Other involves, no less than the desire for immortality, the paradox of perfection in change, the eternal growth of beauty. This paradox precludes meaning, or to put it another way, it precludes love as communication:

> I used to watch—if I be he that watch'd—
> The lucid outline forming round thee; saw
> The dim curls kindle into sunny rings;
> Changed with thy mystic change, and felt my blood
> Glow with the glow that slowly crimson'd all
> Thy presence and thy portals, while I lay,
> Mouth, forehead, eyelids, growing dewy-warm
> With kisses balmier than half-opening buds
> Of April, and could hear the lips that kiss'd
> Whispering I knew not what of wild and sweet,
> Like that strange song I heard Apollo sing,
> While Ilion like a mist rose into towers.
>
> (52-63)

This irresistibly seductive vision of boundless change stands in the best tradition of Victorian verbal progressivity and the dramatic monologue. But this is "mystic change," without loss, without displacement or foreboding. In such a vision, speech can be only sensual sound, only a whispering without content. As soon as there is meaning or exchange, there is loss and death, and to imagine otherwise is to imagine a contradictory immortality such as that produced by the impossible exchange between Tithonus and Eos, which leads to distance and silence—the nothingness that alone can signify the impossible.

I have said that Tennyson has implicitly associated the silent realm of immortality with the abstract beauty of poetic music. The sound artifice, along with the imagery of glimmering diffused light is fully displayed in the central erotic passage, and Thithonus likens the whispers of the loving goddess to Apollo's song. The paradox, then, of being at once human and like the gods is a paradox for poetry as well. The imagination's Romantic request for intimations of perfect beauty or perfect truth—indeed for intimations of immortality—is analogous to Tithonus's request for his own immortality and to the poem's tantalizing fantasy of perfect sexual union with the Perfect Woman in human time. All are paradoxical, and the only escape from the paradox is the realization that what we call Beauty can exist only in its attachment to meaning, a kind of meaning that must be interpersonal and therefore always partial and in the process of being lost—not, in other words, the written "Being" but the "Being Written." Such loss is a loss, not only of meaning, but of identity, that part of the Romantic self that participates in "the eternal, the infinite and the one." Even the immortal Tithonus can know the love of Eos only as memory, and the self remembering has displaced the self that loved. Hence he must qualify even his own subjectivity: "I used to watch—if I be he that watch'd." The speaker in the dramatic monologue is never "he that began," and this is just another way of stating Tithonus's paradox. He lives because he cannot die, and yet the "he" that lives is dead because he cannot live his memory, his youth. Only in a perfect changeless youth would this be possible, and that is not even the kind of immortal youth attributed to the goddess.

II

An adequate history of the Victorian dramatic monologue would need to consider minor as well as major experiments in the form; it would attend to the poems of E. H. Bickersteth or Archer T. Gurney alongside those of Tennyson and Browning. And it would treat the problem of derivative or openly imitative monologues, such as George W. Thornbury's "The Two Musicians after the Opera," which directly apes "A Toccata of Galuppi's." Finding the interesting minor poems is a demanding research project in itself, and we are indebted in particular to K. E. Faas's excellent "Notes Towards a History of the Dramatic Monologue."[6] Faas's article is really just a list, but his judgment and thoroughness are exemplary. He recognizes the need for formal distinctions of a finer resolving power than those of his main predecessor, B. W. Fuson, and though he accepts the traditional abstract definition of the monologue as an "utterance not of the poet but of another individualized speaker," this category cannot begin to account for the shrewdness of his actual selections.[7] In the case of William Morris, for example, Faas passes over the many narrative poems supposedly spoken by medieval knights and identifies unambiguous monologues like "Concerning Geffray Teste Noire" and "The Judgment of God." The former poem displays with a special clarity all of the features that Faas must intuitively have sensed as affinities with the acknowledged masters of the form.

The poem is spoken by one John of Castel Neuf, and it begins in the usual manner of speech as progressive fragment:

And if you meet the Canon of Chimay,
    As going to Ortaise you well may do,
Greet him from John of Castel Neuf, and say,
    All that I tell you, for all this is true.

The beginning in mid-sentence, the heavy initial ostensive reference, and the promise of information unfolding are all familiar enough. Morris soon introduces the pattern of questioning and acknowledgment with his listener:

When first I joined the little army there
    With ten good spears; Auvergne is hot, each day
We sweated armed before the barrier;
    Good feats of arms were done there often—eh?

Your brother was slain there? I mind me now,
    A right good man-at-arms, God pardon him!

                                                    (17–22)

From this point on, the poem is very little like anything we find in Browning and Tennyson. Morris's genius is for narrative. In poems like "Sir Galahad: A Christmas Mystery," this narrative purpose prevails, and whatever echoes of monologue conventions appear seem to serve no real purpose beyond giving a sense of immediate speech. In "Concerning Geffray Teste Noire," however, the initial exchange between John of Castel Neuf and his listener becomes central to the poem's interpretation of the need for historical fictions.

John tells how, joining the army of the duke of Berry, he was sent to ambush the bandits, Sir Geffray and one Blackhead, in the wood of Verville. Arriving near the place where the outlaw company is expected to pass, John and his companions discover the skeletons of a knight and his lady. John tells how his friend Aldovrand asked him then whether he had ever seen a woman's bones before, a question that recalls to his mind a time in his youth when he participated in the massacre of Beauvais with his father, an experience that sickened him at the time and that clearly haunts him still. Virtually without interruption, his attention returns to the discovered skeletons where he sees that the woman has an arrow piercing her throat and a broken wrist. From these details, along with the fact that the lady is wearing a "war-coat," John infers a complete story of how the two came to die in the Verville forest: "Their story came out clear without a flaw." He sits and dreams and thinks over the bones "for hours," and his monologue recalling this revery seems toward the end to be addressed to another lady, a living one who has proven false to him. At the end, he gives a brief account of how he and his band slew the bandits without apprehending either Sir Geffray or Blackhead. These two are known to have died since, however, and John states his intention of adding his tale as an adjunct to their history:

> And much bad living kill'd Teste Noire at last;
>   John Froissart knoweth he is dead by now,
> No doubt, but knoweth not this tale just past;
>   Perchance then you can tell him what I show.

(189–92)

Clearly now John is once again talking to the original listener for whom he had initially insisted that "all this is true." This "all" is probably meant at first to refer to the tale of Verville wood, but the tale as told includes the details from John's youth, reference to his unfortunate adult love affair, and his fantasy about a truer love that led a knight and lady to die together. This subordinate tale is by no means "true" in the sense of being documentable. What John of Castel Neuf has done is to deliver a kind of Thucydidean history in which lost continuities are filled in by likely fictions. It is appropriate that he should intend his tale to supplement Froissart's knowledge since Froissart also wrote this kind of history and defended its value. The epistemological framework for the poem, then, is the blending of fiction and history, a blending explicitly signified by the offer of the fictional John's narrative as a contribution to the history of a real medieval historian.

The monologue seems to assert that the human desire for history is a desire for continuity and that what counts as continuity will depend on the terms of personal involvement brought to bear by the teller of the historical tale: in this case, the adolescent trauma over the killing of women and the later disappointment in love. Both are interfused in John's "explanation" of the skeletons he finds. This requirement of personal involvement in the narrative of history also makes sense of John's relation to his designated listener, whose engagement is secured by creating an initial historical continuity between the events John is to tell and the death of the listener's brother, an event over which John lingers with some of the grim detail that he later employs in his historical fiction. Thus the form of the dramatic monologue justifies the act of fictionalizing history for the consumer as well as the producer of historical texts, and it does so through a rhetorical logic that extends to the act of writing poems of the "medieval" kind, which is Morris's preferred mode. In the end, this logic invites the reader to employ his own personal concerns and experiences to help the poet repair the discontinuities of a distant historical epoch in fiction.

I began this account by saying that Morris's dramatic monologues have very little in common with those of Browning and Tennyson. Still, the results are remarkably compatible. The monologue seeks to imply lines of hidden continuity within a fragmented past. It denies the alienation of past from present by signifying a reciprocal relation between a speaker and listener, it challenges the sharp division between the specialist (the historian in this case) and the nonspecialist (the man who fantasizes), and it insists on the reader's active role in bringing about the poem's special force and value. Morris's other narratives may sometimes have great charm, but few display the complexity of self-criticism or awareness of the psychological basis of Victorian medievalism as richly as the monologue "Concerning Geffray Teste Noire."

The narrative element is important to nearly all of Morris's monologues, and he continued to write them well into the 1890s. There are a few exceptions like "Love's Gleaning-Tide," which adopts ballad conventions, but most of the poems tell continuous tales framed by the devices of continuity, reciprocity, and the overlay of explicitly poetic convention and independent measures of speech. Here, for example, is the beginning of "Mother and Son," published in 1891:

> Now sleeps the land of houses, and dead night holds
>   the street,
> And there thou liest, my baby, and sleepest soft and sweet;
> My man is away for a while, but safe and alone we lie,
> And none heareth thy breath but thy mother, and the moon
>   looking down from the sky
> On the weary waste of the town, as it looked on the
>   grass-edged road
> Still warm with yesterday's sun, when I left my old abode.

The mother goes on to tell the story of her life, her pride and her sorrows, to the baby as though he could understand and respond. The fact that he cannot merely underscores her loneliness in the absence of her husband, and she makes a point of saying things to her son that she could never say in her husband's presence. In the weaker poems, the reason for combining narrative and monologue is unclear or, as in "Mother and Son," simplistically sentimental. Historically, however, this development in the uses of the monologue is important.

Morris's monologues share with those of other late Victorian poets a dependence on plot as a central structuring principle. There are plenty of narrative passages in the monologues of Browning and Tennyson, but the chief temporal continuity is typically in the psychological and social moment of the telling and only in the time referred to by the narrative sequences insofar as they are contiguous with the telling itself.[8] For Morris, both Rossettis, and Swinburne, the episode of the monologue's exchange remains relatively static, and the poem's piecemeal unfolding can be described mainly in terms of "narrative suspense." A good example might be Dante Gabriel Rossetti's "A Last Confession," a poem superficially similar to "Prophyria's Lover" or "My Last Duchess," which also gradually reveal murders committed by the speakers. What marks Rossetti's poem off from at least the latter of these predecessors is the fact that although the relation between the murderer and the priest who takes his confession can be called reciprocal, that relation undergoes no development or change in its own right. The suspense or arrestment of the final revelation is entirely a function of the plot as it unfolds in the narrative.

One exception to the dominance of narrative in Dante Rossetti's work occurs in "Jenny," a meditation and address to a young prostitute. This poem, probably written between 1847 and 1853 (revised c. 1858), is much more similar to the monologues of Browning and is, in my view, Rossetti's finest poem in the genre. This is not to say I want to claim that narrative emphasis necessarily destroys or denigrates the monologue form. Indeed, I consider Christina Rossetti the most successful Victorian master of the dramatic monologue aside from Browning and Tennyson; and the best of her poems, like "A Royal Princess," are of the narrative type, while works that focus more directly on the exchange in progress, such as "The Convent Threshold," often seem melodramatic.

If the closer affinity of the dramatic monologue and narrative verse does not, in itself, lead to inferior poems, it does seem to me an important precondition of the genre's deterioration in the earlier part of the twentieth century. The nineteenth century might well be called the century of plots or scenarios, not only in its incidental fictions, but in its most pervasive cultural myths. Myths of progress, decline, and value-free process all had their characteristic "storylines" of cause and effect sequences. One thinks of rational narrative sequences that organize, for example, nineteenth-century physics, economics, the study of population, international politics, and biology. The century was, in one sense, devoted to a group of exhaustive experiments in the applications of these plots, and one of the things that all of them share is their various degrees of discreditation toward the end of the nineteenth and the beginning decades of the twentieth centuries. This more or less simultaneous failure of various majestic narratives in which had been invested many of Western capitalism's claims to truth and the natural coherence of its world may well have helped to produce, for the twentieth century, a distrust of sequential, cause-and-effect narrative as a mode of rationality in general. If this is true, it might be considered one of the really important conditions of the breakdown of fictional plot structures at the same time, and it might also suggest that a growing alliance between the dramatic monologue and the conventions of romance narrative cannot augur well for the future of the monologue itself. It is at least true that romance narrative does not survive the nineteenth century, and it is true that twentieth-century approximations to the dramatic monologue have virtually no narrative dimension.

III

Important as the alliance between the dramatic monologue and narrative may have been in the monologue's later history, it can be only one among many factors in the disappearance of the form in the early twentieth century. The main early modern imitators of the Victorian monologue were Americans: Robinson, Masters, Pound, and Eliot. They look back, not just to Browning and Tennyson and Swinburne, but to Emerson and Whitman as well. Poems like Emerson's "Alphonse of Castile" or Whitman's "The Wound-Dresser" indicate a specifically American tradition of dramatic monologues, one that does not become predominantly a narrative tradition as it does in Britain.

It is, of course, the modern writers who bring British and American language and literature closer again than they had been since colonial days. The name we think of most readily in connection with the dramatic monologue is Ezra Pound. Pound's imagistic or "ideogrammic" method of composition has been studied thoroughly enough, but its immediate linguistic basis has been surprisingly misconstrued at times. The best example is the widespread overestimation of the influence on Pound of Ernest Fenollosa's essay "The Chinese Written Character as a Medium for Poetry." The essay is mainly about syntax and is based on Fenollosa's acute observation of the most modern poetry he knew in 1902, that is to say, it is based on the syntax of Victorian poetry. The main center of force in language, and thus in poetry, is, according to Fenollosa, the transitive verb, and I have shown in detail elsewhere that the poetics that derives from this premise is inappropriate to both Pound's habitual syntax and his poetry.[9] The modes of forming linguistic relationships that Fenollosa dismisses as "weakened" transformations of primal verbs—the copula and the prepositional phrase in particular—bear a much heavier burden in imagistic writing than do transitive verbs and their adverbial elaboration in complicated predicates. Here is an example from one of the "short, so-called dramatic lyric[s]," which Pound told Williams is the "sort of thing I do":

We have no rest, three battles a month.
By heaven, his horses are tired.
The generals are on them, the soldiers are by them.
The horses are well trained, the generals have ivory arrows

and quivers ornamented with fish-skin.
The enemy is swift, we must be careful.
                              ("Song of the Bowmen of Shu," 16–20)

Six copulas appear in five lines, and the stative verb "have," is used twice, one to introduce a negative, which according to Fenollosa, constitutes another "weakening" of the verb. The copulas create discrete, static categories rather than the fluid interactions we have observed in Victorian monologues: "His horses are tired," "The enemy is swift, we must be careful." They are employed, moreover, in conjunction with prepositional phrases that denote proximity: "The generals are on them, the soldiers are by them." The parallelism of the phrasing is important here too, as it was in Shelley, since it contributes to an appositional or juxtapositional structure in the syntax. The purpose for Pound is different from Shelley's, however. Shelley uses apposition to reveal similitudes that are inherent in the world but previously unnoticed, but Pound uses even simile itself to create surprising juxtapositions and thus call attention to his own facility in forging a reality that in no way exists "in the world" as he finds it. This procedure lies at the center of Pound's technique, whether the end is the lovely "apparitions" of imagist poems like "In a Station of the Metro," "Alba," "The Coming of War: Actaeon" or the stinging satirical wit of "Les Millwins" or "Meditatio." Syntactic parallelism for the purpose of surprising semantic juxtaposition is not, moreover, merely a poetic technique; Pound's "nonliterary" prose depends on it too:

> Have had two opulent weeks as dramatic critic on *The Outlook* and have been fired in most caddish possible manner. Have had my work turned down by about every editor in England and America, but have never before felt a desire for vengeance.[10]

This kind of syntax encapsulates each experience, regardless of duration (two opulent weeks or an instantaneous firing), as a discrete unit to be compared to another such unit, generating between them "an intellectual and emotional complex in an instant of time."

An image, whether visual or not, is above all a *thing,* and writers like Pound are very little concerned with spatial or temporal continuities beyond the boundaries of the entity. The same can, of course, be said of Pound's historical vision. He juxtaposes fragments from the ages of Homer, Confucius, Dante, and Shakespeare in an ideal (often prepositional) proximity to one another and to his own age in what Hugh Kenner has aptly called "nonconsecutive arrays."[11] But extensions beyond the borders of the fragments into their own contexts do not interest Pound. His own sense of alienation from his immediate Anglo-American community leads to the assumption, which he shares with most of his contemporaries, that all great thinkers in all eras experience a similar estrangement. Most of his "short, so-called dramatic lyrics" portray poets, singers, and other men of genius in like predicaments. Hence the truth of Pound's famous statement that the poet is continually "casting off masks of the self."

All of this is, of course, not very congenial to the literary project of Browning as I have described it here, and it is not surprising that Pound chooses to celebrate Browning's most alienated and alienating poem, *Sordello,* as a monument to the affinity that he felt throughout his career. Ignoring Browning's painstaking attempt to reconstruct the bewildering complexity of linkages that explain Sordello's life as he perceives it, Pound makes Sordello into a static, painted image of Browning himself, invoking the desire

> To paint, more real than any dead Sordello,
> The half or third of your intensest life
> And call that third Sordello.[12]

While alienation and its potential repair are for Browning the central problem of the dramatic monologue, alienation is the inalterable, even desirable, *donnée* for Pound. It assures the vacuum that Pound's images need to figure forth his own intensest life, and that vacuum surrounds his so-called dramatic monologues as well.

Poems like "La Fraisne," "Cino," "Marvoil," and "Sestina: Altaforte" furnish good examples of what the dramatic monologue has become in Pound's hands. The speakers are troubadours and other singers who are isolated from any community and estranged from ladies they have loved. Other human beings exist for them only as free-floating fragments. Sometimes, as in "La Fraisne," the fragmentation is temporal:

> Once when I was among the young men . . .
> And they said I was quite strong, among the young men.
> Once there was a woman . . .
> . . . but I forget . . . she was . .
> . . . I hope she will not come again.
> . . . I do not remember . . . . .
>
> I think she hurt me once, but . .
> That was very long ago.
>
> (40-47)

Elsewhere, as in "Cino," the woman herself is remembered only as a collection of physical fragments:

> Eyes, dreams, lips, and the night goes.
> Being upon the road once more,
> They are not.
>
> (10-12)

What is the subject modified by the participial phrase? It is not "they"; it is an unspoken "I," Cino himself, identified in proximity to the road and to his memories. Grammatically, the sentence is a paradox. In the contiguous "real" world, "they" both exist ("Being upon the road") and do not exist ("They are not"). Only by recognizing a solecism can we discover what "is": the speaking subject. This subjectivity, which is the only reality of imagist poetry, is usually not unspoken. "Cino" ends with a perfect imagist poem:

> I will sing of the white birds
> In the blue waters of heaven,
> The clouds that are spray to its sea.

The indesseverable mixing of images is matched perhaps only by H. D. in poems like "Oread," but in all such poems, the agent of fusion is the individual poetic mind, the "I will sing."

That "I" is, of course, a fragment itself, but it is not the kind of fragment that we have found the subject to be in Browning. There the self is a fragment because it is incomplete without the other. For Pound, the subject-as-fragment is not problematically incomplete or divided; it is uncompletable. We find in these poems no devices of reciprocity in their various stages of repair; we find no contingent community either tragically lost, deceptively alienated, or fully intimate. The only community is either the ideal communion of great minds (Sophocles, Dante, Homer, Shakespeare) or, what amounts to the same thing, the many "masks of the self" that sometimes seem to hold coloquy together:

> O strange face there in the glass!
> O ribald company, O saintly host,
> O sorrow-swept my fool,
> What answer? O ye myriad
> That strive and play and pass,
> Jest, challenge, counterlie!
> I? I? I?
>   And ye?
>
> ("On His Own Face in a Glass")

The "I" and the "Thou" have become one for Pound, a condition that amounts to the fullest possible acceptance of alienation and a denial of the very problem addressed in such different ways by both Romantic and Victorian poets.

All of this has radical consequences for the dramatic monologue, and the center of the historical shift from the Victorian monologue to a kind of poetry that I consider to be generically distinguishable lies in the nature of fragmentation, both conceptually and linguistically. When Browning employs sentence fragments, he almost always does so in such a way that the fragment is easily and unambiguously convertible into a complete sentence. Here are some examples in which I have supplied the words necessary to make the fragment a sentence:

What [is] so wild as words are?
    I and thou [are]
In debate, as birds are,
    Hawk on bough!

                     ("A Woman's Last Word," 5–8)

And so along the wall, over the bridge,
By the straight cut to the convent [we went]. Six
    words [were spoken] there,
While I stood munching my first bread that month.

                     ("Fra Lippo Lippi," 90–92)

John of Douay shall effect my plan,
Set me on horseback here aloft,
[As] alive, as the crafty sculptor can [make me].

                     ("The Statue and the Bust," 202–4)

Fragmentation of this kind works as one of those invitations to the reader to collaborate in the making of the poem's meaning that I discussed in chapter 5, a collaboration based on the assumption of a linguistic familiarity fused into whatever esoteric features the poem has. But sentence fragmentation, when it occurs in Pound's writing, is quite a different matter.

The opening lines of canto 5 illustrate what happens to a language heavily laden with progressive forms of verbs when syntax becomes fragmented as Pound does it:

Great bulk, huge mass, thesaurus;
Ecbatan, the clock ticks and fades out
The bride awaiting the god's touch; Ecbatan,
City of patterned streets; again the vision:
Down in the viae stradae, toga'd the crowd, and arm'd,
Rushing on populous business,
    and from parapet looked down
and North was Egypt,
    the celestial Nile, blue deep,
    cutting low barren land,
Old men and camels working the water-wheels;
Measureless seas and stars,
Iamblichus' light,
    the souls ascending,

> Sparks like a partridge covey,
>   Like the "ciocco", brand struck in the game.
> "Et omniformis": Air, fire, the pale soft light.

One way of describing sequences like "Old men and camels working the water-wheels" or "the souls ascending" is to say that they are transformations of progressive sentences and thus fragments that the reader completes by adding the copula to make the *be + verb + ing* progressive formula. But this is not the kind of syntagmatic associations the reader is asked to make. The first line suggests, and the succeeding lines confirm, that the passage is a series or list of noun phrases unconnected by the syntax of predicates—a metaphoric set of variations on a theme akin to the order of a single heading in a thesaurus. A thesaurus, however, depends on a culturally shared or agreed-on set of semantic equivalences. "Great bulk" and "huge mass" are of this kind, but from the second line onward, Pound's "thesaurian" elaborations become unpredictable. The list of noun phrases becomes an increasingly private "vision," to use Pound's own term, and the reader, far from being asked to confirm the justness of the series in communal categories, must merely accept and marvel at the unique historical vision of the man of genius. Hence the potential progressive forms can make sense, not through syntagmatic completion, but only through paradigmatic accretion. "Old men and camels working the water-wheels" is a noun phrase, a visual image in ideal space without movement. The participles work like prepositions for Pound, establishing proximity but not process. If we say that the celestial Nile "is cutting" low barren land, we are using "to cut" in its stative sense of marking a visible boundary, and stative verbs do not normally take progressive aspect.

What we have in Pound, then, is a form of sentence fragmentation that does not invite completion by the reader into sentences. It does not, indeed, invite the reader's active collaboration at all and must therefore be interpreted very differently from Browning's most common mode of fragmentation. The reader of the ideogrammic poem must strain to re-create in his own mind a semblance of metaphoric relations unexpectedly created out of nothing in the mind of the master. This is a kind of cynical romanticism. The Romantic poet, according to Shelley, discovers similitudes, which he asks his reader to recognize, thus discovering an ontological affinity between himself and the poet and, in the most ambitious moments, with all men. Pound creates relations that nowhere preexist awaiting discovery and challenges the reader to keep pace with his imagination. The reader who succeeds, far from joining a wider community of men, accedes to a smaller elite. Like the Coleridgean Romantic poet, the imagist abstracts from the temporal dimension of linear history into a timeless ideal space, but the modern version quickly becomes a celebration of alienation and not, as Coleridge proclaimed, a remedy for it.

The dramatic monologue itself presents a putative fragment in time, and in his earlier poems, Pound imitates some of its devices:

> For I was a gaunt, grave councillor
> Being in all things wise, and very old,
> But I have put aside this folly and the cold
> That old age weareth for a cloak.
>
> I was quite strong—at least they said so—
> The Young men at the sword-play
> But I have put aside this folly, being gay
> In another fashion that more suiteth me.
>
> ("La Fraisne," 1–8)

This poem, like several of Browning's monologues, begins with the coordinating conjunction, suggesting the unbroken flow of linear speech begun at some time prior to, but contiguous with, the poem itself. For Browning, a line like "But do not let us quarrel any more" signifies an unfolding conversation, an interaction between Andrea del Sarto and his wife that, bit by bit, reveals Andrea's emotional and epistemological disabilities. For the characteristic mode of opening a monologue to be integral to the poem's meaning, in other words, it must cooperate with other distinguishing features of the form, in this case, opportunities for reciprocity that Andrea repeatedly fails to understand. In "La Fraisne," the initial "for" signifies no meaningful continuity with something said before; it is little more than a verbal affectation. And the rest of the poem, though it retains vestiges of monologue conventions, assigns no real function to any of them:

> But I have seen the sorrow of men, and am glad,
> For I know that the wailing and bitterness are a folly.
> And I? I have put aside all folly and all grief.

(22–24)

The question "And I?" seems to acknowledge, by repeating, a question asked of the speaker. But no context supports this construction. No evidence of an interlocutor appears elsewhere, and no other markers of exchange, even of the kind that indicate an isolated speaker's projection of a desired interlocutor, confer an integral function on this unique instance. The poem is really no more than a faint allusion to the dramatic monologue as the Victorians used it, and in my view the same is true for all of Pound's "short, so-called dramatic lyrics."

The speaker of "La Fraisne" is a former man of wisdom who has turned himself into an ash tree. This metamorphosis has allowed him to admire the absolute beauty of the dogwood instead of loving women, which has brought him pain. His withdrawal, however, explicitly repudiates more than just the fortunes of love. He has also left behind the activity of the counciling and his comradeship with "the young men at sword-play" who have admired him. Each of these he dismisses with the repeating formula, "But I have put aside this folly." The poem, which appears to begin with a gesture toward syntagmatic continuity traditionally associated with the poetic representation of conversation, quickly denies this kind of structure both formally in its ritualistic repetitions and thematically through its denial of community. For Pound, this "persona" is an ideal mask of the self, and the imagistic fantasy of a self outside of time and human interaction is the poem's project. For such a project, the dramatic monologue is an inappropriate form, and for the producers of that genre, Pound's fantasy would be literally a self-destructive one. Indeed, much of the power of Pound's poetry comes from this willing destruction of the human self and his fierce and unblinking scrutiny of its death. After centuries of a Western cultural tradition devoted to understanding what it means to be human, Pound, with other modern writers, initiates the revolutionary project of imagining a liberation from the entire enterprise by becoming, in the crucial communal sense, no longer human:

> Being no longer human, why should I
> Pretend humanity or don the frail attire?
> Men have I known and men, but never one
> Was grown so free an essence, or become
> So simply element as what I am.
>
> ("Paracelsus in Excelsis," 1–5)

Ironically, the speaker of this poem is Paracelsus, that mystical alchemist who, in Browning's early treatment, endured the agony of discovering the poverty of aspirations toward a pure essence of self-containment.

When Pound sets out to write dramatic monologues, the genre is difficult for him to realize. The difficulty is not superficial; it inheres in his perceived relation to his possible audience and in the terms habitual in him for conceptualizing selfhood or subjectivity. Nevertheless, it is possible to make a serious overstatement of the discontinuity between Pound and his predecessors, since in one important regard, he follows the example of Browning consistently and substantially expands the possibilities of Browning's technique. I refer here to Browning's practice of fusing poetic with ordinary language and the languages of distant cultures with the most familiar rhythms and conventions of contemporary English speech. Pound recognizes Browning as a predecessor in exactly this category when he points, in "Paracelsus," to Browning's "mixing" of eras:

> you mix your eras
> For that great font Sordello sat beside—
> 'Tis an immortal passage, but the font?—
> Is some two centuries outside the picture.

Pound's own technique for mixing eras is well known, and I shall give only one example, one brilliantly analyzed by Hugh Kenner:

> Though my house is not propped up by Taenarian columns from
>   Laconia (associated with Neptune and Cerberus),
> Though it is not stretched upon gilded beams;
> My orchards do not lie level and wide
>   as the forests of Phaeacia
>   the luxurious and Ionian,
> Nor are my caverns stuffed stiff with a Marcian vintage,
> My cellar does not date from Numa Pompilius,
> Nor bristle with wine jars,
> Nor is it equipped with a frigidaire patent;
> Yet the companions of the Muses
>   will keep their collective nose in my books,
> And weary with historical data, they will turn to my dance tune.
>   ("Homage to Sextus Propertius," 1.51–63)

I can do no better than to quote Kenner's remarks to illustrate Pound's affinity with Browning:

> Something had happened; the tone of time has vanished, and aerial perspective. There is no "point of view" that will relate these idioms: neither a modern voice ("bristle"; "frigidaire patent"; "collective nose") nor an ancient one ("Phaeacia"; "Marcian") can be assigned this long sentence; moreover "Laconia" has acquired what looks like a sotto voce footnote, while the modernisms ("frigidaire," "data") sound plausibly Latin. In transparent overlay, two times have become as one and we are meant to be equally aware of both dictions (and yet they seem the same diction). The words lie flat like the forms on a Cubist surface. The archaizing sensibility of James's time and Beardsley's has simply dissolved.[13]

These remarks might easily describe the effect of Browning's dual idioms, though Browning concentrates somewhat less on diction than Pound does. The point is that this possible influence—certainly an affinity—remains as a bond between Browning and Pound throughout Pound's career. Long after the dramatic monologue itself disappears from Pound's repertoire, the curious ability to blend disparate voices into one timeless idiolect marks Pound's unmistakable style.

But one aspect of Kenner's description—as well as his example—
is too limited to point to the more radical experiments of this kind
in the *Cantos*. Browning always limited himself to the fusion of two
modes of discourse: the poetic and the ordinary, the exotic and
the plain, the culturally remote and the insistently Victorian. Within these pairs, each element remains consistent or continuous
throughout a given poem. In Pound, it is seldom that we have just
"ancient Latin" and "modern English"; more often, he gives us
what Kenner calls an "array" of fragments denoting different
origins. Such arrays diminish the prominence of the present. For
Browning, the problem is to rehumanize the poetic present by
connecting it with a particular past or a particular distance. In the
Cantos, the colloquial present is only one of a great range of times
and places accumulated; the juxtaposition of Rome and Renaissance Italy and the China of Confucius is fully as important as the
juxtaposition of any of these and the present. There are a number
of important reasons for the difference. First, the order of history
for Pound is a wholly subjective order based on affective principles
("Only emotion endures") rather than a lost order that has become
an object of desire, as it is in Browning. Second, the principle of
association among elements of the past and present is comparative
or metaphoric instead of developmental. Hence Pound objects to
nineteenth-century literary scholarship because "English novelists
were not compared with the French. 'Sources' were discussed."[14]
Pound's literary history is a simultaneous order, a museum in
which the spatial order of texts governs and the linear reality of
time is left outside. His age is the age of anthologies, and its
literary sensibility is that of Forster, who wished to imagine all
novelists from all periods sitting together writing in the same
room.[15]

This way of thinking produced great literary richness, but it is
not Browning's way, and it does not easily profit from the full
range of opportunities offered by the dramatic monologue. Browning's project, we may recall, was to de-specialize the poet, to
affirm his linkages with that full "British Public who may like
[him] yet." Not only has Pound given up being "liked" by the
public at large, he actively repels both its participation and its

curiosity by multiplying the pieces and disguising the welds that make them into whole poems. For Pound, the poet's entire value lies in his role as a specialized scientist or investigator. His discoveries are esoteric and generally unnoticed. He exists parallel to but not interacting with the other specialists of his generation:

> And we could, presumably, apply to the study of literature a little of the common sense that we currently apply to physics or to biology. In poetry there are simple procedures, and there are known discoveries, clearly marked. As I have said in various places in my unorganized and fragmentary volumes: in each age one or two men of genius find something, and express it. It may be in only a line or in two lines, or in some quality of a cadence; and thereafter two dozen, or two hundred, or two or more thousand followers repeat and dilute and modify. [16]

These formulas are well known and need no explication. My point here is that they account for the selective adoption of conventions from past literary genres that become the bases for new genres quite different from the old. The multiple fragmentations of the "historical voice" in Pound's poems leave the dramatic monologue behind, and in so doing, they create a new genre capable of creating a kind of composite mythic voice with no past or future and no capacity for human interaction. Pound's ultimate persona, well anticipated by his earlier "masks of the self," presents in poetry perhaps the purest version we have of what Derrida calls the "myth of absolute presence." In this, Pound is not alone among his contemporaries. Those few writers, like Frost, who experiment with the dramatic monologue never truly realize the form in the Victorian sense, and they soon give over the attempt. Most modern poets never begin it.

IV

One who did, of course, is T. S. Eliot, and no treatment of the dramatic monologue's history, however sketchy, can ignore "The Love Song of J. Alfred Prufrock" and some of the minor poems in Eliot's early canon. It is useful to trace the development of the dramatic monologue in Eliot's career through three poems, "Prufrock" (1917), "Gerontion" (1920), and "The Waste Land" (1922).

The revolutionary "Waste Land" represents to me the end point in a process of generic disintegration identical to, though more efficient than, the process that brought Pound from *A Lume Spento* to the *Pisan Cantos.* In "The Waste Land," the monologue voice has become a composite, fusing multiple idioms into a subjective unity subsumed in the figure of Tiresias, an embodiment of speech beyond communication or displacement who has "foresuffered all" though he can "connect / nothing with nothing." Tiresias is a transformation of Gerontion, who is a more singular speaker (and thus more appropriate to the monologue) but already an abstraction (his name means simply "old man"). He speaks to no one and no one replies. History has betrayed him, and he has repudiated its continuities as "contrived corridors." Gerontion thus has no past and no future, only a kind of emptied and dried out abstract present. He anticipates "The Waste Land," but he also, in my view, carries forward and exaggerates some of the latent features of "Prufrock" that make that poem mark the twentieth century's symbolic leave-taking of the dramatic monologue.

The paradox of the mythic voice is that it combines the extremes of the personal and the impersonal. Eliot's recommendation of impersonality for the poet in "Tradition and the Individual Talent" has led many to read that essay as a repudiation of "Prufrock" with its inner dialogue: the self speaking to the self. This may indeed have been Eliot's intent, but we have already seen in Pound how the structure of the poems he was writing, in his early books, as only thinly veiled "masks of the self," persists as he discovers his own "impersonal" mythic voice in "Hugh Selwyn Mauberly" and the *Cantos.* We need only concentrate and fuse idioms along with images to achieve a similar, if richer, effect, which might still be called "an intellectual and emotional complex in an instant of time." At one level, the personal and the impersonal form a valid antithesis, but both equally exclude a third term, the interpersonal, the preferred medium of the dramatic monologue. To illustrate this exclusion, we need only compare the first line of "The Love Song of J. Alfred Prufrock" to the first line of "Andrea Del Sarto." They are on the surface very similar:

Prufrock: "Let us go then you and I,"
Andrea: "But do not let us quarrel any more"

However, the entities "you" and "I" and their combination to make an "us" are simply not of the same kind in the two cases. Eliot's are both internal, and part of the poem's meaning is that to externalize them would be paradoxical, as in Pound's little poem on looking at his image in a mirror. Browning's "you" and "I" are external and interactive. This perception, simple and obvious as it is, is what we need to criticize those readers, like Robert Langbaum, who see in speakers like Childe Roland the prototypes of Prufrock. Roland's "I" remains always an agent of interaction despite the fact that the required other does not exist for him. Prufrock's situation is the opposite; he is surrounded by human company but he has no externalized identity capable of communication. The voice of his monologue is like the voice of "The Tomb at Akr Khar" in which the soul "speaks" to the dead man, who has already left the world, the only place where speech can have function and meaning. This conceit works for Pound by rendering language purely textual, timeless, and artifactual, something free of context to be found in tombs and placed in museums or anthologies. Such artifacts are valued for their concentrated intensity, and for Eliot the failure of speech to achieve an intensity of significance is the tragedy of its impoverishment.

Seeking to validate his own myth of absolute presence, Prufrock finds only a gap, an emptiness. The first seventy-two lines of the poem project Prufrock's heroic / erotic moment only in the future tense, and he continually reassures himself that the relevant future is of a comfortable duration:

There will be time, there will be time
To prepare a face to meet the faces that you meet.

Making his enterprise at times trivial and at times preposterously grandiose, he employs his inner nonspeech to defer. Lines 87–111 refer to Prufrock's opportunity in the past tense, as a moment vanished: "And would it have been worth it after all?" The moment sought is a moment of speech, a question, yet the most conspicuous present tense verbs in the poem signify speech that is meaningless:

> In the room the women come and go
> Talking of Michelangelo.

Prufrock, in other words, is a man without a present, at least in terms of meaningful uses of language. The absolute present he seeks is, in the end, only a contradictory ideal, mermaids singing in the silence of the sea. Prufrock himself "should have been a pair of ragged claws / Scuttling across the floors of silent seas," but when he leaves the realm of silence for the realm of actual speech, the plurality within him is destroyed:

> We have lingered in the chambers of the sea
> By sea-girls wreathed with seaweed red and brown
> Till human voices wake us, and we drown.

Prufrock aspires to be nonhuman just as Pound's Paracelsus does. Pound as a poet might be said to be relatively optimistic; he continues to produce poems designed to approximate, re-present, or at least assert the epiphanic absolute present. Eliot depicts the tragic absence of such a nexus, and he focuses on the inadequacy of speech for realizing it. His pessimism might be summarized in Prufrock's elegantly simple "It is impossible to say just what I mean."

To say just what one means would be to achieve presentness in language, and much later, in his greatest poem, Eliot is still regretting the absence of that impossible intersection of time with the timeless:

> So here I am, in the middle way, having had twenty years—
> Twenty years largely wasted, the years of l'entre deux guerres—
> Trying to learn to use words, and every attempt
> Is a wholly new start, and a different kind of failure
> Because one has only learnt to get the better of words
> For the thing one no longer has to say, or the way in which

One is no longer disposed to say it. And so each venture
Is a new beginning, a raid on the inarticulate
With shabby equipment always deteriorating
In the general mess of imprecision of feeling,
Undisciplined squads of emotion . . .

The Four Quartets is a kind of textual metaspeech, a text that, like
Pound's hard images, will stay still long enough to mean. It can
therefore be about the paradoxes of speech that "The Love Song
of J. Alfred Prufrock" tried to depict directly through the vehicle
of the dramatic monologue. Even "Gerontion" was a beginning in
this direction. Pound and Eliot seem to disagree on the possibility
of achieving the desired state of essence in time, but together they
define a dialectical field of value. Similarly, two poems like "Fra
Lippo Lippi" and "Childe Roland to the Dark Tower Came" present the extremes of optimism and pessimism regarding speech as a
medium of human exchange, and they too establish a bivalent field
of value. But the Victorian and modern fields of value themselves
are radically different, and by some kinds of description, they
mutually exclude one another. From the Victorians came the
dramatic monologue. Modern poets, sometimes finding the genre
a convenient source of conventions to transform, soon discarded it.

Historical change, of course, always takes place more gradually
and erratically than subsequent schemata acknowledge. My own
account of a major literary disjunction has been necessarily selective and schematic. In talking about differences between the
Romantic poets and the Victorians, one is aided in the task of
"periodization" by the early deaths of most of the major Romantics and the distinct gap in time before the full emergence of
Browning and Tennyson. The division between the nineteenth
century and the twentieth is nowhere near so neat, and perhaps
the most important factor in complicating the picture is the inter-
penetration of British and American language and literature.
Pound's early debts to Yeats worked to shape Williams and Eliot.
Frost and Hemingway, as well as countless minor writers, took
instruction from Europe. Joyce and Conrad affected everyone
who read them and tried to write afterward. But these influences

came on different schedules for different writers, and a few Americans remained provincial both in their language communities and their literary experiences. It is not therefore surprising that the last great master of the dramatic monologue should be an American who never became a part of the "modernist" network.

This is not the place for an extensive treatment of the poetry of E. A. Robinson; but no proper study of the monologue's history can fail to pay him his due. That Robinson differs sharply from other modern poets is clear to anyone who reads him. As James Dickey puts it, "Robinson has been perhaps the only American poet—certainly the only one of major status—interested exclusively in human beings as subject matter for poetry."[17] He is interested, not just in human beings, but in the fragile social exchanges among them; hence many of his poems are verse portraits of individuals presented from the gently assertive point of view of one who has known and observed them *in communitas.* Robinson's point of interest is nearly always the mysterious semipermeable membrane between the world of the private self and the world in which that self can be known and acknowledged by others:

> We tell you, tapping on our brows,
>   The story as it should be,—
> As if the story of a house
>   Were told, or ever could be;
> We'll have no kindly veil between
> Her visions and those we have seen,—
> As if we guessed what hers have been,
>   Or what they are or would be.

("Eros Turannos," 33–40)

In other poems, Robinson makes a very slight shift to involve the speaker as more than an observer, and when he does, he writes fully realized dramatic monologues. In "Bokardo," for example, the speaker addresses a man who has been his friend and who has betrayed him for money. The poem unveils the past piecemeal just as so many of Browning's do, and when the speaker attacks Bokardo most fiercely, he acknowledges a ghostly response:

Friends, I gather, are small things
In an age when coins are kings;
Even at that, one hardly flings
    Friends before swine.

Rather strong? I knew as much,
    For it made you speak.
No offense to swine, as such,
    But why this hide-and-seek?
You have something on your side,
And you wish you might have died,
So you tell me. And you tried
    One night last week?

                                        (13–24)

Robinson, at least in a great many poems, lacks Browning's skill in
the overlay of verse forms and the rhythms of speech, but even in
his nearest approaches to doggerel rhythm, he achieves an effective
kind of ironic slyness that is peculiar to his style. At his best,
though, Robinson displays his virtuosity as subtlety, through the
modulation of conversational tones in blank verse, such as we find
in "Ben Jonson Entertains a Man from Stratford" or "Toussaint
L'Ouverture (Chateau de Joux, 1803)." The latter poem makes
explicit what might be said about all of the figures in Robinson's
fictional communities: that they are always both terrifyingly
alone and yet not alone:

Am I alone—or is it you, my friend?
I call you friend, but let it not be known
That such a word was uttered in this place.
You are the first that has forgotten duty
So far as to be sorry—and perilously,
For you—that I am not so frozen yet,
Or starved, or blasted, that I cannot feel.
Yes, I can feel, and hear. I can hear something
Behind me. Is it you? There is no light,
But there's a gray place where a window was
Before the sun went down. Was there a sun?

                                        (1–11)

What Robinson so profoundly shares with Browning is his awareness of the disturbing uncertainty of the existence of human beings for each other—the fragility, in other words, of communication. And like Browning, he writes a few poems in which the required interlocutor is genuinely not there, though all of the apparatus of interaction remains. Such a poem is "Rembrandt to Rembrandt," perhaps Robinson's most ambitious monologue. "Rembrandt to Rembrandt" is worth mentioning also because although the speaker speaks to himself, the implications are not what they are in "Prufrock," for Rembrandt is really all the time talking to his dead wife. All of the structures of reciprocity and exchange are there, and it is only fate that has removed the interlocutor necessary to complete the circuit.

V

I have not tried to map a comprehensive history of the dramatic monologue, but I have wished to point out the locations of a few important landmarks. I have done scant justice to the thousands of poems in and near the genre written by minor poets, and I have taken the blurred edges of generic categories fairly well for granted. My main effort in this chapter has been to show something of the range of the monologue's richness and to indicate the literary historical directions of its deterioration. The social context of that deterioration is, of course, complex and would require a more extensive treatment than I could hope to give it here. For the rest of these pages, I want to turn to a different kind of issue. I want partially to divert attention toward the activity of inquiring into a history as distant from us as that of the Victorian period. Why do we ask the questions we ask? Why do we recover history in the way that we do? What do the struggles made manifest in the dramatic monologue have to do with us now? Because I am only one person writing this one book, the only appropriate answer is a personal one. I admit that I am hoping for its wider resonance, but to represent this last critical movement's explicit claim to validity, I have chosen merely to call it "A Personal Epilogue."

EIGHT

A Personal Epilogue

Always historicize!" cries Fredric Jameson on the first page of *The Political Unconscious*. But almost immediately, in good dialectical fashion, he reminds us that there are always two historicities, two "paths": "the path of the object and the path of the subject, the historical origins of the things themselves and that more intangible historicity of the concepts and categories by which we attempt to understand those things.[1] *The Political Unconscious,* as Jameson announces at the outset, takes the second path, concentrating on "the interpretive categories or codes through which we read and receive the text in question." The present book has, thus far, taken the first path, it has examined the text of the dramatic monologue, "the historicity of its forms and of its content, the historical moment of emergence of its linguistic possibilities, the situation-specific function of its aesthetic."[2] But to take this "objective" path without at least acknowledging the situation-specific historicity of the inquiry itself is to risk that nondialectical "historicism" that Althusser has so forcefully shown us Marxism is not.

This is not to say that I conceive of the book as homogeneously "Marxist." Its argument strives to be dialectical, but to me, the first step in the historical self-consciousness of the historian is the recognition of the impossibility of springing wholly free of the ideology of one's own culture. For me, as for everyone living in the West, to think dialectically is a struggle only intermittently successful. The power of Marxist thought today derives from its fierce opposition to the logic of the middle-class rationality that is embodied in each sentence that we speak without consciously re-fashioning our thought in an alternative syntax. The bioenergetic transfer of unitary forces among unitary "subjects" and "objects" supplies a fundamental structure to the simplest sentences in Western languages, the subject-verb-object relations upon which we build linguistically all of our more complicated and contradictory thought.

In this book, I have not attempted to revise the basic thought structures of the prevailing ideology in every sentence or on every page. Such a feat, even if it were possible, would surely produce an unreadable book. Instead, I have alternated between the empiricist methods of traditional scholarship and hermeneutics and a discourse that deprives the object poems of their noncontradictory fixity in historical time and space. The former passages may be considered reactionary or "idealist" by some Marxist critics, while the latter will doubtless strike traditional scholars as too "theoretical" or "speculative." These two movements derive from a split desire: on the one hand, the desire to know and understand "the text" in its historical objectivity, to "possess" it and "teach" it as part of my own professional and intellectual domain, while on the other, the desire to make of that text's interpretation a political gesture that seeks to free it from the oppressive institutional, intellectual, and psychological boundaries that now constrain it. This contradiction is the same contradiction that so many of us feel when we urge our students to think for themselves about a text and yet end by telling them what the text means. The student who thinks for herself, who thinks naively, who knows nothing of the codes and methods of interpretation that are separately sanctioned by separate disciplines or academic departments both delights us and stands in need of our "teaching." She, like her teachers, will reach a point in time when she knows the difference between "thinking like a literary critic" and "thinking like a philosopher" and "thinking like a historian." She will know and practice these divisions, and yet she, again like some of her teachers, will also know that the divisions oppress, that they preclude other kinds of contradictory or speculative or paradoxical thought that seem necessary to the understanding of the total lives we lead.

As the writer of this book, I am still that student. I have said things about dramatic monologues that I think are historically true, that can be defended according to the empiricist rules of the disciplines in which I have been trained. But I have also realized that these historical "truths" have emerged only in response to questions I have asked and that these questions have not always been those sanctioned by my training. In this chapter, therefore, I have chosen to combine a final reflection on the nineteenth century with a self-reflection, a discussion that springs from my own cultural moment and that helps explain the historical questions I had to ask of the nineteenth century in order to write this book.

I want to reflect one last time on the dramatic monologue by indulging in three excurses, one brief one on Charles Darwin's theory of evolution, a longer one on Karl Marx's theory of alienation, and one on the therapeutic principles of Alcoholics Anonymous. This is not a random choice, but it is a personal choice. My interest in alcohol addiction and in a few individual alcoholics has helped me to understand my own culture better, and that understanding has also been liberated in part by what I have learned about the nineteenth century. I do not think this connection is either whimsical or intellectually accidental. Without attempting a full historical explanation of how modern alcoholism developed in advanced capitalist societies, however, I want to suggest that Darwin and Marx, in their very different contexts and idioms, formulate a central epistemological paradox that was also a major concern of the poets who invented the dramatic monologue. That paradox, focused in the concept of alienation, can also clarify the alcoholic's dilemma and his surprising affinity with the "normal," sober epistemology of the world he lives in. I believe that the alcoholics who founded Alcoholics Anonymous came to understand this dilemma through the logic of their own suffering; and I therefore think it no accident that a critical link in their method of recovery has always been the dramatic monologue.

The fragility of lines of verbal connection between the individual and his possible interlocutors seems to me one of the central problems of the dramatic monologue. The open-ended time schemes of these poems, the doubleness of their language, and their partial structures of reciprocity all help to raise a single general question in a wide range of circumstances: Is the individual complete in himself, a self-sustaining monad, the "captain of his soul," and responsible for his fate? Or does the individual have existence only as part of a system, a circuitry of exchange constituted in the communal language that he must speak in order even to express his individuality?[3] The ideology of Victorian England seeks to naturalize or reconcile these contradictory descriptions, but I believe Browning wishes powerfully to assert the latter.[4] Whether he does or not, though, he never oversimplifies. His special poetic invention, the dramatic monologue, presents the problem in all its complexity and ambiguity, and it is only because the problem is finally impossible to solve in the real world that it can be such a rich source of poetic discovery.

The Victorian age with its powerful new emphasis on competition, enterprise, and personal mobility seems to demand, for survival, a strong sense of the self as a discrete entity. Yet with the immense growth of population, decentralized government, industry, and world trade, a compelling anxiety emerges as each person feels swept ever more helplessly by great collective forces that threaten to act and change beyond any singular human control. Hence two new lines of inquiry often appear to supplant the ancient dual question about freedom of the will and divine foreknowledge or predestination: an inquiry into the potential of the individual to control, conquer, or reshape his environment and an inquiry into the nature of the social and biological systems themselves of which the individual increasingly seems so inextricably a part.

For the advent of complexity and its threat to the individual, I can think of no better emblem than Lily Dale's departure for London from Allington in *The Last Chronicle of Barset*. Lily "was never away from home a month in her life," and yet she must plunge into a virtual labyrinth of social pathways and experiences in which her own personal powers seem bound to prove negligible. The question in Lily's mind is a question of control:

> When Crosbie had written to her mother, making a renewed offer which had been rejected, Lily had felt that she certainly need not see him unless

it pleased her to do so. He could hardly force himself upon her at Allington. And as to John Eames, though he would, of course, be welcome at
Allington as often as he pleased to show himself, still there was a security
in the place. She was so much at home there that she could always be
mistress of the occasion. She knew that she could talk to him at Allington
as though from higher ground than that on which he stood himself; but
she felt that this would hardly be the case if she should chance to meet
him in London.[5]

The security of Allington is what the English nineteenth century
feels itself to be losing, and Trollope joins other Victorian novelists
in questioning the purpose of personal understanding in this context: Does man strive to understand his environment in order to
dominate and refashion it or in order to dissolve his individuality
into it without fearing his own extinction? Lily Dale clings to the
ideal of control and may seem heroic at the end. Dorothea Brooke
in *Middlemarch* makes the other choice, and George Eliot invites
us to pass judgment on her at the end. Both novelists, it seems to
me, are gently taunting their reader's most likely assumptions
about independence and personal worth.

When we speak in these terms of an individual's relation to his
or her environment, and that environment is social, we introduce a
central issue in much of Victorian literature, both fiction and
poetry. When the environment is natural, we have, of course,
posed the crucial dilemma of Darwin's *The Origin of Species*. When
we think of Darwin now, we perhaps only think of a catch phrase
like "natural selection" or "the survival of the fittest" (a phrase
Darwin himself never used). Or perhaps we recall an argument
something like the following: The world at any time has a great
many species in it, competing for control of the world's resources.
Variations in a species that increase a strength needed for local
survival tend to be preserved in the species and help that species
displace others. When the variation is marked enough and effective
enough, we get a new species. Hence we have explained both the
extinction of weaker existing forms of life and the emergence of
stronger new ones.

Recently, modern ecologists have perceived a fatal flaw in this scenario. Darwin's basic unit of survival, they argue, is the individual species, subspecies, or family of organisms. Everything outside this unit is designated as an environment to be conquered, appropriated, or, if it consists of other, competing, species, to be displaced or vanquished. The model works well enough when the competition among these entities called species remains fairly well balanced, but a strange thing happens when one species becomes extremely successful. The process of displacement proves to be reflexive. The most conspicuous example of unbalanced competition arises from the unique ability of the human species to dominate its environment through the development of technology. The cerebral variation commonly called rational thought, along with modern methods of production, has resulted in a power of adaptation so destructive of competing forms of life that the effects threaten to vanquish the vanquisher in his moment of greatest strength. Humankind is beginning to learn the hard way that a species that destroys its environment destroys itself, that the human organism is inextricably part of his environment, and that it is forever part of him. If it is defeated or conquered, he is defeated or conquered. Hence, some ecologists argue, we must reject a major premise of Darwin's theory and say that the unit that survives or fails to survive is not the single species or organism but a set of relations among species that constitutes an environment.[6]

From the point of view of the human individual, this means something like what Gregory Bateson says in his *Steps to an Ecology of Mind:* "The total self-corrective unit which processes information, or, as I say, 'thinks' and 'acts' and 'decides,' is a *system* whose boundaries do not at all coincide with the boundaries either of the body or of what is popularly called the 'self' or 'consciousness.' "[7] If I have been right about the dramatic monologue, Bateson's comment might well describe the awareness Browning is trying to set against that of the individual or unitary subject. But I would argue that writers like Bateson are at least partially unfair in their homogeneous interpretations of Darwin. It is true that *The Origin of Species* is liberally laced with passages like the following that are responsible for popular notions of Darwin's thought:

As many more individuals of each species are born than can possibly survive; and as, consequently, there is a frequently recurring struggle for
existence, it follows that any being, if it vary however slightly in any manner profitable to itself, under the complex and sometimes varying conditions of life, will have a better chance of surviving, and thus be *naturally
selected*. From the strong principle of inheritance, any selected variety will
tend to propagate its new and modified form.[8]

Nearly as often, though, we find visions of natural cooperation that
are strikingly modern in their awareness of the complexity of
ecological systems:

In the case of the misseltoe, which draws its nourishment from certain
trees, which has seeds that must be transported by certain birds, and which
has flowers with separate sexes absolutely requiring the agency of certain
insects to bring pollen from one flower to the other, it is equally prepos-
terous to account for the structure of this parasite, with its relations to
several distinct organic beings, by the effects of external conditions, or of
habit, or of the volition of the plant itself.[9]

These two passages occur within a page of one another, and they
represent two opposing poles of thought for Darwin. Just as for
Browning, the dramatic monologist's listener is both there and not
there, both part of the self and an alien otherness, Darwin's "environment" is both part of the very life of the individual organism
or species and a potentially threatening competitor for the resources needed for survival. But the natural world is not neatly
divided into the support systems and adversaries that Darwin's two
statements invoke. The same elephant that keeps a certain tree's
foliage ideally pruned at one time may, in a drought year or in the
case of its own unaccustomed confinement or overpopulation, deci-
mate the landscape and destroy the same species altogether. How
do we know in nature when to view the individual in isolated struggle and when to view it in such a texture of cooperation that only
a statement like Bateson's can suffice to describe the phenomenon?

Far from taking the unilateral individualist / competitive position, Darwin's treatise does no more than pose the question. Darwin is troubled throughout, and with a refreshing candor, precisely
because he cannot reconcile these two epistemological poles:

The missletoe is dependent on the apple and a few other trees, but can only in a far-fetched sense be said to struggle with these trees, for if too many of these parasites grow on the same tree, it will languish and die. But several seedling missletoes, growing close together on the same branch, may more truly be said to struggle with each other. As the missletoe is disseminated by birds, its existence depends on birds; and it may metaphorically be said to struggle with other fruit-bearing plants, in order to tempt birds to devour and thus disseminate its seeds rather than those of other plants. In these several senses, which pass into each other, I use for convenience sake the general term of struggle for existence.[10]

Here he acknowledges the disquieting (and dialectical) fact that the antitheses, competition and cooperation, tend to "pass into each other" and may, at times, be sustained only "metaphorically." The missletoe's competition with fruit-bearing plants cannot reasonably be extended to describe its relation to the apple tree, and the most intense competition of all may be between organisms of the same species in close proximity. All of these worried observations tend to devalue the boundaries that mark off species as individual competing units. Yet Darwin's analysis as a whole requires the discrete existence of these units for its logic.[11]

Discreteness, or what we might call "entityship," is essential in Darwin's world; relationship is accidental. It does not really matter whether the entity in question is an individual or a collective. Darwin does warn against affixing terms like "habit" or "volition" onto collective entities. He sees rightly that these concepts are only appropriate to individuals. But why does he face or anticipate the temptation to make such a confusion? It is because he fundamentally treats collectives as individuals in that his main points of reference are their internal uniformity and the boundaries that distinguish them from other species and from the "conditions of life."

I want to stress that in neither Darwin's case nor in Browning's is the interesting problem one of choosing between the individual and the collective, between self-interest and dependence, the organism and its environment. The agonizing question in its general form is whether to preserve these dualisms as a basis for knowledge and action or to abolish them; whether to accept the ancient philosophical distinction between mind and matter, the inside and the outside, the self and the other, or to insist that mind and matter are always inextricably part of one another, that the world is made up, not of essential entities, but of essential relationships. When Darwin worries about terms like "volition" and the implications of discrete will inherent in a phrase like "struggle for existence," his field of anxiety is wider than the biological sciences. Knowing that his ideas are new and inevitably controversial, he must use a language that is ideologically acceptable to his audience. It is also his own most comfortable language, yet at times, he seems to see that it imposes an excessively digital structure on the world, that it quickly becomes "metaphorical." Indeed, Darwin's whole theory of natural selection is a metaphor. It is based on the model of the selective breeding of domestic plants and animals, a process in which the determining singular will is provided by the human breeder. Breeders create ecologies that are controlled closed systems with clear boundaries, just as Lily Dale could create a controlled and closed social system at Allington. Further, both Darwin and Lily Dale sense that the greater complexity of open systems like natural ecologies or London can be neither ignored nor equated wth more limited and familiar spaces. In the end, both probably lean back toward the safety of their Cartesian metaphors as templates for the world. Browning, I think, distinctly leans toward the systemic view. In the case of Karl Marx, our final great observer of the nineteenth century's world, there can be no uncertainty.

For Marx, the isolation of the discrete individual as captain of his soul and imaginary master of a fate that, in reality, increasingly masters him is perhaps the central contradiction of capitalist economies. Under capitalism, the chief mode of material progress is the division of wage-labor. The worker who produces can no longer see his life and his labor as part of an integral product and as part of the lives that consume that product. Instead of making a cart that his neighbor uses to bring food back to the cartmaker's family and community, the modern worker under capitalism fastens rivets into steel plates that become boilers that become parts of locomotives that bring food to distributors who sell to merchants who sell at crushingly inflated values to the exploited worker. Hence, not only for that worker but for the manager and the capitalist too, life and work become "estranged" or "alienated." The worker, as an integral human being, becomes alienated from the product of his labor, and he becomes alienated from other workers whose labor in turn produces only a meaningless fragment under the increasing division of labor. Marx says that this process of fragmentation or alienation obscures in the consciousness of worker and capitalist alike the reality of work and productivity as central to human nature. Hence the worker begins to think of himself as no more than a thing, one more commodity to be bought and sold by the capitalist. Capitalism attempts to assuage the alienated worker by creating a mystique of the so-called sovereignty of the individual and of the imaginary opportunities opened to each individual by free competition in the marketplace.

What the individualist myth obscures is the fact that all of the life-relations in which the individual participates are part of what that individual is. The individual, at least according to Marx's early writings, is made up of all of the relations and interactions in which he participates, relations that define him, not as a private person or as one of the people, but as a member of a specific class. He has no free identity apart from these relations, and the illusion that he does is merely a trick designed by those who rule him to conceal the fact that the system of relations under capitalism exploits and dehumanizes his labor and his life.[12]

This is what Marx calls alienation, the myth that the individual is a self-sustaining enterprise engaged in an equally matched struggle for existence (to use Darwin's term) with other such individuals. The deception is simple but elegant in the way it deals with the inevitable perception that the struggle is not evenly matched. Misled by the ideology of the individual "private person," the worker feels that he is losing the struggle for survival because the adversary, the wealthy manager or capitalist, begins, as an individual, with an initial and insuperable advantage in strength. Thus the worker's anger is directed at his immediate oppressor, and if he is sufficiently moved to rebel, he tries to remove that oppressor's strength as though it were a discrete commodity or attribute.

A ready example of such logic would be the various forms of Luddite violence in England during the first half of the nineteenth century. Pressed into poverty by increased capital in the form of machines acquired by factory owners, the workers expressed their frustrations and hostility by smashing the machines. This response is naive, not because mechanized industry was inevitable and the machines replaceable, but because it represents a failure to avoid a basic epistemological mistake. The workers, accepting the myth of individual struggle, misidentified their adversaries as the individual capitalists represented materially by their capital (the machines). But the struggle for survival is unequal precisely because the adversary is not an individual but a class system, a system of which the worker is ironically himself an integral part in the very form of his rebellion. The worker is taught to regard the self as the unit that survives in the material world, while as in ecology, the real unit of survival is the systemic self-plus-environment, and only by altering the total system can the material lot of the real self be improved.

When the individual believes that he struggles against other individuals but in fact struggles vainly against a system, he confronts a power intrinsically and logically different from selfhood, and the imaginary self thus becomes what Marx called an abstraction. This competing unitary self does not really exist; it is merely an idea, a disguise for a dominant network of relations. The result is contradiction, a struggle simultaneously against and in behalf of a thing called "self." The paradox is logical and similar to that of Epimenides the Cretan when he stated "All statements by Cretans are lies." If Epimenides is telling the truth, he must be lying, and if he is lying, he must be telling the truth. Bertrand Russell solved this paradox by dividing propositions into a hierarchy of logical types. A proposition about a category (second order proposition) is, according to Russell, of a higher logical type than a proposition about a member of the category (first order proposition). And since a category cannot be a member of itself, these two orders of proposition cannot logically either affirm or contradict one another. Therefore, Epimenides' statement amounts to saying that "all first order propositions by Cretans are lies." In saying this, he makes a second order statement, leaving open the possibility that he is now telling the truth, and that we can expect that all first order propositions by Epimenides, a Cretan, will be lies.[13]

By this kind of logic, it becomes possible to say that the Luddite rebellions failed because of a confusion of logical types. The concept "individual" is, at one level, the name for a particular system of relations under capitalism. As such, it is the worker's natural enemy. But "individual" is also a name for the self who suffers in the material world. These two applications, like the two applications of the name "Cretan," are of different logical types, but the worker is prevented from knowing this. To escape the paralyzing contradiction, he must ignore one of these concepts. Feeling the individual-as-self to be the more "real," or "universal," the worker implicitly discards the individual-as-part-of-system and searches out the other individuals-as-selves to struggle against. The problem Marx saw so clearly is that, under the tutelage of the bourgeoisie, the worker has learned unwittingly to invert the order, taking the individual-as-self to be of a higher (more universal) type than the individual-as-part-of-system.

These illusions arise under particular historical conditions, among others, the awareness on the part of the individual of powerful and mysterious new forces that seem to dominate his life but elude his understanding. Such conditions enhance the prestige of "chance" in the common vocabulary and spawn elaborate machineries of thought designed to displace "chance" in the chain of causal explanation. In *The German Ideology,* Marx writes, "In the present epoch, the domination of material conditions over individuals, and the suppression of individuality by chance, has assumed its sharpest and most universal form, thereby setting existing individuals a very definite task. It has set them the task of replacing the domination of circumstances and of chance over individuals by the domination of individuals over chance and circumstances."[14] This is, in part, Darwin's task, but Darwin could only partly accept the myth on which the task is based. Thus he created, or adapted, a fictional entity, the species, as a kind of quasi individual: part individual-as-self, acquiring the power to dominate "chance and circumstances," and part individual-as-part-of-system, escaping the contradictions of that imaginary autonomy. In this

uneasy balance, his fictions are like those of Browning and Tennyson; Browning and Tennyson, in turn, continually struggle with
the contradictions that Marx so brilliantly analyzed.

In order to show why Marx's formulation of the concept of
alienation is so closely related in my own thinking to Browning,
we need to refine a bit on the idea of a cybernetic system that I
introduced in chapter 5. First, we can say that a cybernetic system
of the kind allowed into the world by the dramatic monologue is a
discursive as opposed to a symbolic system. These are the terms
that I used in chapter 2 to distinguish between two modes of relating ideal and material realities. It may be recalled that in that discussion, I used the example of the Greek and Egyptian methods of
representing the gods: the Greek believes that the representation
should resemble its ideal object in a way that can be discursively
explained, while the Egyptian rejects human claims to know the
gods directly and therefore represents them with arbitrary symbols.
Romantic poetic forms, as I argued, attempt to signify symbolically "the eternal, the infinite and the one"; Victorian dramatic
monologues also line up with an ideal reality larger than their
own moment, but that reality is not an ideal wholeness. Moreover,
the link is always discursive and explicable.

If we now return to our logical terms for a moment and define
a system as a reality of a higher logical type (in Russell's sense)
than its constituent parts, we can see that the problem posed by
the Egyptian and the Greek has its application to the problem of
relating any ideal whole to the material parts that compose it.
This brings us back to Marx and the role of abstraction in alienation. Despite many of the tenets of "vulgar Marxism," Marx did
not insist on a simple bipolar choice between material and ideal
values. Rather, he called into question the prevailing mode of relating the two: positing ideal (or spiritual or legal or political)
values as being of a logically higher order than material or economic
values. Logically, Marx demanded an inversion of this order,
recognizing it as an ideology designed to protect those already in
control of material production and wealth. But Marx's challenge
was more than an inversion; by making the material and economic
order the logical context for the ideal, he also changed the relation

between them from a symbolic to a discursive one. This is what Louis Althusser calls Marx's "theoretical revolution."

Althusser designates the problematic relation between the whole, or higher reality, and the parts, or material components, by the name "effectivity." This effectivity is determined, according to Althusser, by the question of whether the higher order phenomenon is conceived as structured. In the terms of the debate between the Egyptian and the Greek, the effectivity of the gods in the world will depend on whether the gods can be formally (i.e., structurally) known. I shall quote at length from Althusser's *Reading Capital* in order to show how he places the issue historically:

> Very schematically, we can say that classical philosophy (the existing Theoretical) had two and only two systems of concepts with which to think effectivity. The mechanistic system, Cartesian in origin, which reduced causality to a *transitive* and analytical effectivity: it could not be made to think the effectivity of a whole on its elements, except at the cost of extraordinary distortions (such as those in Descartes' "psychology" and biology). But a second system was available, one conceived precisely in order to deal with the effectivity of a whole on its elements: the Leibnizian concept of expression. This is the model that dominates all Hegel's thought. But it presupposes in principle that the whole in question be reducible to an inner essence, of which the elements of the whole are then no more than the phenomenal forms of expression, the inner principle of the essence being present at each point in the whole, such that at each moment it is possible to write the immediately adequate equation; such and such an element (economic, political, legal, literary, religious, etc., in Hegel) = the inner essence *of the whole*. Here was a model which made it possible to think the effectivity of the whole on each of its elements, but if this category—inner essence / outer phenomenon—was to be applicable everywhere and at every moment to each of the phenomena arising in the totality in question, *it pre-supposed that the whole had a certain nature, precisely the nature of a "spiritual" whole in which each element was expressive of the entire totality as an "ars totalis".* In other words, Leibniz and Hegel did have a category for the effectivity of the whole on its elements or parts, but on the absolute condition that the whole was not a structure.
>
> If the whole is posed as *structured*, i.e., as possessing a type of unity quite different from the type of unity of the spiritual whole, this is no longer the case: not only does it become impossible to think the determination of the elements by the structure in the categories of analytical and

transitive causality, it also becomes impossible to think in the category of the global expressive causality of a universal inner essence immanent in its phenomenon. The proposal to think the determination of the elements of a whole by the structure of the whole posed an absolutely new problem in the most theoretically embarrassing circumstances, for there were no philosophical concepts available for its resolution.[15]

The passage is long and knotty, but in the canon of recent interpretations of Marx, it seems to me one of the most important moments. Althusser has shown that it was Marx who disturbed the prestige of symbolic world views with the fundamentally different concept of the world as a discursive system. In the two main philosophical options discussed by Althusser, whether the whole is said to cause or to express its constituent phenomena, the relation is a symbolic one. The verbs "cause" and "express" can no more found a discourse of effectivity than the verb "symbolize" can. Because they denote all possible relations between part and whole, they resemble the Saussurian "signify," which Derrida has so effectively "deconstructed" to show its dependence on a transcendent unity or logos. All such verbs, whether they point to a scholastic "final cause," a Hegelian "absolute Spirit," or a transcendent "signified," stand for an unarticulated gap between individual elements and their inclusive context or "whole." This is part of the reason why, in a symbolic writer like Shelley, transcendental metaphysics and necessitarianism are not logically incompatible.

For Marx, on the other hand, the whole is not an absolute presence ontologically apart from all of those partial realities that are always emerging and disappearing in time and space. Rather, the whole is an immanent order, articulated, being written, itself always disappearing and reforming. This immanent order is what cybernetics calls a pattern, what Althusser calls a structure. In a symbolic system, the primary distinction is between material things and the ideal "essence" that includes those things. In a cybernetic system, the distinction is between differences and the pattern of those differences. The system does not, of course, organize all measurable differences. Between the cat and the mat, the mat and the earth, the earth and the universe, there exist an infinite number of differences. To incorporate these items into a system, to recognize a pattern that relates them, we say that certain differences "make a difference," become "information," while other differences become irrelevant, become "noise" in the system.[16] Moreover, the difference that makes a difference between the cat and the mat is not a material entity; it is not "in" either the cat or the mat, any more than the difference called "poverty" resides either in the worker's personal deprivations or in the capitalist's machines. In a cybernetic system, some differences may correspond to the boundaries between objects or entities, and some, like temperature or time or exploitation, may not. Thus, the "parts" of a cybernetic system may be either "things" or relationships or both. Symbolic systems are defined by single-valued relationships among "particulars"; whether identity / difference, cause / effect, employer / employee, competitor species / supporting species, or something else.

The theory of alienation, it seems to me, is both a critique of symbolic relations between the material and the ideal and the presentation of a discourse that offers an alternative. Althusser is no doubt correct in his assertion that this theoretical revolution belongs chiefly to Marx. But Marx would be the first to insist that his own individual innovation must be systematically "part of" more general historical changes. These changes include less formally theoretical experiments in "thinking the effectivity" of discursive or structured systems, experiments that emerge in languages as disparate as those of science and poetry in the late nineteenth century. Let us look at a literary example of our two kinds of systems.

For novelists, people exist in systems or communities. Here is one kind of system:

> Did it matter then, she asked herself, walking towards Bond Street, did it matter that she must inevitably cease completely; all this must go on without her; did she resent it; or did it not become consoling to believe that death ended absolutely: but that somehow in the streets of London, on the ebb and flow of things, here, there, she survived, Peter survived, lived in each other, she being part, she was positive, of the trees at home; of the house there, ugly rambling all to bits and pieces as it was; part of people she had never met; being laid out like a mist between the people she knew best, who lifted her on their branches as she had seen the trees lift the mist, but it spread ever so far, her life, herself.[17]

At first glance, this meditation seems worthy of the most thorough-going "ecology of mind." It comes early in Virginia Woolf's *Mrs. Dalloway,* and its principle is repeated several times in the novel, nearly always attended by metaphors of all-connecting mists, threads, and spider's webs. People here are not isolated; they are part of a larger whole, and they feel this "being part of" as "life." It is not just a system that Clarissa Dalloway senses, however; it is a symbolic system, since the nature of particular interactions among its members is incidental to the felt relation "part of." Between Clarissa and Peter Walsh, relations exist that can be described dis-cursively in finely articulated detail, but Clarissa feels equally "part of people she had never met," like the war-maddened suicide, Septimus Warren Smith, or the unknown old lady whom Clarissa watches through a window across the street from her own house. "Part of" is an immaterial essence that allows Mrs. Dalloway to hope for a kind of immortality.

A different kind of system governs the novels of George Eliot. Her entire task is to articulate the differences in time and space that create the finely calibrated constraints and liberties implicit in the pattern of life as interaction. Musing on the leisure of a writer like Fielding to expand on the universal significance of events, George Eliot's narrator concludes,

> We belated historians must not linger after his example; and if we did so, it is probable that our chat would be thin and eager, as if delivered from a camp-stool in a parrot-house. I at least have so much to do in unravelling certain human lots, and seeing how they were woven and interwoven, that all the light I can command must be concentrated on this particular web, and not dispersed over that tempting range of relevancies called the universe. [18]

The metaphor of the spider's web is important to George Eliot, as it is to Virginia Woolf, but here the web indicates a complexity of interactions and exchanges in time and space, a pattern of "dif-ferences that make a difference" in the relations that are part of the immanent human system called *Middlemarch.* When George Eliot reviewed Browning's *Men and Women,* she commented on his abandonment of Romantic "feelings too deep for expression" in favor of "dramatic indication." Both may be vehicles for exploring the individual's participation in forces greater than the self, but these higher order contexts are of fundamentally different kinds in the two cases of symbolic and discursive wholes. Fred Vincy, in *Middlemarch,* can displace his own alienation because he can finally relinquish a concept of his own "self" that is wholly abstract or symbolic. The result is a partial return to nonalienated labor and an effectivity of interaction within a structured whole. Fra Lippo Lippi achieves a similar disalienation of labor in painting because he inverts the authoritative logical typing that places the nonmaterial God in the role of creating material man. For Lippo, the artist creates God with his labor, thus establishing a reciprocity and structuring a system—a community—that relates the material to the ideal discursively.

In discussing the morphology of alienation, I have been deliberately using a hybrid language. The language of logical typing, derived from Russell, has been invoked in recent years by communication theorists to understand acute modern problems that Marx could not have foreseen, but it indicates a continuity in the structure of alternative epistemologies from the nineteenth century to the present. By way of illustrating this continuity, I have chosen to offer a final excursus on the methods of Alcoholics Anonymous. This choice has been made for several reasons. First, alcoholism affects everyone who might read this book. Second, the methods of Alcoholics Anonymous claim, in combating the problem, a strikingly superior rate of success than that of more traditional forms of individual treatment such as psychoanalysis. Third, a theory of alcoholism exists that is compatible with the methods of Alcoholics Anonymous and that employs the tools of logical typing much as I have used them in discussing Marxian alienation. Fourth, to bring our argument full circle, Alcoholics Anonymous uses in its treatment a device that is formally very like the dramatic monologue. I think that my own analysis of the monologue in this book can explain why coming to terms with its conventions helps the alcoholic to recover.

I have said that when the individual struggles against a system, he confronts a power intrinsically and logically greater than selfhood, and the imaginary self thus becomes what Marx called an abstraction. In saying this, I have already begun to use the carefully chosen language of Alcoholics Anonymous. Once recognize that your life is dominated by a power greater than selfhood, and, according to Marx, social change has already begun. With this premise in mind, I want to introduce the first three of the "Twelve Steps" that, in the program of Alcoholics Anonymous, are necessary for the movement toward sobriety to begin. The other nine are really all implied by these three:

1. We admitted we were powerless over alcohol—that our lives had become unmanageable.
2. Came to believe that a Power greater than ourselves could restore us to sanity.
3. Made a decision to turn our will and our lives over to the care of God *as we understood Him.* (emphasis mine)

Alcoholics Anonymous has often been criticized for its sham religiosity, but the irreducible fact is that it works to help alcoholics achieve and retain sobriety. For some time, I have been interested in trying to explain why AA works, and I have been convinced that these phrases, "God as we understood Him" and "a Power greater than ourselves," are essential to one stage of its success. In brief, for sustained sobriety to be possible, I think the alcoholic must achieve a two-phase shift away from a state of mind in which the essential materials of the world are discrete individual entities. This shift requires first a displacement of the individual prestige by a symbolic system and, second, the transformation of that symbolic system into a discursive one. I think the religious language signifies the intermediate symbolic phase.

The passage about systems that I quoted earlier from Gregory Bateson is actually taken from an essay on alcoholism in which Bateson argues that addiction to alcohol is based, in this particular moment of Western culture, on what he calls alcoholic pride. The alcoholic perpetuates his drinking by a "cycle of risk" in which he repeatedly tests the power of his unaided individual will to resist excessive drinking. After a brief period of being "on the wagon," the drinker must prove to himself and to others that he can take "just one drink" and no more. He is, in his pride, the "captain of his soul"—the AA literature actually uses this term—and he attempts to assert his independence in a competition for dominance with the bottle. Often, the discourse of the alcoholic personifies the bottle. It becomes alternately the lover, as when the drinker invites it to "kiss and make up," and the enemy. As enemy, the bottle is sometimes given relatively neutral male names, such as "John Barleycorn" or "Mr. Gin," or more overtly adversarial ones like "Demon Rum." Indeed, the richness of alcoholic demonology points both to the need for an initial counterforce conceived in supernatural terms and to the central epistemological contradiction underlying alcoholic pride.

The problem is that the bottle is not a real adversary; it is not another individual as the alcoholic imagines himself to be. It is not "this bottle"; it is "The Bottle." It is an abstraction, and as such it cannot be defeated or vanquished in direct competition. The alcoholic always eventually loses the struggle of wills between himself and the bottle, thus setting up a new cycle of testing and failing. This is because The Bottle has no will and no soul to be subdued; it is a part of the alcoholic's self, but it is also a power greater than the self.

The key to Bateson's theory is his perception that the epistemology of drunkenness is not an aberration, not a rejection of the epistemology of sobriety in the alcoholic's world. Rather, the alcoholic carries to one kind of logical conclusion the pattern of thought that is the most persistent norm of his culture. It is often said that people drink for escape, that the "pressures" of business, of marriage, or of parenthood are too much to bear without anesthesia. But alcohol is more than a physical anesthetic. It is a transference of the logic of individual competition and defeat into a region where the individual's "defeat" is not so readily contrasted with an imaginary myth of victory. The alcoholic can usually laugh off his defeats at the hand of John Barleycorn, and he continues "not to take them too seriously" long past the time when everyone who knows him knows that he has a drinking problem. Typically, it is far down the road of physical deterioration that the alcoholic accepts the fact that his failure to be "captain of his soul" in confrontation with The Bottle has had consequences more serious than all of those other "failures" of his imaginary individuality.

Alcoholics Anonymous understands all of this, and from it comes one of its most important premises: that the alcoholic cannot recover from his disease by himself. He must first admit that he, as an individual, is powerless over alcohol, and this is the most important and most difficult step: giving up the myth of the unitary self upon which all of his pride and all of his life's strivings have been based. Then, having seen that alcohol is really a power greater than the self, the alcoholic must perform an act of substitution. For a destructive power he must substitute a sustaining power that, in the words of the second step, "can restore him to sanity." At first the substitution is an ideal one, with a spiritual God replacing The Bottle as the symbolic repository of the drinker's will. It allows him to relinquish the myth of control by making, as AA puts it, "a decision to turn our will and our lives over to the care of God as we understand Him." This "letting go" initiates a process of disalienation, but the first step is extremely difficult. Alcoholics Anonymous has found that the alcoholic must usually be very sick in body and spirit to be able to take the first step—and he or she can almost never do it alone. Hence the absolutely crucial importance of the AA meeting and its particular format.

My own view is that the AA meeting itself is the real power greater than the self, and the catalytic ingredient that facilitates the disalienation of the individual alcoholic is the dramatic monologue. In every AA meeting, one member stands before the group and tells the story of his drunkenness and, where appropriate, his progress toward recovery. The story is always exactly the same story, with only the most minor rearrangements of episodes as formulaic as those of a Russian folktale. Occasionally the story is funny, but usually it is painfully boring. A writer like Browning, not wishing to be boring, takes great pains to de-familiarize his monologues, but AA "drunkalogues," as they call them, have a different purpose. That purpose is to destroy the illusion of the uniqueness of the self and to impress each member with the fact that he or she has become no more than the embodiment of the most predictable of types. Just as during the growth of capitalism, the maker of carts becomes only an undifferentiated "laborer," the alcoholic has become an empty abstraction.

The creation of this awareness is, of course, only half the function of the drunkalogue; the other half is restorative. The structure of the drunkalogue is very nearly that of the dramatic monologue, including the tentative trying out of fragile interconnections between the speaker and interlocutors whose responses are sometimes hard to interpret. Gradually, though, the speaker becomes less and less an isolated individual and more part of a community of unusually open communicative pathways. He learns, in other words, to turn his will and his life over to the care of a power greater than the self, and that power is none other than the system of communication and exchange that is the AA community itself. This sense of being "part of" remains with him and interrupts the cycle of alcoholic pride in risk. The higher power is no longer an adversary external to the self (The Bottle); it is now internal to the self through the creation of a certain kind of community founded on the mechanism of the drunkalogue and its social environment. The drunkalogue represents, in other words, a moment of transition between an epistemology based on a symbolic inclusion of the self within the other—the religious conversion of the Twelve Steps—and one based on communicative participation in a discursive system. At the beginning of the alcoholic's experience of the drunkalogue, he is learning to accept a single-valued mode of relation: his own typicality. Later, as he accepts more of the responsibility of helping other alcoholics recover, articulated distinctions reappear in his relations within the group. But these distinctions are now systemic measures of dynamic "difference" and not signifiers of the static boundaries that alienate the self. God remains in the discourse of Alcoholics Anonymous, but the qualifying phrase "as we understood Him" takes on a new importance as the alcoholic experiences the full restorative cycle of his new community. I would argue that "God as we understood Him" in Alcoholics Anonymous is very near to God as Lippo understands him in "Fra Lippo Lippi." I would also argue that the recovering alcoholic goes through a process quite analogous to the evolution of Lippo's relation to the constable who apprehends him. We may recall that Lippo begins by attempting to survive by matching the abstract power of his patron's prestige against the systemic legal power of the constable, a symmetrical competition. But he soon realizes that his real success depends on transforming this power relationship into a solidarity relationship with the officer based on the establishment of reciprocal circuits of communication. This establishment is the dramatic monologue. We might say that in doing this, Lippo is giving his will and his life over to the care of God as he understands him, and this way of putting it would be supported by the vision of God-as-part-of-system that Lippo gives us near the poem's closing.

Alcoholism is only one conspicuous way of displaying a disease that afflicts us all to some degree. Marx called it a contradiction, not a disease, and he gave it the general name of alienation. But while Marx and the founders of Alcoholics Anonymous address the problem in its most destructive manifestations, the vision of writers like Browning and Darwin is more ambivalent and, at times, more subtle. If we are wise, we do not read them seeking social or physical cures, but this does not mean that we can only read them as disconnected artifacts of a lost and irrelevant age. What Browning and Tennyson and Darwin and Marx and Bateson all see so clearly is that we are always "part of" the system of history that we ourselves write, and that our opportunity as listeners and readers who also speak and write is not just to "learn" this lesson but to participate in unfolding its continuities.

"Always historicize!" This chapter has, of course, made no attempt to look deeply into the methods of the chapters that precede it. Jameson is right to say that a practical choice must be made, and this book's choice has been to look hardest at the dramatic monologue itself. To be more self-reflexive would be to analyze at length the work of those contemporary writers who have helped to shape and sharpen my own procedures. Only in Marx do the nineteenth century and the discourse of this book about the nineteenth century truly meet. Nevertheless, the purpose of this epilogue, if not to analyze the subject of the book's discourse, has at least been to acknowledge the presence of such a subject, one that is not omniscient but historically fixed by the questions it can find to ask about the past.

Notes

ONE   Toward the Subject of the Dramatic Monologue

1. Karl Marx, *Selected Writings*, ed. David McClellan (Oxford: Oxford University Press, 1977), p. 164.
2. Ibid., pp. 359–60.
3. See, for example, Engels's letter to Starkenburg of January 25, 1894, in Marx and Engels, *Basic Writings on Politics and Philosophy*, ed. L. Feuer (New York: Doubleday, 1959), pp. 411–12. For an elaboration of the implication of Engels's view, see Georg Lukacs, "Marx and Engels on Aesthetics," in *Writer and Critic and Other Essays* (New York: Grosset and Dunlap, 1970), pp. 61ff.
4. Marx, *Selected Writings*, p. 359.
5. Hans Robert Jauss, "The Idealist Embarrassment: Observations on Marxist Aesthetics," *New Literary History* 7, no. 1 (1975): 191–208.
6. Marx, *Selected Writings*, p. 389.
7. See Lukacs, "Marx and Engels on Aesthetics," p. 79: "The Marxist conception of realism is realism in which the essence of reality is exposed perceptually and artistically. This represents the dialectical application of the theory of reflection to the field of aesthetics." The most energetic defense of Lukacs has been made by Fredric Jameson in "The Case for Georg Lukacs," in *Marxism and Form* (Princeton: Princeton University Press, 1971), pp. 160–205.
8. That the reflection theory neglected questions of form and of the production of aesthetic objects was explicitly acknowledged by Engels in a letter to Franz Mehring, July 14, 1893: "There is only one point lacking, which, however, Marx and I always failed to stress enough in our writings and in regard to which we are all equally guilty. That is to say, we all laid, and *were bound* to lay, the main emphasis in the first place, on the *derivation* of political juridical and other ideological notions, and of actions arising through the medium of these notions, from basic economic facts. But in so doing we neglected the formal side—the ways and means by

265

which these notions, etc., come about—for the sake of the content" (quoted in Marx and Engels, *On Literature and Art,* ed. Lee Baxandall and Stefan Morawski [St. Louis: Telos Press, 1973], p. 99).

9. Lucien Goldmann, *Towards a Sociology of the Novel* (London: Tavistock Publications, 1975), p. 6.

10. Ibid., p. 7.

11. Jameson, *Marxism and Form,* p. 375. For Jameson's contention that Goldmann's theory is no more than a "rearrangement within the model" that includes reflection theories, see especially p. 382.

12. Ibid., pp. 327–59.

13. Robert Weimann, *Structure and Society in Literary History* (Charlottesville: University of Virginia Press, 1976; Baltimore: Johns Hopkins University Press, 1984) p. 162.

14. Ibid., p. 171.

15. Louis Althusser and Etienne Balibar, *Reading Capital,* trans. Ben Brewster (London: NLB, 1977), p. 95.

16. Ibid., p. 99.

17. Ibid., p. 100.

18. See Fernand Braudel, *On History,* trans. Sarah Matthews (Chicago: University of Chicago Press, 1980); Lucien Febvre, *A New Kind of History,* ed. Peter Burke, trans. K. Folka (London: Routledge and Kegan Paul, 1973), esp. the title essay, pp. 27–43; George Kubler, "Period Style and Meaning in Ancient American Art," *New Literary History* 1, no. 2 (1970): 127–44; Claudio Guillen, *Literature as System* (Princeton: Princeton University Press, 1971); F. P. Pickering, *Literature and Art in the Middle Ages* (Coral Gables, Fla: University of Miami Press, 1970).

19. Althusser and Balibar, *Reading Capital,* p. 100.

20. Ibid., pp. 184–93. In *The Political Unconscious* (Ithaca: Cornell University Press, 1980), Fredric Jameson treats Althusser's position in terms that are somewhat similar to my own.

21. Althusser and Balibar, *Reading Capital,* p. 100.

22. E. P. Thompson, *The Poverty of Theory and Other Essays* (New York: Monthly Review Press, 1978), pp. 1–210.

23. Loy D. Martin, "Literary Invention: The Illusion of the Individual Talent," *Critical Inquiry* 6, no. 4 (1980). 649–67.

24. Raymond Williams, *Marxism and Literature* (Oxford: Oxford University Press, 1977), p. 59.

25. Ibid., p. 19.

26. Ibid., p. 59.

27. Ibid.

28. Ibid., p. 60.

29. Ibid., p. 38. This is also consistent with Althusser, for whom "there is no

practice except by and in ideology" (*Lenin and Philosophy* [London: New Left Books, 1971], p. 159).

30. Jacques Lacan, response to Charles Morazé, quoted in Richard Macksey and Eugenio Donato, eds., *The Structuralist Controversy, The Languages of Criticism, and the Sciences of Man* (Baltimore: Johns Hopkins University Press, 1972), p. 194.

31. Rosalind Coward and John Ellis, *Language and Materialism* (London: Routledge and Kegan Paul, 1977), p. 23.

32. Ibid., p. 73. In *The Political Unconscious* (p. 45), Jameson has objected to considering language production as material production.

33. Marx, *Selected Writings*, p. 183.

34. Coward and Ellis, *Language and Materialism*, p. 76.

35. Ibid., p. 77.

36. Ibid., p. 78.

37. Ibid., p. 77.

38. Ibid., p. 100.

39. Wolfgang Iser, for example, makes the argument that literary works can both represent and call into question their dominant "repertoire" of social norms and ideological habits of thought. See "The Reality of Fiction: A Functionalist Approach to Literature," *New Literary History* 7, no. 1 (1975): 7–38.

40. Coward and Ellis, *Language and Materialism*, p. 60.

41. Ibid., p. 47.

42. Julia Kristeva, *Desire in Language*, ed. Leon S. Roudiez (New York: Columbia University Press, 1980), pp. 36–63.

43. See M. M. Bakhtin, *The Dialogical Imagination: Four Essays by M. M. Bakhtin*, ed. Michael Holquist, trans. Caryl Emerson and Michael Holquist (London and Austin, Texas: University of Texas Press, 1981), esp. pp. 262ff.

44. M. H. Abrams, *Natural Supernaturalism* (New York: Norton, 1973), p. 145.

45. *Collected Letters of Samuel Taylor Coleridge*, ed. E. L. Griggs (Oxford: Oxford University Press, 1956ff.), 4: 545.

TWO The Genesis of the Monologue

1. The powerful concept of a text's "intertextuality" is based on such an intersection. Adapting Bakhtin, Julia Kristeva maintains that "the word's status is . . . defined *horizontally* (the word in the text belongs to both writing subject and addressee) as well as *vertically* (the word in the text is oriented toward an anterior or synchronic literary corpus)." It is from these two kinds of texts, the social and the literary, that the literary work

constructs its "mosaic of quotations." The idea of intersecting axes Kristeva takes from Bakhtin, who calls them axes of "dialogue" and "ambivalence." See *Desire in Language,* p. 66.

2. Critics have traditionally located the monologue primarily in relation to the lyric and the drama. My own view is that it is related in an equally important way to the nineteenth century's major literary form, the novel. To detail the complex interrelation of genres at a particular conjuncture would, however, require a separate study in itself.

3. See, for example, Herbert Tucker, *Browning's Beginnings* (Minneapolis: University of Minnesota Press, 1980), p. 9.

4. For a fuller elaboration of this logical structure, see Michael H. Bright, "Browning's 'Pictor Ignotus': An Interpretation," *Studies in Browning and his Circle* 4, no. 1 (1976): 54–55.

5. George Bornstein notices the relevance of the parable but does not give it central importance in the poem's strategy. See "The Structure of Browning's 'Pictor Ignotus,'" *Victorian Poetry* 19, no. 1 (1980): 70.

6. Matt. 25: 14–30.

7. For the comparison with Vasari, see Leonee Ormond, "Browning and Painting," in *Robert Browning,* ed. Isobel Armstrong (Athens: Ohio University Press, 1975), pp. 184–210, esp. pp. 195–96. J. B. Bullen believes that Browning's model for the Pictor Ignotus was Fra Bartolommeo di San Marco. His speculation is interesting but is based on fragmentary similarities between the life of Fra Bartolommeo and details in the poem. Bullen offers no argument that Browning is using a single source, however. It now seems more likely that Browning has in mind a generalized dilemma of a particular historical period of which several different painters might serve as examples. See J. B. Bullen, "Browning's 'Pictor Ignotus' and Vasari's 'Life of Fra Bartolommeo di San Marco,'" *Review of English Studies,* n.s., 23, no. 91 (1972): 313–19.

8. Cited in Michael Baxandall, *Painting and Experience in Fifteenth-Century Italy* (Oxford: Oxford University Press, 1974), p. 4.

9. See Kristeva, "The Bounded Text," in *Desire in Language,* pp. 36–63.

10. David Hume, "Of the Standard of Taste," in *Critical Theory since Plato,* ed. Hazard Adams (New York: Harcourt Brace Jovanovich, 1971), p. 314.

11. E. D. H. Johnson, *The Alien Vision of Victorian Poetry* (Princeton: Princeton University Press, 1952), p. 111; Ormond, "Browning and Painting," p. 188. William Clyde DeVane, of course, defended the speaker in *A Browning Handbook* ([2d ed.; New York: Appleton-Century-Crofts, 1955], p. 155), but recent critics have tended to take the hard individualist line. Richard Altick asserts the speaker's inability "to compete with the bright new stars of Renaissance painting" ("'Andrea del Sarto': The Kingdom of Hell Is Within," in *Browning's Mind and Art,* ed. Clarence Tracy [New York: Barnes and Nobe, 1970], p. 18). More recent

appraisals are those of Herbert Tucker (*Browning's Beginnings,* pp. 165–71), George Bornstein ("The Structure of Browning's 'Pictor Ignotus'"), and Constance W. Hassett (*The Elusive Self in the Poetry of Robert Browning* [Athens: University of Ohio Press, 1982], pp. 71ff). Tucker writes of the pictor's "perverse consciousness" and argues that in the poem, he "chooses to repeat his self-crippling choice" (p. 168). Bornstein agrees that "the pictor's discourse both describes and reenacts his abortive career" (p. 78), as it reveals the cause of his failure: "Pictor fears his own powers of imagination." Hassett calls the poem a "confession manqué" and asserts of its speaker: "His entire meditation attempts to justify a failure it does not fully acknowledge, his terrified refusal to 'all express' ('One Word More,' l. 111) himself" (p. 77). All of these critics, whether friendly or hostile, read the monologue as a transparent rationalization of a pitiable or contemptible personal failure.

12. The modern critic who most nearly has seen the full dialogical significance of the monologue is J. Hillis Miller: "Since [the poet] commits himself only for a time to each life, he will not be petrifying himself in a false self, but will live in a constant process of temporary crystallization, followed by breakup, followed by reorganization in a different form" (*The Disappearance of God* [Cambridge: Harvard University Press, 1963], p. 102).

13. For a sensitive account of this stage, one much more extensive than I can give here, see Tucker, *Browning's Beginnings,* chaps. 2–4.

14. Robert Preyer, "A Reading of the Early Narratives," in *The Browning Critics,* ed. Boyd Litzinger and K. L. Knickerbocker (Lexington: University of Kentucky Press, 1967), pp. 352–53.

15. For recent revaluations of Shelley's influence on Browning, see Richard C. Keenan, "Browning and Shelley," *Browning Institute Studies* 1 (1973): 119–45; William Irvine and Park Honan, *The Book, the Ring, and the Poet* (New York: McGraw-Hill, 1974), pp. 13–29; and John Maynard, *Browning's Youth* (Cambridge: Harvard University Press, 1977), pp. 193–237. For A. Dwight Culler's account of the monodrama, see "Monodrama and the Dramatic Monologue," *PMLA* 90, no. 3 (1975): 366–85.

16. *The Collected Essays of J. V. Cunningham* (Chicago: University of Chicago Press, 1976), p. 277. Donald S. Hair, in *Browning's Experiments with Genre* (Toronto: University of Toronto Press, 1972), finds *Pauline* a spasmodic poem (see pp. 4–19). But Clyde de L. Ryalls's more judicious treatment reaches the sort of conclusion I am assuming here. See "Browning's *Pauline:* The Question of Genre," *Genre* 9 (1976): 231–46.

17. I owe this example to a lecture by Wesley Trimpi, "The Ancient Dilemma of Knowledge and Representation," delivered in 1977 at Brandeis University and the University of Michigan.

18. Ormond, "Browning and Painting," p. 188.

19. "A Defence of Poetry," in *Shelley's Prose,* ed. David Lee Clark (Albuquerque: University of New Mexico Press, 1966), p. 277.

20. Ibid., p. 278.

21. Ibid.

22. I am convinced that this is the same contradiction that Harold Bloom observes in his latest reading (or misreading) of *Prometheus Unbound.* According to Bloom, in act 4 "Shelley attempted a humanistic apocalypse, which may be an oxymoron" (*Poetry and Repression* [New Haven: Yale University Press, 1976] p. 96).

23. Kristeva, *Desire in Language,* p. 73. See also Bakhtin, *The Dialogical Imagination,* pp. 43ff.

24. Kristeva, *Desire in Language,* p. 74.

25. A poem like "To a Skylark" occupies the opening between Wordsworth and Browning that Lawrence Poston III calls a "displacement": "In the last book of *The Prelude,* Wordsworth's famous description of the ascent of Snowdon turns on the sudden appearance of the moon in a cloudless sky, illuminating the hills that upheave their 'dusky backs' over the 'still ocean' of mist. The vision of the moon partly dissolves, but from it the poet derives 'the emblem of a mind / That feeds upon infinity,' 'a mind sustained / By recognitions of transcendent power.' The experience itself does not last forever, but it endures long enough to induce a reflective calm from which the poet extrapolates a sense of permanence, a recognition that there are minds whose 'consciousness of Whom they are' is 'habitually infused / Through every image and through every thought.' By contrast, Browning's technique for dwelling on such moments of illumination is to stress not only their transience but the uncertainties associated with the individual consciousness that registers them" ("Browning and the Romantic Landscape," in *Nature and the Victorian Imagination* ed. U. C. Knoepflmacher and G. B. Tennyson [Berkeley: University of California Press, 1977], p. 427).

26. The interpretation that most nearly "splits" the subject of this poem is that which sees Julian and Maddalo as representing opposing tendencies within Shelly or within the discourse of Shelley's poetry. Stuart Curran takes this line, identifying Julian with the optimism of *Prometheus Unbound* and Maddalo with the pessimism of *The Cenci.* The poem's chronological place lends support to this view, although it leaves open important questions about Shelley's relation to Byron. See Curran's *Shelley's Annus Mirabilis* (San Marion: Huntington Library, 1975), esp. p. 137. See also Earl Wasserman's claim that for Shelley, Byron "represented an opposing aspect within his own mind" (*Shelley: A Critical Reading* [Baltimore: Johns Hopkins University Press, 1971], p. 60).

27. Critics have often based their commentaries on the question of whether the maniac's speech supports Julian's or Maddalo's argument. A good

example of this type of interpretation is Donald H. Reiman's *Percy Bysshe Shelley* (New York: Twayne Publishers, 1969), pp. 69–73. Kenneth Neill Cameron, on the other hand, maintains that the maniac himself is to be identified with Shelley. See *Shelley: The Golden Years* (Cambridge: Harvard University Press, 1974), pp. 255–66. On the general issue of the opposition between views of life as passive or dependent on the active will, see Judith Chernaik, *The Lyrics of Shelley* (Cleveland: Case Western Reserve Press, 1972), pp. 26–27.

28. Stuart Curran, in a complementary reading, says that Julian " 'shows his wisdom' by pursu[ing] his obligations to a human and humane community" (*Shelley's Annus Mirabilis*, p. 137). This interpretation contrasts with that of Earl Wasserman who finds in Julian's abdication a "moral failing" (see *Shelley: A Critical Reading*, pp. 80–81).

29. We can, of course, argue that in poems like *Alastor, Adonais,* or *Laon and Cythna,* two distinct perspectives are laid before us (a "double perspective"). But such is also the case in the monological epic where "narrator" and "character" are distinct. It is only when the character is cited (in the novel) that discourse itself becomes split or dialogical. Similarly, the monologue bifurcates its discourse as whole poems of Shelley do not. For the double perspective in Shelley, see Chernaik, *The Lyrics of Shelley,* p. 19.

30. Richard Ohmann, "Modes of Order," in *Linguistics and Literary Style,* ed. Donald C. Freeman (New York: Holt, Rinehart and Winston, 1970), p. 210.

31. Quoted in ibid., p. 213.

32. In *Shelley's Prose,* p. 315.

33. Ibid., p. 281.

34. Shelley, "A Defence of Poetry," pp. 296–97.

35. "The Poetical Works of Robert Southey," *Edinburgh Review,* 67 (1839): 355.

36. Ibid.

37. See Loy D. Martin, "Changing the Past: Theories of Imitation and Invention, 1680–1830," *Dispositio* 4, nos. 11–12 (1979): 189–212. See also Matthew Arnold, "The Function of Criticism at the Present Time," in *Poetry and Criticism of Matthew Arnold,* ed. A. Dwight Culler (Boston: Houghton, Mifflin, 1961), pp. 240–41.

38. Mrs. Sutherland Orr, *A Handbook to the Works of Robert Browning,* 3d ed. rev. (London, 1887), p. 21.

39. The idea of Shelley's poetry as spontaneous and uncrafted has long been discredited, but in early statements of this former commonplace, we can see how the accurately observed discontinuities among Shelley's images might lead to a mistaken inference. F. R. Leavis, for example, was sensitive to the arbitrariness of the individual particulars in many

of Shelley's catalogues. "To a Skylark," he says, "is a mere tumbled out spate ('spontaneous overflow') of poeticalities, the place of each one of which Shelley could have filled with another without the least difficulty and without making any essential difference" (*Revaluation: Tradition and Development in English Poetry* [London: Chatto and Windus, 1947], p. 215).

40. Quoted in Jameson, *Marxism and Form,* p. 73.

41. Preface to *Paracelsus* in *Complete Works of Robert Browning,* ed. Roma A. King, Jr., et al. (Athens: Ohio University Press, 1969), 1: 65.

42. Herbert Tucker, who offers the best interpretation of *Pauline* in print, declines to accept my reading of Browning's desire to repair continuity (*Browning's Beginnings,* p. 226, n. 6). Tucker's entire book presents Browning as an "anti-closural" poet, one who continuously projects beyond the present to an uncertain future. This would seem to contradict his claim about *Pauline* that Browning "chooses to make his poem a discontinuous fragment." Perhaps Tucker's argument is somewhat distorted here as elsewhere by his allegiance to the theories of Harold Bloom, for whom the "strong poet" must always be desperately striving to open up space that the predecessor cannot occupy. My own argument, on the other hand, might well support Tucker's general thesis better than Bloom's theory does. For Bloom, all strong poets fear too much continuity, but this form of anxiety seems less appropriate to the 1830s than the form outlined in this chapter. In a recent article, Tucker has developed his own idea of the dramatic monologue in ways that seem responsive to the same features I am trying to explain. See "From Monomania to Monologue: 'St. Simeon Stylites' and the Rise of the Victorian Dramatic Monologue," *Victorian Poetry* 22, no. 2 (1984): 121–37.

43. "The School of the Heart and Other Poems by Henry Alford," *Edinburgh Review* 62 (1836): 299.

44. Frederick Pottle, *Shelley and Browning: A Myth and Some Facts* (Chicago: Pembroke Press, 1923), p. 33.

THREE   The Being Written

1. Thomas Weiskel, *The Romantic Sublime* (Baltimore: Johns Hopkins University Press, 1976), p. 59.

2. Jacques Derrida, *Of Grammatology,* trans. Gayatri Spivak (Baltimore: Johns Hopkins University Press, 1976), pp. 18–26.

3. Bernard Comrie, *Aspect* (Cambridge: Cambridge University Press, 1976), p. 16.

4. Ibid.

5. Ibid., p. 4.

6. Ibid.

7. Martin, "Literary Invention."

8. Coward and Ellis, *Language and Materialism*, p. 77.

9. Ibid.

10. Elizabeth Closs Traugott, *A History of English Syntax* (New York: Holt, Rinehart and Winston, 1972), pp. 40–41.

11. Paul Ricoeur, "The Model of the Text: Meaningful Action Considered as a Text," *New Literary History* 5, no. 1 (1973): 91–120; and "Metaphor and the Main Problem of Hermeneutics," *New Literary History* 6 (1974): 95–110.

12. Also related is Browning's often-remarked "particularity of detail." One purpose of the type of analysis offered here is to prevent misreadings of Browning like that of Carol Christ in *The Finer Optic: The Aesthetic of Particularity in Victorian Poetry* (New Haven: Yale University Press, 1975). Christ, noting Browning's power of particularized designation, finds in him "an insistence upon the priority of the individual over classification" (p. 69), arguing that he sees "a word composed of peculiar self-contained bodies, each soliloquizing its way through life." (p. 71). By opposing "the individual" to "classification," Christ fails to notice that dramatic monologues are not soliloquies, that Browning's speakers confidently employ their "particularized" discourse in speaking to someone, thus implying shared, rather than idiosyncratic, knowledge.

13. Herbert Tucker convincingly finds the seeds of this strategy in the "dialectic of anticipation and deferment" that structures early poems like *Paracelsus (Browning's Beginnings*, p. 63).

14. J. McH. Sinclair, "Taking a Poem to Pieces," in *Linguistics and Literary Style*, ed. Donald C. Freeman (New York: Holt, Rinehart and Winston, 1970), pp. 129–42.

15. Browning, *The Complete Works* 1: 65.

16. William Cadbury, "Lyric and Anti-Lyric Forms: A Method for Judging Browning," in *Browning's Mind and Art*, p. 41.

17. Robert Langbaum, *The Poetry of Experience* (New York: Norton, 1957), p. 82.

18. The contradiction or irony pointed out here bears a close affinity to the "double frame" of aesthetic fixity and dynamic social convention that Joshua Adler finds governing the poem. For a departure from that perception that is somewhat different from my own, see Adler's "Structure and Meaning in Browning's 'My Last Duchess,'" *Victorian Poetry* 15, no. 3 (1977): 219–27.

19. Shiv K. Kumar, "The Moment in the Dramatic Monologues of Robert Browning," in *British Victorian Literature: Recent Revaluations*, ed. Shiv K. Kumar (New York: New York University Press, 1969), p. 93.

20. *The Works of John Ruskin*, ed. E. T. Cook and Alexander Wedderburn (London, 1909), p. xxxiv.

21. Roma A. King, Jr., *The Focusing Artifice* (Athens: Ohio University Press, 1968), p. xix.
22. Gerald R. Bruns, "The Formal Nature of Victorian Thinking," *PMLA* 90, no. 5 (1975): 904-18. Quotation is from the Abstract, p. 811.
23. Ibid.
24. Jacques Lacan, response to Charles Morazé, in Macksey and Donato, *The Structuralist Controversy*, p. 42.
25. I think I am describing the aspects of the monologue that lead Harold Bloom to find a reader's ambivalence over the question of whether the "strong" monologues display ruined quests or good moments. Bloom finds these poems occasions for *aporia* on the part of the reader; their speakers "abide in our uncertainty." This seems to me true of the best poems, but not true for poems like "My Last Duchess." See Bloom, *Poetry and Repression*, pp. 180-81.

FOUR   The Divided Subject

1. For a useful summary of these attitudes in the Victorian decades, see Jerome H. Buckley, *The Triumph of Time* (Cambridge: Harvard University Press, 1966).
2. Walter Pater, *The Renaissance* (London, 1914), p. 234.
3. Ibid., pp. 235-36. The recognition of this dialectic of attitudes toward the "self" now seems preferable to J. Hillis Miller's claim that "in Browning's day, and in England the idea of the indeterminacy of self-hood was a scandalous notion." Nevertheless, Miller's discussion of Browning's lack of a "definite, solid self" is one of the best moments in modern Browning criticism. See *The Disappearance of God*, pp. 103ff.
4. John Stuart Mill, *Essays on Politics and Culture*, ed. Gertrude Himmelfarb (New York: Doubleday, 1962), p. 3.
5. Thomas Carlyle, *Sartor Resartus* (New York: Dutton, 1975), p. 57.
6. In his chapter on Browning in *The Disappearance of God*, Miller properly perceives these qualities as functions of subjectivity. Furthermore, he also sees that Browning never finally repudiates the ideal of wholeness: "The habit of 'Still beginning, ending never' is one of the central characteristics of Browning's thought. Even at the last minute of life he will still be moving, still rejecting the latest expression of the indivisible whole, and still starting over indefatigably to make another, which will only be rejected in its turn" (p. 87). Miller also approaches an apprehension of the splitting of the subject in Browning, but by saying that the poet himself "oscillates within the poem back and forth between contradictory impulses," Miller cannot finally abolish the unitary subject; he merely moves it around.

7. See Browning's note to *Dramatic Lyrics* in *The Complete Works* 3:197. The second remark is quoted in DeVane, *A Browning Handbook,* p. 430.

8. B. W. Fuson, *Browning and His English Predecessors in the Dramatic Monologue* (Iowa City: University of Iowa Press, 1948), pp. 11–12; Michael Mason, "Browning and the Dramatic Monologue," in Armstrong, *Robert Browning,* p. 232. See also Park Honan, *Browning's Characters* (New Haven: Yale University Press, 1961), p. 122. An interesting group of recent theoretical statements on the nature of the dramatic monologue may be found in *Victorian Poetry* 22, no. 2 (1984). The most thorough and efficient collections of Browning's own statements supporting the conventional view appears in Philip Drew, *The Poetry of Browning: A Critical Introduction* (London: Methuen, 1970), pp. 12–14.

9. For an illuminating account of the origins of Browning's split subject in earlier poems, see Herbert Tucker's reading of the recognition of Eglamor at the end of *Sordello* in *Browning's Beginnings,* pp. 16–29.

10. Ralph W. Rader, "The Concept of Genre and Eighteenth-Century Studies," in *New Approaches to Eighteenth-Century Literature,* ed. Philip Harth (New York: Columbia University Press, 1974), pp. 91–92. Rader's observation is, of course, simply an elaboration of a commonplace familiar at least since William Lyon Phelps compared Browning's couplets to those of Pope and Keats in 1912. See Phelps, *Robert Browning* (New York: Archon Books, 1968), pp. 170–72.

11. Ralph W. Rader, "The Dramatic Monologue and Related Lyric Forms," *Critical Inquiry* 3, no. 1 (1976): 139.

12. Browning's early uneasiness about these oppositions is expressed in his explanation of the title, *Bells and Pomegranates:* "I only meant by that title to indicate an endeavor towards something like an alternation, or mixture, of music with discoursing, sound with sense, poetry with thought" (from the preface to *A Soul's Tragedy* in *The Complete Works,* 5:4).

13. Cadbury, "Lyric and Anti-Lyric Forms," p. 38.

14. This question is, of course, a transformation of the Shelleyan questions about the skylark's song that I discussed in chapter 2. For a transitional example, where the "meaning" of the music is, as for Shelley, more metaphysical than textual, see *Pauline,* lines 413–16, where Browning characterizes the task of reading Shelley: "To disentangle, gather sense from song; / Since, song-inwoven, lurked there sense which seemed / A key to a new world, the muttering / Of angels, something yet unguessed by man" (quoted in John Hollander, "Robert Browning: The Music of Music," in *Robert Browning: A Collection of Critical Essays,* ed. Harold Bloom and Adrienne Munich [New York: Prentice-Hall, 1979], p. 102). Hollander's essay is especially useful on the subject of Browning's music

poems, as is George M. Ridenour's "Browning's Music Poems: Fancy and Fact," *PMLA* 78, no. 4 (1963): 369–77. See also Wendell Story Johnson, "Browning's Music," *Journal of Aesthetic and Art Criticism* 12, no. 2 (1963): 203–7.

15. For the relation between dialogical literary language and the presentation of open-ended time frames of the kind I have described in chapter 3, see Bakhtin, *The Dialogical Imagination,* pp. 7ff.

16. Langbaum, *The Poetry of Experience,* esp. chap. 6.

17. Herwin Schaefer, *Nineteenth-Century Modern* (New York: Praeger, 1970), p. 66.

18. Traugott, *The History of English Syntax,* p. 163.

19. Charles Morazé, *The Triumph of the Middle Classes* (New York: Doubleday, 1968), pp. 114–15.

20. Williams, *Marxism and Literature,* p. 51.

FIVE   The Cooperating Fancy

1. The classic statement, and still in some ways the most sensitive, is that of William Lyon Phelps in *Robert Browning,* pp. 169ff.

2. Langbaum, *The Poetry of Experience,* p. 182.

3. Malcolm Coulthard, *An Introduction to Discourse Analysis* (London: Longman, 1977), p. 65.

4. See Starkey Duncan, "Towards a Grammar for Dyadic Conversation," *Semiotica* 9, no. 1 (1973): 29–46, and "On the Structure of Speaker-Auditor Interaction during Speaking Turns," *Language in Society* 3, no. 2 (1974): 161–80; Harvey Sacks, Emanuel Schegloff, and Gail Jefferson, "A Simplest Systematics for the Organization of Turn-taking for Conversation," *Language* 50, no. 4 (1974): 696–735; Emanuel Schegloff and Harvey Sacks, "Opening up Closings," *Semiotica* 8, no. 4 (1973): 289–327.

5. See Sacks, Schegloff, and Jefferson, "Simplest Systematics," and Duncan, "Towards a Grammar for Dyadic Conversation."

6. Coulthard, *Introduction to Discourse Analysis,* p. 70.

7. For a different interpretation of "gold" in this poem, see Barbara Melchiori, *Browning's Poetry of Reticence* (London: Oliver and Boyd, 1968), pp. 67–89.

8. Images of enclosure have long been recognized as central to the poem. For treatments somewhat different from mine, see Eleanor Cook, *Browning's Lyrics: An Exploration* (Toronto: University of Toronto Press, 1974), pp. 126–27; Tucker, *Browning's Beginnings,* pp. 198–200; and, more recently, Lee Erickson, *Robert Browning: His Poetry and His Audiences* (Ithaca: Cornell University Press, 1984), pp. 166–70. Erickson's entire fifth chapter treats the issue of reciprocity in the monologues

of *Men and Women* but does not distinguish the Romantic or Hegelian understanding of the self and the other from the Victorian emphasis on discursive reciprocity.

9. See Gregory Bateson, "Minimal Requirements for a Theory of Schizophrenia," in *Steps to an Ecology of Mind* (New York: Ballantine Books, 1972), pp. 244–270.

10. Ibid., p. 317.

11. Ibid., pp. 331–32.

12. Browning, *The Complete Works*, 1: 65.

13. See Edward Bostetter, *The Romantic Ventriloquists* (Seattle: University of Washington Press, 1963), pp. 1–11, 302–6; and Earl R. Wasserman, *The Subtler Language* (Baltimore: Johns Hopkins University Press, 1959), pp. 3–12, 169–88.

14. Wasserman, *The Subtler Language*, p. 11.

15. See Tucker, *Browning's Beginnings*, p. 11.

16. Boyd Litzinger and Donald Smalley, eds. (New York: Barnes and Noble, 1970), p. 166.

17. Maisie Ward, *Robert Browning and His World: The Private Face* (New York: Holt, Rinehart and Winston, 1967), p. 112.

18. Among modern critics, perhaps the most sensitive to the monologue's claim on the reader's capacity to supply missing material is Philip Drew in "How to Read a Dramatic Monologue," in *The Poetry of Robert Browning: A Critical Introduction* (London: Methuen, 1970), pp. 12–38.

19. Litzinger and Smalley, *Browning: The Critical Heritage*, p. 157 (emphasis mine).

20. Ibid., p. 174.

21. George Eliot, *Middlemarch*, ed. Gordon S. Haight (Boston: Riverside, 1968), p. 298.

SIX Browning, Childe Roland, and the Speech of Dreams

1. J. W. Lever, *The Elizabethan Love Sonnet* (London, 1968), p. 53.

2. A full account of these works would need to treat lyric sequences in which the poems are not formally sonnets, such as Meredith's *Modern Love*.

3. *The Letters of Robert Browning and Elizabeth Barrett 1845–1846*, ed. Elvan Kinter (Cambridge: Harvard University Press, 1969), 1: 239.

4. Ibid., p. 342.

5. DeVane, *A Browning Handbook*, p. 276.

6. Quoted in ibid., p. 229.

7. Sigmund Freud, *The Interpretation of Dreams*, trans. James Strachey (New York: Avon Books, 1965), p. 197.

8. Ibid., p. 187.

9. DeVane, *A Browning Handbook,* pp. 231-32.

10. Freud, *Interpretation of Dreams,* pp. 311-12.

11. Quoted in Anthony Wilden, *System and Structure: Essays in Communication and Exchange,* 2d ed. (London: Tavistock Publications, 1980), p. 43.

12. Freud, *Interpretation of Dreams,* p. 352.

13. See William Lyon Phelps, *Browning: How to Know Him* (Indianapolis: Bobbs-Merrill, 1937), pp. 232, 237, and Langbaum, *The Poetry of Experience,* p. 195.

14. Freud, *Interpretation of Dreams,* p. 354.

15. For a more traditional, but still freshly provocative, reading of this landscape's significance in the poem, see "Browning and the Romantic Landscape," pp. 426-39, esp. pp. 433ff.

16. For an even more obviously related, though much later, example, see *Bad Dreams III* and Harold Bloom's brief commentary on it in *Poetry and Repression,* pp. 197-99.

17. Freud, *Interpretation of Dreams,* p. 358.

18. Quoted in Irvine and Honan, *The Book, the Ring, and the Poet,* p. 290.

19. Ibid., pp. 287-91.

20. Ibid., p. 289.

21. E. D. H. Johnson seemed to sense this affinity when he wrote, "The dramatic technique, as [Browning] employed it, became simply a process of sublimation equivalent in stylistic terms to Tennyson's thematic use of dream, madness, vision and the quest" (*The Alien Vision of Victorian Poetry,* p. 92).

22. Coward and Ellis, *Language and Materialism,* pp. 94-95.

SEVEN   Others: Using and Losing Connection

1. Cited in A. Dwight Culler, *The Poetry of Tennyson* (New Haven: Yale University Press, 1977), p. 202.

2. Because this is not a full interpretation of the poem, these remarks may seem to read the ending too optimistically. In his very satisfying detailed treatment of *Maud,* James Kincaid insists that "the war is therapy, not a final solution" (*Tennyson's Major Poems* [New Haven: Yale University press, 1975], p. 115).

3. Culler, "Monodrama and the Dramatic Monologue," pp. 366-85.

4. Robert Pattison says the poem "builds on the convention of the dramatic monologue" but "moves well beyond that convention in anticipation of the form that would be needed for the Arthurian epic" (*Tennyson and Tradition* [Cambridge: Harvard University Press, 1979], p. 129).

5. For an alternative reading of the poem, see Kincaid, *Tennyson's Major Poems,* pp. 41ff. For Kincaid, the poem "seems to insist absolutely on the final separation of the individual from communal values" (p. 43).

He reads Ulysses' address to his mariners as "mere cajolery," though he also calls it "eloquent persuasion" (p. 44). Kincaid's book is excellent, and he does perceive a doubleness in Ulysses' portrayal, but I do find his reading more "individualist" than I find the poem. In a less detailed reading, Robert Pattison follows Kincaid, finding that "in *Ulysses* all human rapport is sacrificed to self and will" (*Tennyson and Tradition*, p. 85). These treatments remain, of course, similar to a conventional view of Ulysses' heartless individualism, perhaps most forcefully expressed by E. J. Chiasson in "Tennyson's 'Ulysses'—A Re-interpretation," *University of Toronto Quarterly* 13 (1954): 402–9. For an interpretation that, though not entirely convincing as a whole, views "Ulysses" as a "poem of communal hope," see Mary Saunders, "Tennyson's 'Ulysses' as Rhetorical Monologue," *Victorian Newsletter* 60 (1981): 20–24.

6. Fass, "Notes Towards a History of the Dramatic Monologue," *Anglia* 88 (1970): 222–32.

7. Ibid., p. 226.

8. After *The Ring and the Book*, Browning's poems become more consistently narrative, and some of the later poems may be considered as monologues. Browning defined a dramatic idyll as "a succinct little story" that "is told by some actor in it," and Mark Siegchrist has stressed the emphasis on plot and other narrative devices in the idylls. See his "Thematic Coherence in Browning's *Dramatic Idylls*," *Victorian Poetry* 15, no. 3 (1977): 229–39.

9. Loy D. Martin, "Pound and Fenollosa: The Problem of Influence," *Critical Quarterly* 20, no. 1 (1978): 48–60.

10. D. D. Paige, ed. *The Letters of Ezra Pound* (New York: Harcourt, Brace and World, 1950), p. 151.

11. Hugh Kenner, *The Pound Era* (Berkeley: University of California Press, 1971), p. 67.

12. Cited in ibid., p. 359.

13. Ibid., p. 29.

14. *The Literary Essays of Ezra Pound*, ed. T. S. Eliot (London: Faber and Faber, 1963), p. 16.

15. E. M. Forster, *Aspects of the Novel* (New York: Harcourt, Brace and Co., 1927), p. 14.

16. Pound, *Literary Essays,* p. 19.

17. *Selected Poems of Edwin Arlington Robinson,* ed. James Dickey (New York: Collier Books, 1965), p. xvi.

EIGHT   A Personal Epilogue

1. Jameson, *The Political Unconscious,* p. 9.

2. Ibid.

3. This question appears to mirror the distinction made by James R. Kincaid between the "ironic" and "comic" poles of Tennyson's poetry. Still, there are problems with such an alignment. I think it would stretch the plausibility of this book's inferences to read Browning's dramatic monologues as depicting ironic lives within comic frames. Kincaid's concept of the ironic is also bifurcated in itself, allowing for an individual to feel either isolated or deterministically fixed, and this would seem to derive ideologically from the dialectical unity of private and public interest that I have discussed in chapters 2 and 4. Thus, the distinctions made here and those made by Kincaid might turn out to be versions of each other, but this hypothesis needs to be tested in greater detail than the present occasion allows. See Kincaid, *Tennyson's Major Poems,* esp. pp. 1–14.

4. The idea of Victorian writers opposing Victorian ideology is not new. Most often the claim is made as Johnson makes it in *The Alien Vision of Victorian Poetry:* "Yet, paradoxically, it becomes increasingly difficult to think of the great Victorians as other than solitary and unassimilated figures within their century. Deeply as they allowed themselves to be involved in the life of the times, familiarity seemed only to breed contempt. Their writings, inspired by a whole-hearted hostility to the progress of industrial culture, locate the centers of authority not in the existing social order, but within the resources of individual being" (p. x). My argument is not merely reversing Johnson's claim. Rather, it locates the phrasing of "allowed themselves to be involved" and "centers of authority" within an ideology that includes both "individual being" and "industrial culture" as homogeneous, nonsystemic entities. The opposition being offered here is between this entire horizon of concepts and a horizon on which both "culture" and "the individual" are conceived as at once part of and constituted by systems of relationships.

5. Anthony Trollope, *The Last Chronicle of Barset,* ed. Arthur Mizener (New York: Riverside, 1964), p. 354.

6. See Bateson, *Steps to an Ecology of Mind,* p. 483.

7. Ibid., p. 319.

8. Charles Darwin, *The Origin of Species,* ed. J. W. Burrow (New York: Penguin Books, 1976), p. 68.

9. Ibid., p. 67.

10. Ibid., p. 116.

11. In *The Disappearance of God,* J. Hillis Miller finds a similar dilemma in the early Browning: "*His* nature is a contradiction. His inner law seems to be a tumultuous need to 'become all natures, yet retain / The law of [his] own nature" (p. 94).

12. See Bertell Ollmann, *Alienation* (New York: Cambridge University Press, 1977), pp. 3–69.

13. See Bertrand Russell "Mathematical Logic as Based on the Theory of Types," in *Logic and Knowledge,* ed. Robert C. Marsh (New York: Putnam's, 1971), pp. 59–102.

14. Karl Marx, *The German Ideology,* ed. C. J. Arthur (New York: International Publishers, 1978), p. 117.

15. Althusser and Balibar, *Reading Capital,* pp. 186–87 (italics in original).

16. The phrase "difference that makes a difference" is Bateson's imprecise but useful invention for making the central concept of information theory accessible.

17. Virginia Woolf, *Mrs. Dalloway* (New York: Harcourt, Brace and World, 1953), p. 12.

18. Eliot, *Middlemarch,* p. 96.

Index

This book was composed in Aldine Roman text
by A. W. Bennett, Inc., Windsor, Vermont,
and Lady display type by The Typeworks, Baltimore, Maryland,
from a design by Cynthia W. Hotvedt.

It was printed on 50-lb. Sebago Eggshell Cream Offset paper
and bound in G.S.B. book cloth by
The Maple Press Company, York, Pennsylvania.